English Constitutional Conflicts
of the Seventeenth Century
1603–1689

English Constitutional Conflicts
of the Seventeenth Century
1603–1689

by

J. R. TANNER

CAMBRIDGE
AT THE UNIVERITY PRESS
1966

PUBLISHED BY

THE SYNDICS OF THE CAMBRIDGE UNIVERSITY PRESS

Bentley House, 200 Euston Road, London, N.W. 1
American Branch: 32 East 57th Street, New York, N.Y. 10022
West African Office: P.M.B. 5181, Ibadan, Nigeria

First Edition 1928
Reprinted 1937
1947
1948
1952
1957
1960
1961
1962
1966

Printed in Great Britain at the University Printing House, Cambridge
(Brooke Crutchley, University Printer)

CONTENTS

PARLIAMENTS, 1603–1689

JAMES I

FIRST PARLIAMENT, 19 March, 1604, to 9 February, 1611.

SECOND PARLIAMENT (The Addled Parliament), 5 April, 1614, to 7 June, 1614.

THIRD PARLIAMENT, 30 January, 1621, to 6 January, 1622.

FOURTH PARLIAMENT, 19 February, 1624, to 27 March, 1625.

[This Parliament was prorogued 29 May, 1624, and dissolved by the King's death, 27 March, 1625.]

CHARLES I

FIRST PARLIAMENT, 18 June, 1625, to 12 August, 1625.

SECOND PARLIAMENT, 6 February, 1626, to 15 June, 1626.

THIRD PARLIAMENT, 17 March, 1628, to 10 March, 1629.

FOURTH PARLIAMENT (The Short Parliament), 13 April, 1640, to 5 May, 1640.

FIFTH PARLIAMENT (The Long Parliament), met 3 November, 1640.

[Pride's Purge, 6 December, 1648.]

THE INTERREGNUM

LONG PARLIAMENT continued as the Purged Parliament, to 20 April, 1653.

PARLIAMENT OF SAINTS (Barebones Parliament or Assembly of Nominees), 4 July, 1653, to 12 December, 1653.

FIRST PARLIAMENT OF THE PROTECTORATE, 3 September, 1654, to 22 January, 1655.

SECOND PARLIAMENT OF THE PROTECTORATE, 17 September, 1656, to 4 February, 1658.

RICHARD CROMWELL'S PARLIAMENT, 27 January, 1659, to 22 April, 1659.

LONG PARLIAMENT restored 7 May, 1659, to 13 October, 1659; and again 26 December, 1659, to 16 March, 1660.

[The members excluded by Pride's Purge were restored to their seats 21 February, 1660.]

CHARLES II

CONVENTION PARLIAMENT OF THE RESTORATION, 25 April, 1660, to 29 December, 1660.

PENSION PARLIAMENT, 8 May, 1661, to 24 January, 1679.

HABEAS CORPUS PARLIAMENT, 6 March, 1679, to 12 July, 1679.

[This Parliament was prorogued 27 May, 1679, and did not meet again.]

EXCLUSION BILL PARLIAMENT, 7 October, 1679, to 18 January, 1681.

[This Parliament was prorogued before it met, and did not sit until 21 October, 1680.]

OXFORD PARLIAMENT, 21 March, 1681, to 28 March, 1681.

JAMES II

JAMES II's PARLIAMENT, 19 May, 1685, to 2 July, 1687.

[This Parliament was prorogued 20 November, 1685, and did not meet again.]

CONVENTION PARLIAMENT OF THE REVOLUTION, 22 January, 1689, to 6 February, 1690.

[The Convention was transformed into a Parliament in 1689 by 1 W. & M. c. 1.]

PREFACE

THE lectures printed in the present volume were delivered in the University of Cambridge by the author as Deputy for the Regius Professor of Modern History during the academical year 1926–27. They have all the characteristic defects of lectures appearing in book form—in particular, the want of architectural proportion due to the necessity of forcing a varied subject-matter into the Procrustean framework of sixteen discourses of equal length—but the lecturer has been advised that an historical summary of this kind is likely to be useful to students reading for the Historical Tripos, and to their service he therefore dedicates it, in memory of the successive generations of their predecessors to whom he taught History for nearly forty years.

Some of the material for these lectures was brought together a long time ago without any idea of publication, and in a few cases no sufficient note was taken of its sources. If therefore adequate acknowledgment has not always been paid to the work of others, the author desires to express his very sincere regret for this unfortunate result of his youthful sins of omission.

Like all other students of the seventeenth century, the writer owes to the late Dr S. R. Gardiner and to Sir C. H. Firth an immense debt; he therefore wishes to pay special acknowledgment to the kindness of Messrs Longmans, Green & Co. in granting him permission to use some of the quotations from original sources printed in the former's *History of England* 1603–1642, *History of the Great Civil War* 1642–1649, and *History of the Commonwealth and Protectorate* 1649–1660, and in the latter's *Last Years of the Protectorate* 1656–1659, and *House of Lords during the Civil War.*

Grateful thanks are also due to the Delegates of the Oxford Press for permission to quote from Sir G. W. Prothero's *Statutes and Constitutional Documents* 1558–1625 and S. R. Gardiner's *Constitutional Documents of the Puritan Revolution* 1625–1660; and to Messrs Methuen & Co. for leave to quote from Sir C. Grant Robertson's *Select Statutes, Cases, and Documents*... 1660–1832, and Mrs S. C. Lomas's edition of Thomas Carlyle's *Letters and Speeches of Oliver Cromwell.*

J. R. T.

ALDEBURGH
March 6, 1928

ENGLISH CONSTITUTIONAL CONFLICTS
OF THE SEVENTEENTH CENTURY
1603–1689

※

LECTURE I : *Introductory*

AN old historian,[1] writing in 1744 of the Revolution of 1688, protests against the habit which prevailed in his day of regarding the Revolution as an isolated event.

"It is usual", he says, "to consider the great Revolution which took place in the year 1688 as a single Act or Interlude which was complete in itself, and needed neither Prologue nor Chorus by way of illustration. But to me it appears rather as the grand Catastrophe of several Acts, consisting of a Multiplicity of Scenes, which began to open soon after the Restoration of King Charles II, and which, through a great Variety of Incidents, in a perplexed and irregular manner, made way almost continually, though insensibly, for that important Event".

Here we have the conception of the historical drama, and this conception can be nowhere more fruitfully applied than to the history of the seventeenth century. Nor need we restrict it to a play which begins with the Restoration. The piece is on the stage for nearly a hundred years. The first Act ends with an execution and the second with an abdication; while between them there is an Interlude of military rule. The character of the Revolution was determined by the Rebellion; while the reign of James I is only the Prologue of the same great play. If we are to understand the history of the seventeenth century, we must begin by grasping its dramatic unity. But this compels the historian of the Constitution to a particular way of treating his subject; he can no longer afford to leave chronology out of account. It is no longer possible for him—as in the Tudor period—to trace the process of organic change as it goes on in separate institutions; it is now necessary to follow a story and to watch

[1] Ralph, *History of England*, i. 1.

an unfolding plot. Nevertheless, it is convenient, in an introductory lecture, to ignore chronology and to group together some of the fundamental facts.

It has been said that as we pass from the sixteenth to the seventeenth century we appear to emerge into a new age. The point is put in a variety of ways.

(1) It is said that the Tudor period reconstructed English civilisation. The two great powers in which medieval civilisation had centred had been the Church and the Baronage, and both these had been overthrown by the Tudor Kings. The Dissolution of the Monasteries was a visible social revolution; and scarcely less of a revolution was involved in the more silent and gradual subsidence of the baronial power. The fresh industrial energy of the towns was everywhere replacing the declining industrial energy of the monastic foundations; and as the Reformation swept away the monasteries, so the Civil War was about to dismantle the baronial strongholds—now only relics of a military power which had long since spent itself. The danger from great lords and retainers had completely passed away; the King's writ ran everywhere; the long arm of the Privy Council reached into every corner of the kingdom. What men needed now was not protection from the great lords, but protection from tyrannical abuse of its authority on the part of the power by which the great lords had been overthrown.

(2) The same strong dynasty which had thus accomplished a social revolution had also achieved an ecclesiastical revolution. The Reformation had been carried through; on the whole, its results were accepted; and the crusade of the Catholic powers against it had had the effect of identifying the cause of national independence with the repudiation of the claims of Rome. The long reign of Elizabeth, by bringing the greater part of the nation into the fold of the national Church, had put an end to the danger of a war of religion within the realm. The adherents of Rome had ceased to be dangerous. They were a small minority which could organise an assassination but could not raise a rebellion.

(3) The Tudors had also lifted the fear of foreign

invasion from the English mind. It was not only that the Spanish Armada had been defeated; but also that there had been an immense improvement in the defensible position of England. The success of the United Provinces against Spain had placed the ports of Holland—the natural base for a flank attack upon the English coasts— in the hands of a friendly power. Somewhat the same thing had happened in Ireland—the most vulnerable point in the dominions of Elizabeth. "Ireland hath very good timber and convenient havens", says a letter-writer of 1580;[1] "if the Spaniard might be master of them, he would in short space be master of the seas". This was clearly understood by Spanish statesmen, and so long as Ireland was full of semi-independent chieftains who were hostile to the Reformation, it was easy for Spain to stir up and co-operate in rebellions. But the relentless suppression of rebellions by Elizabeth's vigorous viceroys had at any rate closed the door to foreign intervention. And now at last the accession of James VI of Scotland to the throne of England had barred another road, and had deprived another foreign power of its traditional opportunity for intervention. The alliance between France and Scotland, which had weighed heavily upon the judgments of English statesmen, now determined in the course of nature, and ceased to affect the direction of English policy. England was finally delivered from the nightmare of the North.

(4) A principal danger of the reign of Elizabeth had been the danger of a disputed succession. At one time it must have appeared doubtful whether a disputed succession would not, after all, follow upon Elizabeth's death; for James of Scotland did not appear then in the light in which we are accustomed to regard him now—as quite the obvious heir. If the succession was to be determined by the will of Henry VIII, the crown would go to the descendants of his younger sister Mary, who had married Charles Brandon, Duke of Suffolk. But if the will of Henry VIII was set aside, and it was held that the descendants of his elder sister Margaret had the prior

[1] Thomas Bawdewyn to the Earl of Shrewsbury (Edmund Lodge, *Illustrations of British History*, ii. 231).

claim, then it was at any rate arguable that James as an
alien could not inherit; and in that case the crown would
pass to the descendants of Margaret's second marriage,
who were represented by Lady Arabella Stuart. But
fortunately for the union between England and Scotland,
the advantages which the accession of James would bring
were present to the minds of English statesmen, and
especially to the mind of the one whose word carried the
greatest weight—the aged Queen herself. As death drew
near, she abandoned her habitual reserve on the succession
question and spoke out plainly in favour of James. "I told
you", she said to Nottingham and others on March 22,
two days before she died, "my seat had been the seat of
Kings, and I will have no rascal to succeed me; who should
succeed me but a King?" Cecil asked her what she meant
by "no rascal shall succeed me"; and she replied, "My
meaning was, a King should succeed me; and who should
that be but our cousin of Scotland?"[1] Thus it came about
that the Stuart House succeeded to the throne of England
without opposition; and when its title was once established, there was an end to disputed successions, for the
curse of childlessness which had descended upon the
House of Tudor spared the House of Stuart. At the time
of his accession James had two sons.

The sense of relief with which the nation saw the
accession of James is described in one of Bacon's Frag-
ments.[2] It had been generally supposed, he tells us,
especially abroad, that when Elizabeth died,

there must follow in England nothing but confusions, interreigns,
and perturbations of estate; likely far to exceed the ancient calamities
of the civil wars between the Houses of Lancaster and York, by
how much more the dissensions were like to be more mortal and
bloody when foreign competition should be added to domestical,
and divisions for religion to matter of title to the crown.

But when it fell out that James succeeded without
opposition, "it rejoiced all men to see so fair a morning

[1] Robert Carey's account, quoted in Creighton, *Queen Elizabeth*, p. 302.
[2] "The Beginning of the History of Great Britain" in *Works* (ed.
Spedding), vi. 277.

of a Kingdom, and to be thoroughly secured of former apprehensions; as a man that awaketh out of a fearful dream".

The considerations which I have mentioned all serve to differentiate the centuries.

"England in 1620", says Seeley,[1] "was not the same state that she had been under the Queen. England and Scotland were united in the person of the King, and united in the Reformation. All those dangerous and terrible discords which in the Queen's time had laid the island open to foreign invasion were extinguished. There were no longer two sovereigns in the island, and two evenly balanced religions; no longer two systems of alliance and of royal affinity. The State ruled by James was as much greater than the State ruled by Elizabeth, as James himself was less great than Elizabeth".

But observe the consequences. In the reign of Elizabeth it was foreign policy that was of transcendent importance, and determined the issues of national life and death. The causes which governed foreign policy lay for the most part outside England, and the whole matter was, from its very nature, bound to be in the hands of the Queen and the group of experts in diplomacy which surrounded her. But in the reign of James the greatest foreign questions have been already settled, and it is therefore possible for constitutional questions to come to the front. Foreign affairs are a region where statecraft may exercise itself, but they no longer involve issues that are vital; the subtle and discerning instinct of the political classes sees that they need no longer eclipse all other questions.

"Just as after the Napoleonic wars", says Seeley,[2] "a period of reform set in, and the kind of stagnation in which legislation had fallen was broken up, so at the end of the long Spanish war, Parliament was relieved from a pressure which had paralysed it".

And this brings us to a new point. The Parliament which was thus let loose upon politics was not the same deferential assembly which had been bullied and browbeaten by Henry VIII. One of the great achievements of the Tudor period on the constitutional side was the consolidation of Parliamentary institutions. The very fact that the Tudor Kings had found Parliaments subservient

---

[1] *Growth of British Policy*, i. 258.   [2] *Ib.* i. 259.

and had therefore used them, had given Parliaments a great place in the State. It might have been possible for Henry VIII to have ignored the authority which Parliament claimed over legislation and taxation; to have accomplished the Reformation by royal Injunction instead of by Act of Parliament; to have recruited his finances by royal writs instead of subsidies; to have discontinued by degrees the practice of summoning the Estates. But the fact that he did not do so mightily strengthened the position of Parliament. The Tudors allowed Parliamentary influence to be confirmed by a whole century of precedents, and thus the road which for the first Tudor had been only an ill-marked track had become to the feet of the first Stuart the beaten way of the Constitution.

"Parliament", says Prothero,[1] "had in fact confirmed its position as an indispensable element in the State. Without the training, the prestige, and the sense of self-importance conferred on it by a century of Tudor legislation, it could never have been styled by Pym, the soul of the body politic".

And in Parliament, the House of Commons was no longer relatively unimportant. The Tudors, seeking a counterpoise to the baronage, had done their best to elevate the country gentry and the commercial classes into political importance; and during the sixteenth century these classes had steadily improved their position. The gentry had been enriched by the practice of enclosure and the spoils of the monasteries, while the commercial classes had profited by the growth of trade and the merchant ventures in the New World at the expense of Spain; and the best of the energy and enterprise of these classes was concentrated in the House of Commons.

So far we have been dealing with general causes; but we must not leave personality altogether out of account. The House which had succeeded to the powers of the Tudor absolutism had not inherited the Tudor political genius. All the Tudors had been dignified and effective personalities, and Henry VIII and Elizabeth had been great statesmen. The Stuarts, coming to power at a time

[1] *Statutes and Constitutional Documents*, 1558–1625, p. xxiv.

when statesmanship was more important than ever to the Crown, displayed qualities of only the ordinary type. They were for the most part conscientious and meritorious, but the dynasty only produced one statesman, and he was neither conscientious nor meritorious—I mean, of course, Charles II. The contrast between the Houses may be measured by comparing Queen Anne with Queen Elizabeth and Charles I with Henry VIII. Set side by side with this decline of statesmanship on the part of the Crown, the advance of Parliament to its new position. If the policy of the Stuart dynasty should seem to be dangerous, if it should appear to threaten the public weal as the country gentry and the commercial classes conceived it, Parliament was now qualified to come forward as a critic of the Government, or even as a rival to the Crown, if any powerful motives should arise to induce it to take up an attitude of independence. It is remarkable that just at the time when Parliament was becoming capable of self-assertion and initiative, motives of almost irresistible strength were beginning to operate in this direction. The controversies between the first two Stuart Kings and their Parliaments turn mainly on the two great questions of Taxation and Religion.

Financially, the Stuart Kings fell on evil days. The permanent revenue of the Crown, even under the careful management of Elizabeth, did not produce enough to meet the ordinary expenses of government, and yet the expenses of government continually tended to increase. It was not that the country as a whole was poorer; in fact the contrary was the case. After the defeat of the Armada, and the clearing of the cloud of uncertainty and danger which had hung so black over England in the earlier years of the great Queen's reign, there had been an immense improvement in the general financial position. This is the period of the manor-house—what someone alludes to as "all that great bravery of building that set in in the times of Elizabeth". It is also pre-eminently the period of plate, in which the savings of all classes were accumulated, almost as a peasant of India lays money by in the form of silver ornaments and jewels. The foreign trade of England

also was making a considerable start. In the earlier years of
James I's reign both the East India Company and the
Levant Company did remarkably well, and later the
Thirty Years' War on the Continent threw a great deal of
trade into English hands. The difficulty was that under
existing constitutional arrangements the Crown did not
sufficiently share in this increase in the country's wealth.
It is true that the revenue of James I benefited through
the customs by the increase in foreign trade, and, as we
shall see later, the remarkable increase in the yield to
custom was his salvation from bankruptcy. But the Crown
gained little from the increasing wealth of the country in
general, because the assessment for subsidy remained
unchanged. We find Sir Walter Raleigh protesting in
Elizabeth's Parliament of 1601 against the absurd under-
assessment of persons of large fortune. "Our estates that
be £30 or £40 in the Queen's books are not the hundredth
part of our wealth."[1] And yet it was not in practice possible
to go behind the subsidy books or to break down the
tenacious custom which governed the entries there.

Although the Stuart Kings succeeded to the poverty of
Elizabeth, they did not inherit her saving spirit. Speaking
generally they were wasteful Kings, and this is true of
James I as well as of Charles II. The ordinary peace
expenditure of Elizabeth had been about £220,000 a year;
in 1607 James spent £500,000. It is true that the Irish
troubles were a constant drain on the Exchequer, and that
the rise in wages and prices was always putting Government, as a large employer and purchaser, at a disadvantage
—but a considerable part of the increase was due to an
extravagant household, pensions to courtiers, and pre-
posterous purchases of plate and jewels. On the whole
we may take it, that where Elizabeth had only been
pressed for money, James and Charles were on the verge
of bankruptcy, and that this sinister change in the
situation was due—in part at least—to wasteful administration.

This poverty of the Stuart Kings is a fundamental fact in
the history of the period, because it established a vicious

[1] *Parliamentary History*, i. 920.

circle. (1) It compelled the Crown to summon frequent
Parliaments, and to ask for subsidies to meet ordinary
expenditure, in violation of the theory of the Constitution,
which made Parliament meet on great occasions only, to
vote supplies for the emergencies of war or rebellion.
(2) Frequent Parliaments meant facilities for Parliamentary organisation and Parliamentary criticism which
had not existed in the days of the Tudors when Parliament
met seldom and sat for a short time. (3) When a Stuart
Parliament met, it found itself confronted by ecclesiastical
grievances of sufficient magnitude to justify it in pressing
the Crown for their redress, and for this a powerful lever
now lay ready to its hand, for it could insist that redress
of grievances should precede supply. (4) It thus became
an object of the first importance with the Crown to increase its ordinary or extra-Parliamentary revenue, even
although in order to do so it was necessary to press its
legal rights against individuals much further than
Elizabeth had done. But (5) this was to make fresh
grievances for Parliament to redress, and so to embitter
still further its relations with the Crown.

Besides these financial grievances, Parliament found
itself confronted by ecclesiastical grievances, and these
were the more important, for religion not only furnished
far more powerful motives of action than did finance, but
it determined the spirit in which the controversy was
carried on. "It is observable in the House of Commons,
as their whole story gives it", wrote Sir John Eliot,[1] who
knew the House better than any other politician of the
day except Pym, "that wherever that mention does break
forth of the fears or dangers in religion, and the increase
of popery, their affections are much stirred; and whatever
is obnoxious in the State, it then is reckoned as an incident
to that".

At two points in particular the policy of the elder
Stuarts was precisely such as to "stir the affections" of
the House of Commons.

(1) It must be remembered that in the seventeenth
century most problems of foreign policy had a religious

---

[1] John Forster, *Sir John Eliot* (edition of 1872), i. 145.

character, and the foreign policy of the Stuarts sometimes appeared to their Parliaments to imperil Protestantism. To us, who look at things from a distance, it is clear that after the defeat of the Armada and the failure of Spain to overwhelm her revolted provinces Protestantism had ceased to be in any serious danger. But it was not possible for the men of the time immediately to grasp their true position, and thus in the first half of the seventeenth century the panic fear of Spain and Popery was liable to periodical revivals, during which it exercised a potent influence upon politics. And the foreign policy of the Stuarts was exactly such as to arouse this fear. The engagements of James with Spain and of Charles with France seemed dangerous to Protestantism, and especially dangerous at a time when the Catholic Powers were carrying all before them in the Thirty Years' War. And where Protestantism was at stake, Parliament was prepared to break out of the circle to which the incantations of the Tudors had confined it, and to claim an influence hitherto denied it upon the foreign policy of the Crown.

But (2) the Stuart period saw also a new internal religious discord, and in this the Crown appeared to have taken the wrong side. On James I's accession Puritanism in the narrower sense—the rejection of the Prayer Book as a whole, and the complete repudiation of episcopal authority—was only represented by a small minority in the country; but Puritanism in the wider sense—the Puritanism which asked for a further reformation of doctrine and ritual than Elizabeth had been willing to allow—was the creed of the greater part of the members of the Church of England itself. Nor was this at all surprising, for the system of doctrine and the system of discipline associated with Puritanism are the result of the necessity that Protestantism should be systematised.[1] If Protestantism was to fight Rome it must be something more positive and coherent than a mere negation of Rome, and it acquired coherence through the work of Calvin, who "shaped the mould in which the bronze of Puritanism was cast", and "by his unbending will, his pride, his severity,

1 S. R. Gardiner, *Cromwell's Place in History*, p. 107.

his French spirit of system, his gift for government, for legislation, for dialectic in every field, his incomparable industry and persistence, had conquered a more than pontifical ascendency in the Protestant world".[1] The spirit of Calvinism had permeated deeply the Church of Elizabeth, and Hooker himself adhered generally to Calvin's doctrine of election and always spoke of him with respect.[2] We might apply to the public teaching of the Church of Elizabeth some words of Fuller's written in a different connexion: "The pulpit spake pure Canterbury in the morning, and Geneva in the afternoon".[3] Thus it had come about that the doctrinal system of Calvin had been very generally taught, both at Cambridge and Oxford, to the rising generation of parish clergy,[4] and although his system of discipline had proved unsuitable to the temper of the English people and had failed to take any root, great numbers of religious men accepted the doctrine which Calvin had stated, almost as if it were self-evident: that by the decree of God and for the manifestation of His glory some men are predestinated to everlasting life and others fore-ordained to eternal death.[5]

But when the days of storm and stress were over—when Protestantism had vindicated its position—it was inevitable that the iron system from the shelter of which the Reformers had defied Rome, should now appear to some thinkers in a new light—as a prison confining religious thought and as a check to the free development of religious life. There were many who declined, in time of peace, to live in a fortress under martial law; and thus in the early seventeenth century a new tendency in religion begins to make its appearance in England. The leader of the new school—at any rate in the realm of

---

[1] John Morley, *Oliver Cromwell*, p. 47.
[2] *Dictionary of National Biography*, xxvii. 290.
[3] *Worthies* (ed. P. A. Nuttall, 1840), i. 423.
[4] G. M. Trevelyan, *England under the Stuarts*, p. 148.
[5] "No one who wishes to think piously will dare simply to deny that predestination by which God adopts some to hope of life and adjudges others to eternal death....For not all are created to a like condition; *sed aliis vita aeterna, aliis damnatio praeordinatur*." Quoted in A. S. Duncan-Jones, *Archbishop Laud*, p. 23.

thought—was Lancelot Andrewes, whose controversial
writings "laid the foundation of the Anglican position" as
the seventeenth century understood it.[1] He, and those
who followed him, contended that the accepted Calvinistic
doctrines were not the doctrines of the Prayer Book, and
were therefore not the doctrines of the Church of England.
They were disposed to fall back instead to the theology of
the early days of the Reformation, before Calvinism had
gathered strength—to the view of Cranmer, that nothing
must be rejected which was supported by the custom and
practice of the Early Church. This appeal to primitive
antiquity was the special characteristic of the work of
Andrewes, and he applied it, not only to doctrine but also
to the worship in which the doctrine was embodied and
expressed, for he attached himself to external rites "as
influencing the spiritual conscience, and mellowing the
ironclad reasoning of the Calvinistic preacher".[2] Thus the
new interest in early practices, combined with a revival of
the artistic taste which Calvinism had stifled, led to the
revival of a number of Church ceremonies which, under
the influence of Calvinism, had gradually fallen into disuse.
To this revolt against Calvinism in England a name was
given which was drawn from the history of a similar revolt
against Calvinism abroad. The Dutch theologian Arminius
had preached in opposition to the more rigid of Calvin's
doctrines, and those who followed him were called
Arminians. From the point of view of doctrine—if you
care for the technical terms—Arminianism met predestination by free will; implacable Necessity by merciful
Contingency; Man the Machine by Man the self-
determining Agent.[3] From the point of view of worship,
at any rate in England, it meant a ceremonial revival in
the Church.

According to the Elizabethan theory of the Constitution,
this new movement in the Church was the business of the
ecclesiastical supremacy—certainly not of Parliament as a
whole, and least of all of the House of Commons—but it
was clearly a matter with which Government was con-

---

[1] W. H. Hutton, in Traill, *Social England*, iv. 25.
[2] Gardiner, *Cromwell*, p. 108.   [3] Morley, *Cromwell*, p. 53.

cerned. In that age it was unthinkable that there should be more than one Church; the discussion centred on the question in whose hands the one Church should be. "Only on the minds of a few lonely thinkers or hunted sectaries had the idea of religious liberty as yet dawned."[1] Every religious party held that the ideal of the Church was inseparably bound up with the ideal of the rightly ordered State,[2] and coercion in religion was applied as a matter of course. The difficulty of the situation was that the Crown and the Parliament were coming to belong to opposite religious parties, for while Parliament was Puritan and Calvinist the Crown was Arminian. Even James I was disposed to favour the Arminians: it is said that in his reign a courtier with a taste for theological enquiry once asked "what the Arminians held", whereupon someone replied that they "held" all the best bishoprics and deaneries in the kingdom.[3] The position of Charles I may be inferred from the fact that when Archbishop Abbot died in 1633—an ecclesiastic "stiffly principled" in Puritan doctrines, who saw in the bishops only a superintending pastorate, and not a separate order in the Church[4]—he replaced him by the most famous of the followers of Lancelot Andrewes—William Laud. And this was not all; not only was Laud himself an Arminian, but unlike Bishop Andrewes, who never forced his ceremonies upon others, "content", as Fuller said, "with the enjoying without the enjoining",[5] he was prepared to go all lengths to establish the Arminian character of the English Church. And in this he was supported by the Crown, for Charles I naturally adopted the universal principle of Europe—that the subject ought to be of the same religion as his sovereign —naturally, because this was the doctrine of his day and after his day; it survived the civil wars, was the main principle of the policy of James II, and was only abandoned when the Revolution of 1688 laid down the converse principle, that the sovereign should be of the

[1] Goldwin Smith, *The United Kingdom*, i. 432.
[2] Morley, *Cromwell*, p. 54.
[3] John Hunt, *Religious Thought in England*, i. 148.
[4] *D.N.B.* i. 6.   [5] *Church History* (edition of 1837), iii. 349.

same religion as his subjects, and England being Protestant should be governed by a Protestant prince.

It may be convenient to sum up for future use the
principal points of controversy between Arminianism and
Calvinism—or, to put it in a different way, between that
tendency of thought in the Church which is called Anglican
and the other tendency of later origin and wider diffusion
which is called Puritan—between those who appealed to
the Bible as interpreted by primitive antiquity and those
who appealed to the Bible interpreted literally and exactly
as it stood.

(1) The great ordinance of Puritanism was preaching,
while the great ordinances of Anglicanism were the
Sacraments. This difference in their conception of religious
life was not a novelty of the seventeenth century, but had
its roots further back, in the reign of Elizabeth. The
Queen herself hated preaching, and she had a short way
with preachers. On Ash Wednesday, 1565, she went to
Paul's Cross to hear the Dean of St Paul's preach. The
Dean had not proceeded far in his sermon, when he came
to the subject of images, which, we are told, he "handled
roughly". "Leave that alone", Elizabeth called from her
seat. The preacher did not hear, and went on with his
sermon. "To your text, Mr Dean", she shouted, "To
your text. Leave that. We have had enough of that".
The Dean was so confused at the interruption that he was
not able to go on with his sermon. Archbishop Parker,
seeing him "utterly dismayed", took him "for pity home
to Lambeth to dinner".[1] On the other hand it was one
of the notable achievements of the Puritan party in
Elizabeth's reign that it succeeded in reviving preaching.
The Puritans complained bitterly of "dumb ministers"
and the Puritan clergy carefully cultivated the art. The
paralysis of the pulpit which was one of the earlier effects
of the Reformation was cured by them, and they reaped
their reward. Man cannot live by bread alone, and power
over the common people fell to the Puritans rather than
to the Anglicans. "What won them most repute", says

---

[1] The story is told in J. A. Froude, *The Reign of Elizabeth* (Everyman's
Library), i. 472.

Fuller,[1] "was their ministers' painful preaching in populous places; it being observed in England that those who hold the helm of the pulpit always steer people's hearts as they please".

Out of this arose very naturally (2) the Altar Controversy—whether the altar should stand "tablewise", in the middle of the church, where men sometimes put their hats upon it, or used it as a writing-table on which to transact parish business; or "altarwise", at the east end of the church, covered, and railed about. Connected with this great fundamental question were a number of minor disputes upon various points of ceremonial; and thus, as Bishop Creighton once remarked in another connexion, "the unfortunate legacy of fighting great principles over outward trifles was bequeathed to the English Church".[2]

(3) Last of all, the Sabbatarian Controversy is vastly more important than it appears to be at first sight. The fundamental conflict was after all between those who contended for the exclusive authority of the Bible and those who contended for the co-ordinate authority of the Church.[3] This expressed itself in worship when one side argued that no ceremonies might be imposed which were not authorised by the Bible, and the other side maintained that such ceremonies might be imposed by the authority of the Church, provided that they were not in opposition to the spirit of the Bible teaching. It was only another application of their principle when the Puritans claimed for Sunday the characteristics of the Jewish Sabbath, and a Puritan House of Commons in 1621 expelled the member for Shaftesbury for maintaining that the Sabbath meant Saturday, and for pointing out with reference to the legality of dancing, that David danced before the ark.[4] In this matter, as in many others, the Crown declared itself to be anti-Puritan, and in 1617 James I issued the declaration which was afterwards embodied in the "Book of Sports", and commanded it to be read in churches.

---

[1] *Church History*, iii. 101.
[2] *Queen Elizabeth*, p. 129.
[3] W. H. Frere, *A History of the English Church* 1558–1625, p. 322.
[4] *Commons' Journals*, i. 521, 524–5.

The Puritan point of view upon this question is indicated by Milton, who accused the bishops of plucking men "from their soberest and saddest thoughts", to "gaming, jigging, wassailing, and mixed dancing", as did "the reprobate hireling priest Balaam" draw the Israelites "from the sanctuary of God to the luxurious and ribald feasts of Baal-peor".[1]

[1] *Of Reformation in England*, Book II.

Religious Questions in the Parliaments of James I

JAMES I was a scholar rather than a statesman. Like his predecessors the Tudors, he had been precocious, being able at the age of ten "extempore to read a chapter out of the Bible out of Latin into French and out of French after into English", and exhibiting a "surprising command of general knowledge".[1] This precocity was the forerunner of a genuine interest in things of the mind, but ever since the days of Pope and the *Dunciad* it has been the fashion to call him a pedant.

> O, cried the goddess, for some pedant reign!
> Some gentle James to bless the land again;
> To stick the doctor's chair into the throne,
> Give law to words, or war with words alone,
> Senates and Courts with Greek and Latin rule,
> And turn the Council to a grammar-school!

It is true that James belonged to an age when scholarship was often pedantic; it would, however, be nearer the mark to speak of him as a scholar.

Although there was nothing about James I to inspire devotion, or to strengthen the hold of the monarchy upon the nation, his ability and learning were both real, and they raised him to a level at which he was capable of appreciating large ideas and taking a statesmanlike view.[2] On two important questions, in particular, he was far in advance of his time—on a union with Scotland which should be real as well as personal,[3] and on toleration for the Roman Catholics. It is true that he was inclined to over-value himself: "I am neither a god nor an angel", he thought it necessary to inform his Council, "but a man like any other";[4] but in the monarchical age in which he lived this defect was not as serious as it seems. Where James really failed was in his want of steadiness of purpose;

---

[1] *D.N.B.* xxix. 161.
[2] *Ib.* ii. 336.
[3] See note on "The Union with Scotland", Appendix, p. 268 below.
[4] *D.N.B.* lviii. 328.

in his imperfect understanding of his English Parliaments
due to his Scotch upbringing and early experience; and
above all, in his unfortunate weakness for favourites.
Someone says of him that he suffered from a "partiality
to worthless Scotsmen, if only they were sprightly and
active",[1] and of this the promotion of Robert Carr is the
most important instance. But Carr was not so dangerous
as Buckingham, for he left affairs in the hands of the
trained administrators, while Buckingham, "brilliant,
ambitious, vain-glorious, impulsive, and passionate, with
just capacity enough to go splendidly astray",[2] would be
satisfied with nothing less than an effective personal
control of both policy and administration. A Government
in which the wise Burghley and the wise Burghley's son
came to be replaced by men of this type, was certain,
sooner or later, to find itself in political difficulties.

Another thing to be noticed about James I is that his
political thought was coloured by the doctrine of the
Divine Right of Kings; and it is convenient for us to ask
at this point what Divine Right meant in the mouths of
the Stuart Kings, and in what way it contributed to widen
the breach between them and their Parliaments. But to
understand Divine Right, we must speak first of Prerogative.

It has been the fashion with some writers to regard
prerogative as if it were something illegitimate and
tyrannical; but, strictly speaking, the royal prerogative is
neither more nor less than the legal exercise of the royal
authority. Its province, at different times in English
history, has varied in extent. Before 1377 it had included
powers of legislation and taxation. It has always included
the power of summoning and dissolving Parliament, of
coining money, of creating peers, and of pardoning
criminals. In the Tudor period its scope was greatly
extended, for by the Reformation the control of the
Church fell to it, and it was even strong enough to develop
permanent institutions, for the Star Chamber and High
Commission Court, although they had a basis in statute
were not limited by statute, but were dependent on and

[1] *D.N.B.* xxix. 171.   [2] Goldwin Smith, i. 453.

controlled by the authority of the Crown. But all this does not exhaust the meaning of prerogative. In every state there must be some ultimate power to deal with emergencies and exceptional situations—the power which modern jurists speak of as "sovereignty". This also was prerogative, and in the seventeenth century the emergency power was unquestionably vested in the Crown.

This doctrine of prerogative was essential to the existence of a civilised State; and it came to the Crown by right of inheritance, for in early days, when the State was as yet imperfectly developed and the province of law small, it was to the right "of *kings* to rule and *princes* to decree justice" that the country owed internal security as well as military glory. And it belonged to the Tudor Kings also because there was no other serious claimant, for in their day no statesman ever dreamed of entrusting emergency powers to an assembly. Thus when James I came to the throne, he succeeded to a prerogative which was stronger than it had ever been before. The Commons read the history of the preceding century rightly when they complained in the *Apology* of 1604: "the prerogatives of princes may easily and do daily grow", although they grossly misrepresented the Parliamentary history of the Tudor period in their next sentence: "The privileges of the subject are for the most part at an everlasting stand".[1]

Now this salutary prerogative, when it fell into the hands of literary persons with a taste for broad philosophical conceptions, could easily be transformed from something necessary into something intolerable. It only required a few touches to convert the Tudor doctrine of "royal prerogative" into the Stuart doctrine of "absolute power". Singularly enough, the first thinker and writer to tamper with the idea of prerogative was James I himself. It has been said of him that he lived in an intellectual world of his own.[2] For him "pompous definitions and sweeping generalities" possessed an "irresistible fascination". And so we find him in his *True Law of Free Monarchies*, published anonymously in 1598, claiming an independent

[1] Prothero, p. 289.
[2] *D.N.B.* xxix. 170.

legislative power for the Crown,[1] and in a speech to the judges in 1616 using this language concerning his own position in the State:[2]

That which concerns the mystery of the King's power is not lawful to be disputed; for that is to wade into the weakness of Princes, and to take away the mystical reverence that belongs unto them that sit in the throne of God....As for the absolute prerogative of the Crown, that is no subject for the tongue of a lawyer, nor is lawful to be disputed. It is atheism and blasphemy to dispute what God can do; good Christians content themselves with His Will revealed in His Word: so it is presumption and high contempt in a subject to dispute what a King can do, or say that a King cannot do this or that, but rest with that which is the King's revealed will in his law.

James himself did not press his own premisses to their logical conclusion—the destruction of the English parliamentary system—but there were others who were quite prepared to do so. In 1607 Dr John Cowell, the Professor of Civil Law in the University of Cambridge, published *The Interpreter*, a kind of law dictionary, in which he took occasion to define various political terms. In the article "King" he wrote: "He is above the law by his absolute power",[3] a phrase that at once converted the constitutional doctrine of prerogative, which gave the King powers *outside* the law—to deal with emergencies for which the law made no provision—into a doctrine by the authority of which the King would be enabled to override the law. Under "Parliament" he stated that "to bind the Prince" by laws made in Parliament "were repugnant to the nature

---

[1] "For albeit the King make daily statutes and ordinances, enjoining such pains thereto as he thinks meet, without any advice of Parliament or estates; yet it lies in the power of no Parliament to make any kind of law or statute without his sceptre be to it, for giving it the force of a law" (*Works*, ed. McIlwain, p. 62).

[2] *Works*, p. 333.

[3] "He is above the law by his absolute power..., and though for the better and equal course in making laws he do admit the 3 estates, that is, Lords spiritual, Lords temporal, and the Commons unto council, yet this, in divers learned men's opinions, is not of constraint but of his own benignity, or by reason of his promise made upon oath at the time of his coronation....And though at his coronation he take an oath not to alter the laws of the land, yet this oath notwithstanding, he may alter or suspend any particular law that seemeth hurtful to the public estate."

and constitution of an absolute monarchy". Under "Prerogative" he held it to be incontrovertible that the King of England is an absolute King;[1] and under "Subsidy" he implied that the King might of his absolute power levy taxes independently of Parliament.[2]

It is not surprising that doctrines such as these were repudiated by the House of Commons, and that Dr Cowell's *Interpreter* was ordered to be burned by the common hangman. But although the House could thus destroy the book, it could not destroy the habit of thought which had produced the book. James himself never went as far as Dr Cowell, for he admitted in a message to Parliament that although "it was dangerous to submit the power of a King to definition", yet "withal he did acknowledge that he had no power to make laws of himself, or to exact any subsidies *de jure* without the consent of his three Estates". But Archbishop Laud in the next reign taught that it was sacrilege to dispute the King's judgments; and Dr Sibthorp in 1626 and Dr Manwaring in 1627 worked out that further refinement of the doctrine which was to play so important a part between the Restoration and the Revolution as the "doctrine of non-resistance". "If a Prince", said Sibthorp, "impose an immoderate, yea, an unjust tax, yet the subject...is bound in conscience to submit".[3] And Manwaring went further: "All the significations of a royal pleasure are and ought to be to all loyal subjects in the nature and force of a command.... No subject may, without hazard of his own damnation in rebelling against God, question or disobey the will and pleasure of his sovereign".[4] And the same principles found their way freely into the sermons of the Arminian

---

[1] "I hold it incontrowlable that the King of England is an absolute king."

[2] "Some hold opinion that this subsidy is granted by the subject to the Prince in recompense or consideration that, whereas the Prince of his absolute power might make laws of himself, he doth of favour admit the consent of his subjects therein, that all things in their own confession may be done with the greater indifference."

[3] *Sermon on Apostolic Obedience*, p. 16.

[4] *First Sermon on Religion and Allegiance*, pp. 10, 11.

clergy, who were unable to resist the temptation offered
them by the first two verses of the thirteenth chapter of
the Epistle to the Romans, lying ready to hand as a text:
"Let every soul be in subjection to the higher powers:
for there is no power but of God; and the powers that be
are ordained of God. Therefore he that resisteth the power,
withstandeth the ordinance of God: and they that with-
stand shall receive to themselves judgment". In this body
of teaching, which might so easily be turned against the
whole parliamentary constitution of the country, we have,
as it were, the philosophical cause of the Great Rebellion.
The ultimate question involved cannot be expressed better
than it was expressed a generation later, on the eve of the
Civil War, in the Protestation of the Lords and Commons
of May 26, 1642: "this erroneous maxim being infused
into princes that their kingdoms are their own, and that
they may do with them what they will, as if their
kingdoms were for them, and not they for their
kingdoms".[1]

The Divine Right of Kings is closely connected with
the doctrine of extraordinary prerogative, but it starts
from a different point. In its earlier seventeenth century
form it is little more than a right of inheritance—the
right of James to succeed Elizabeth. As her life drew to
a close, it came to be realised more clearly than before
what possibilities of mischief lay in a disputed succession.
Yet in 1594 a Jesuit was proving in an able book[2] how
uncertain the succession was. James, he said, was a
reigning monarch who was an alien; the whole House of
Suffolk was illegitimate, for Charles Brandon had a wife
alive when he married the sister of Henry VIII—and so,
by a series of plausible disqualifications, he traced the
inheritance to a Roman Catholic heir, pronouncing finally
in favour of the Infanta of Spain. These arguments had
the effect of calling into existence a set of counter-arguments
in defence of James's title.

"The King is barred by being an alien", say the Jesuits;

---

[1] Quoted in Traill, iv. 204.

[2] *A Conference about the next succession to the Crown of England*, by
Robert Parsons, writing under the pseudonym of R. Doleman.

but his hereditary claim overrides this. "He is barred by the Act of Parliament which gave Henry VIII power to devise the Crown by will"; but his right to the throne is derived from a higher source than an Act of Parliament. Heaven has given him, as next in the succession, an indefeasible Divine Right. Thus the doctrine of Divine Right comes into existence as the only answer which would be a valid one to the Roman Catholic controversialists who attacked James I's title to the throne; and it was supported by the practice of touching for the King's evil, which was to the common people a visible sign of the sanctity of the royal House.

Nor was it long before the doctrine of the Divine Right of inheritance was brought to bear upon the doctrine of extraordinary prerogative and absolute power. If the King succeeded by Divine Right, he held his power of God, and therefore to disobey him was to disobey the ordinance of God. Such a logical inference was all the easier because there was a line of earlier thought which made in the same direction. In the Middle Ages the Popes had claimed sovereignty by Divine Right, disobedience to which was a mortal sin; and this claim had called into existence a counter-claim on behalf of the Emperors—that their authority existed by Divine Right, and had come to them, not by grace of the Pope, but by grace of God alone.[1] It was now easy to make the same claim on behalf of monarchy—in France in defence of Henry IV, and in England in defence of James I, for they both obtained their thrones by right of birth alone, and without the sanction of the Papacy.[2]

The development of the principles of Divine Right and absolute power was the special business of the clergy, who were always convinced and earnest supporters of authority. As Fuller puts it: "In all state alterations, be they never so bad, the pulpit will be of the same wood with the Council Board".[3] "Severed from the Roman centre of

---

[1] J. N. Figgis, *The Divine Right of Kings*, p. 65.
[2] *Ib.* p. 173.
[3] Quoted in G. P. Gooch, *Democratic Ideas in the Seventeenth Century.* p. 62.

ecclesiastical authority", as a modern writer remarks,[1] they

"had no support but the throne", to which they "clung with a loyalty often servile, giving to the King...more than a Catholic in the middle ages would have given to the Pope. Jesuitism, with a centre of support above monarchies, had preached tyrannicide: Anglicanism, having no centre of support but the monarchy, preached passive obedience and Divine Right".

The enemies of monarchy and the foes of episcopacy were the same, and "No Bishop, no King"[2] was one of the wisest of James's *obiter dicta*.[3] If men began to enquire into the origin of monarchy, they were very likely to reach a conclusion which derived its authority from the consent of the governed, and this involved the inference that so far from being a divine institution it was not worth maintaining unless it was useful. But the same critics who were attacking monarchy might very well attack the English episcopacy, using the same weapons; and in fact the Roman Catholic writers had already marshalled their forces, while a different kind of criticism was shaping itself on the Puritan side. It was therefore natural that the clergy, led rather by instinct than by logic, should take a lively interest in the problem of monarchy as it was now being stated afresh. Thus from the principle of the Divine Right of inheritance they were led to enquire into the whole nature of political authority. In opposition to the Roman Catholic writers, who derived power from the people, they argued that resistance, even to an unjust King, was sinful, and they expounded the whole course of Old Testament history in accordance with these views.

It is curious that the most important single contribution to the literature of Divine Right in the seventeenth century should have proceeded from a layman. In 1642 Sir Robert Filmer wrote a treatise called *Patriarcha, or the Natural Power of Kings*, which was published posthumously in 1680 as an argument against the Exclusion Bill. It is

---

[1] Goldwin Smith, i. 429.

[2] "His Majesty concluded this point...and closed it up with this short aphorism, No Bishop, no King" (William Barlow, *The Sum of the Conference*, edition of 1625, p. 36).

[3] W. H. Hutton, in Traill, iv. 18.

difficult to condense Filmer's reasoning without carica-
turing it, but it is practically this: Power in its origin was
patriarchal. The earliest government was that of Adam
over his family, succeeded by that of Noah over his sons.
The confusion of tongues was the beginning of *kingly*
power, for in all the nations formed at Babel "God was
careful to preserve the fatherly authority by distributing
the diversity of languages according to the diversity of
families"[1]—as in the Scriptures may be plainly seen. The
history of the world was then expounded on the same lines
and carried by implication down to Charles I who,
although not their "natural parent", exercised over his
people the same absolute patriarchal power which Noah
had exercised over his sons in the ark. But the patriarchs
did not receive their power by vote of their children; they
derived it direct from God. And so with the power of
Kings. It is not derived from the people but is a Divine
Right.

We are too ready in these days to regard the whole
system of argument by which Divine Right was defended
in the seventeenth century as simply absurd, and to think
little of the intelligence of the generation which accepted
it. But like the equally unhistorical theory of the original
contract between King and people, which was the philosophical justification of the Revolution of 1688, Divine
Right played a necessary part in the history of political
thought.[2] It began by providing a form under which the
Reformation could fight the Papal claims to sovereignty;
and it gave an intellectual justification to the claims of the
Stuart House to the throne. It was only after the Revolution, when all danger from the side of Rome was finally
removed, that the theory ceased to be useful and therefore
began to appear absurd. If in the seventeenth century the
danger from Rome had been greater, the doctrine might
have carried everything before it; but under the Stuarts
England was safe enough for a Parliamentary revolt
against it to be possible, and here again the Crown and
Parliament were on opposite sides.

[1] *Patriarcha*, p. 14.
[2] On this see Figgis, chapter x.

The first Parliament of the reign of James met on March 19, 1604, but trouble was already brewing in the sphere of religion. The Puritan party within the Church of England had a strong hold upon the nation; and soon after the new King's accession the leading clergy of this school made an attempt to obtain from James what Elizabeth had always denied them—a further reformation in doctrine and worship. Their views were set out in the Millenary Petition[1]—so called because a thousand clergy were supposed to have signed it. This Petition, which was the more important because it really emanated, as it professed to do, not from "factious men, affecting a popular parity in the Church", nor from "schismatics aiming at the dissolution of the State ecclesiastical", but from "faithful servants of Christ and loyal subjects" of the King—made certain moderate demands which may be assigned to four heads: (1) Modifications in *ceremonial*, the most important of which were: the discontinuance of the use of the sign of the cross in baptism, of confirmation, of the ring in marriage, and of the use of the terms "priest" and "absolution"; the wearing of the surplice "not to be urged"; "church songs and music moderated to better edification"; and the "longsomeness" of the service "abridged". (2) *Preaching*: the abridging of the service was only to make more room for the sermon, and in accordance with the Puritan conception of its importance, the petitioners prayed that none be hereafter admitted to the ministry but "able and sufficient men, and those to preach diligently, and especially upon the Lord's Day". (3) *Livings*: that bishops be not allowed to hold livings *in commendam* with their bishoprics; and that "double-beneficed men" be not allowed. (4) *Church discipline*: that excommunication should not be in the name of lay officials; that "men be not excommunicated for trifles and twelvepenny matters"; that the delays of ecclesiastical courts be restrained; and that "the oath *ex officio*, whereby men are forced to accuse themselves, be more sparingly used". The petitioners also asked for greater strictness in keeping the Sabbath.

[1] Printed in Prothero, pp. 413–16.

Bacon, whose statesmanship enabled him to perceive the danger that lay in a breach between the Crown and the Commons,[1] was in favour of concessions to the Puritans in order to preserve the unity of English religious life. And James himself, always disposed to be tolerant, read the Petition with sympathy, and called a Conference on January 14, 1604, at Hampton Court, at which a deputation of the Puritan clergy met the bishops and argued the question of Church reform with them in the King's own presence. The ecclesiastical supremacy, regarded hitherto as a defence against Puritan innovations, was deeply concerned in the controversy, and the ultimate decision rested with the theologian on the throne, who took the keenest interest in the discussions. One of the disputants at the Conference incautiously used the word "presbytery", and James, rich in experience of Scotland, at once put himself in a passion.

"A Scottish Presbytery", he said, inverting in his wrath the proper order of the comparison, "a Scottish Presbytery...agreeth as well with a monarchy as God and the Devil. Then Jack and Tom and Will and Dick shall meet, and at their pleasures censure me and my Council....Stay, I pray you, for one seven years, before you demand that of me; and if then you find me pursy and fat, and my windpipes stuffed, I will perhaps hearken unto you".[2]

The bishops were delighted, and one of them said that "his Majesty spake by the instinct of the spirit of God".[3] The King himself was no less pleased, and in a letter written the day after the Conference closed, he expressed his satisfaction thus:

We have kept such a revel with the Puritans here these two days as we never heard the like, where I have peppered them...soundly.... They fled me so from argument to argument without ever answering me directly, *ut est eorum mos*, as I was forced at last to say unto them that if any of them had been in a College disputing with their scholars, if any of their disciples had answered them in that sort, they would have fetched him up in place of a reply, and so should the rod have plied upon the poor boy's buttocks.[4]

[1] See *D.N.B.* ii. 336.
[2] William Barlow, *The Sum of the Conference* (edition of 1625), p. 81.
[3] *Ib.* p. 85.
[4] J. O. Halliwell, *Letters of the Kings of England*, ii. 109.

In the end there were a few minor concessions, but the King refused to meet the petitioners on any of the main points; and the only important practical result of the Conference grew out of the famous resolution: "One uniform translation of the Bible to be made, and only to be used in all the churches of England". It is to this that we owe the Authorised Version of 1611. The Conference only shewed the Puritan clergy how little they had to expect from James, who on these matters was proving himself to be almost as inflexible as Elizabeth. In a proclamation of July 16, 1604,[1] he warned them that "what untractable men do not perform upon admonition they must be compelled unto by authority"; and the enforcement of the King's policy by Archbishop Bancroft led to the ejection of some 300 clergy from their livings for refusing to subscribe *ex animo* to the Book of Common Prayer.[2]

Near the beginning of James's first Parliament a secular question arose which was to disturb the cordiality of the relations between the Commons and the Crown. Before the election, James issued a proclamation,[3] in which he described in general terms the persons to be chosen, and required in particular

that an express care be had that there be not chosen any persons bankrupts or outlawed, but men of known good behaviour and sufficient livelihood, and such as are not only taxed to the payment of subsidies and other like charges but also have ordinarily paid and satisfied the same.

Returns of the persons elected were to be made to Chancery, and warning was given in the proclamation that "if any shall be found to be made contrary to this proclamation, the same is to be rejected as unlawful and insufficient, and the city or borough to be fined for the same". The electors for the County of Bucks returned Sir Francis Goodwin, an outlaw, but his election was declared null and void in Chancery, in accordance with the terms of the proclamation, and a second writ was issued, under which Sir John

---

[1] The substance of this is printed in Prothero, pp. 420–1.
[2] See also *D.N.B.* iii. 111.   [3] Printed in Prothero, p. 280.

Fortescue was chosen. As soon as Parliament met, the whole question was raised in the House of Commons, and Goodwin was declared to have been lawfully elected, on the ground that he had been wrongly described as an outlaw at the time of the election, and even if he had been an outlaw, there were precedents for outlaws sitting in the House. The King replied with the statement that the Commons derived all their privileges from him, and they ought not to meddle with the returns; as to whether an outlaw was eligible or not, he advised them to consult the judges. The Commons drew up a memorial defending their action,[1] and asked the Lords to lay it before the King, but they refused to confer with the judges. James, now thoroughly angry, demanded a conference between the judges and a Committee of the House in the presence of the Council, and when the Commons hesitated, he took— not exactly the Elizabethan tone, but the tone which Elizabeth might have taken if she had expressed herself in terms of the Stuart doctrine of prerogative—he "desired and commanded" it "as an absolute King".

Upon this unexpected message there grew some amazement and silence: but at last one[2] stood up and said, "The Prince's command is like a thunderbolt, his command upon our allegiance like the roaring of a lion; to his command there is no contradiction".[3]

The House, not yet grown to its full stature, surrendered to this argument, and the conference took place. The result was a compromise, for at the personal request of the King both elections were annulled and a new writ was issued for the County of Bucks. But on April 11 it was reported to the House that the King had acknowledged that the House of Commons was a court of record, and a proper, though not the exclusive, judge of the returns; and as a matter of fact the right of the House was not again called in question.

Their differences with the King led the Commons to draw up in June, 1604, the first of the striking constitutional documents of the Stuart period—*The Form of Apology*

---

[1] The greater part of this is printed in Prothero, pp. 327–30.
[2] Yelverton.   [3] Prothero, p. 330.

and Satisfaction to be presented to his Majesty.[1] This document, in which the Commons "with great thankfulness to God acknowledge that he hath given us a King of such understanding and wisdom as is rare to find in any prince in the world", is profoundly respectful in form, but in substance it is a lecture to a foreign King on the constitutional customs of the realm which he had come to govern, but which he so imperfectly understood. The King, they say, has been misinformed in three things pertaining to their privileges:

First, that we hold not privileges of right, but of grace only, renewed every parliament by way of donature upon petition, and so to be limited. Secondly, that we are no Court of Record, nor yet a court that can command view of records; but that our proceedings here are only to acts and memorials, and that the attendance with the records is courtesy, not duty. Thirdly and lastly, that the examination of the return of writs for knights and burgesses is without our compass, and due to the chancery.... Against which assertions, most gracious Sovereign, tending directly and apparently to the utter overthrow of the very fundamental privileges of our House, and therein of the rights and liberties of the whole Commons of your realm of England, which they and their ancestors from time immemorable have undoubtedly enjoyed under your Majesty's most noble progenitors, we, the knights, citizens, and burgesses of the House of Commons assembled in parliament, and in the name of the whole Commons of the realm of England, with uniform consent for ourselves and our posterity, do expressly protest, as being derogatory in the highest degree to the true dignity, liberty, and authority of your Majesty's high court of parliament, and consequently to the rights of all your Majesty's said subjects and the whole body of this your kingdom; and desire that this our protestation may be recorded to all posterity.

The Form of Apology was not principally concerned with matters of religion, but the sympathies of the Commons were with the Puritan ministers in their conflict with the King and the bishops, and in significant references to the subject they took occasion to state—in opposition to the ecclesiastical supremacy and to the Tudor position generally—what may be called the parliamentary position in matters of religion.

"For matter of religion", they say, "it will appear, by examination of truth and right that your Majesty should be misinformed if any

---

[1] The greater part of this document is printed in Prothero, pp. 286–93.

man should deliver that the Kings of England have any absolute power in themselves, either to alter religion (which God defend should be in the power of any mortal man whatsoever), or to make any laws concerning the same, otherwise than as in temporal causes, by consent of parliament".

But the language of the *Apology* will serve to disabuse our minds of any idea that the ecclesiastical system which the Commons contemplated allowed of anything of the nature of religious liberty, or "toleration".

Neither desire we so much that any man, in regard of weakness of conscience, may be exempted after parliament from obedience to laws established, as that in this parliament such laws may be enacted as by relinquishment of some few ceremonies of small importance, or by any way better, a perpetual uniformity may be enjoyed and observed.

Thus the Commons proposed to take the religious settlement out of the hands of the King, and to make by statute those concessions to the Puritans which he had refused to make by an exercise of the Supremacy; but after that, conformity was to be enforced, and where James chastised with whips, the Commons were prepared to chastise with scorpions. This explains why there was always a minority in the country ready to support the supremacy of the Crown. Thus the wise lawyer Bacon objected to the transfer of power over religion from the King to Parliament, and regarded the Crown as the proper depositary of existing constitutional authority; and on this particular question it was James who represented the future and stood far in advance of his age.

The religious controversy did not end with the *Apology* of 1604; for a Petition from the Commons in 1610[1] takes up once more the cause of the "deprived and silenced ministers". Nor was it the King's first Parliament only that was of a Puritan complexion. The Parliament of 1614 insisted on going in a body to receive the Communion at St Margaret's, Westminster, avoiding the Abbey for fear of "copes and wafer cakes".[2] The grievance concerning

---

[1] Prothero, pp. 300–1.
[2] "The Communion to be received at the Abbey: not at the Abbey, but at the Parish Church. That in the Abbey they administer not with common bread, contrary [to the] 20th Canon and the Book of Common Prayer"

ceremonies, throughout the reign, poisoned the relations between James and his Parliaments.

If the King's attitude towards the Puritans roused the hostility of his Parliaments against him, still more did his attitude towards the Roman Catholics. Here he was betrayed by his very virtues. At his speech at the opening of his first Parliament in 1604, he said,

My mind was ever so free from persecution or thralling of my subjects in matters of conscience, as I hope that those of that profession within this kingdom have a proof since my coming, that I was so far from increasing their burdens with Rehoboam, as I have, so much as either time, occasion, or law could permit, lightened them.[1]

And this claim was justified, for although Parliament had passed an Act to confirm the penal laws of Elizabeth's reign,[2] the pressure of them in practice was relaxed by lenient administration. At this point, however, the cause of the many was prejudiced by the fanaticism of the few. First the Bye Treason, and then the Main Treason, had set up a reaction in the mind of James which brought to an untimely end the first attempt ever made by any English Government towards toleration for the Catholics. In February, 1605, he announced a change of policy in the Council, "protesting his utter detestation of" the "superstitious religion" of the Papists, and that "he was so far from favouring it, as if he thought his son and heir after him would give any toleration thereunto, he would wish him fairly buried before his eyes".[3] The resolute enforcement of the penal laws which followed, led to Gunpowder Plot, and this in turn to the Acts of 1606,[4] which represent the extreme limit of anti-Catholic legislation. But as soon as the immediate danger was over, James was disposed once more to relax the severity of their administration;

(*Commons' Journals*, April 13, 1614, i. 463). It is from this time that the close connexion between the House of Commons and St Margaret's may be said to date (Gardiner, *History of England* 1603–1642, ii. 237).

[1] Prothero, p. 283.   [2] *Ib.* p. 252.
[3] Henry Ellis, *Original Letters*, 2nd Series, iii. 216.
[4] 3 Jac. I, cc. 4 and 5.

and this involved him in a fresh quarrel with his Parliaments. In 1610 he was urged by the Commons to cause to be executed, "without dread or delay", the "good and provident laws" against the priests, "who are the corrupters of the people in religion and loyalty";[1] and similar demands appear in a petition of 1621.[2]

[1] Prothero, p. 300.   [2] *Ib.* p. 307.

LECTURE III

Constitutional Questions in the Parliaments of James I

IN my last lecture I grouped together certain religious questions arising in the earlier part of the reign of James I, and tried to shew how they contributed to destroy, under the earlier Stuarts, that good understanding between Crown and Parliament which had made the Tudor constitution workable. Something was then said of the alliance between James and the clergy; and the way from the religious to the constitutional questions of his reign lies through a consideration of certain events which brought the King-supported clergy into collision, first with Parliament and afterwards with the courts of common law.

In 1604 an attempt was made by the clergy to recover the legislative power of which the Reformation had deprived them by issuing a code of 141 canons, compiled by the Archbishop, passed in Convocation, and approved by the King. The question was raised again in 1606, when fresh canons were approved by Convocation, but the Commons viewed with peculiar jealousy anything which trenched upon their legislative province, and early in 1607 a bill passed their House "to restrain the execution of canons ecclesiastical not confirmed by Parliament",[1] although the influence of the bishops secured its rejection in the Lords. This is the basis of subsequent legal opinion that ecclesiastical canons are not binding on the laity unless confirmed by Parliament, and it thus inflicted a serious blow upon the authority of Convocation, and prepared the way for "the divorce which later history was to pronounce between the corporate life of the nation and the corporate life of the Church".

Just as the attempt of Convocation to legislate failed in 1604, so the attempt of the ecclesiastical courts to maintain their judicial independence failed in 1605 and subsequent years. The conflict between the ecclesiastical courts and

[1] *Commons' Journals*, i. 326, 348.

the courts of common law was no new thing; it was only that in the reign of James I it came to a head. The temporal courts had been accustomed to enforce their monopoly of temporal jurisdiction by sending out "writs of prohibition" forbidding the spiritual courts to proceed further in particular cases which might come before them until the judges had satisfied themselves that the case raised a spiritual question and did not fall within temporal jurisdiction. Thus the courts of common law claimed an unqualified superiority, for they asserted their right to decide what the limits of ecclesiastical jurisdiction were. The action of the judges was resisted by the Archbishop, who in 1605 presented a formal protest to the King which was named by Coke *Articuli Cleri*, after the articles of grievances presented to Henry III by Archbishop Boniface on behalf of the clergy in 1267. The interest of this protest for our purposes lies in the fact that the arguments used on both sides foreshadow, in relation to this smaller question, the Royalist and Parliamentarian positions in the greater controversy which was soon to arise. It was necessary for the argument of the clergy that they should exalt the authority of the Crown. All jurisdiction, they said, "flowed originally from the King", and it flowed in two separate streams. The King possessed in his own person all spiritual and all temporal jurisdiction; the one he delegated to the bishops and the other to the judges. Thus if there was any dispute as to what was and what was not matter for the spiritual courts, the proper arbiter was the King. The task of answering Bancroft fell upon Coke, who had just been made Chief Justice of the Common Pleas, and he brought to it vast legal learning, an exaggerated respect for technicalities, a strong professional feeling, and lying somewhere behind all this, a genuine sense of the danger of this attempt to extend the royal and ecclesiastical authority.[1] The technicalities of his argument would not interest and do not concern us: the important point is that he took occasion to assert, in language of remarkable breadth and simplicity, the legislative supremacy of Parliament. The right of issuing

[1] *D.N.B.* xi. 231.

prohibitions, he said in effect, is an ancient and established custom; it is therefore part of the law of the realm; as such, the King cannot touch it, for he is not above the Law. "The law of the realm cannot be changed but by Parliament."

In 1607 the question of prohibitions was raised again by Bancroft in rather a different form. He carried his previous argument a step further, and represented to James that as he was the source of all jurisdiction, spiritual as well as temporal, it was within his power to withdraw spiritual causes from the jurisdiction of the bishops and temporal causes from the jurisdiction of the judges, and to hear and determine them himself as the supreme judge of the realm. It must be remembered that in the seventeenth century the judges of the courts of common law were the recognised legal advisers of the Crown, and it was to these experts—as to the Attorney-General or Solicitor-General by modern usage—that all political questions involving points of law would naturally be referred. Bancroft's suggestion attracted James and, in accordance with the practice of the day, he referred it to the judges, only to encounter the uncompromising resistance of Coke.

"Nothing can be more pedantic", says Dicey,[1] "nothing more artificial, nothing more unhistorical, than the reasoning by which Coke induced or compelled James to forego the attempt to withdraw cases from the courts for his Majesty's personal determination. But no achievement of sound argument, no stroke of enlightened statesmanship, ever established a rule more essential to the very existence of the Constitution than the principle enforced by the obstinacy and the fallacies of the great Chief Justice".

Of the argument itself,[2] it will be enough to quote the concluding passage, because we find there also, as it were caught up and entangled in what is mainly technical, the two opposing principles of the Stuart controversy. Coke is himself describing the interview between the King and the judges:

Then the King said that he thought the law was founded upon reason and that he and others had reason as well as the judges. To

---

[1] *The Law of the Constitution*, p. 18.
[2] See Coke, 12*th Report*, pp. 63–5.

which it was answered by me that true it was God had endowed his Majesty with excellent science and great endowments of nature, but his Majesty was not learned in the laws of his realm of England, and causes which concern the life, or inheritance, or goods, or fortunes of his subjects, are not to be decided by natural reason but by the artificial reason and judgment of law, which law is an act which requires long study and experience before that a man can attain to the cognisance of it; and that the law was the golden met-wand and measure to try the causes of the subjects, and which protected his Majesty in safety and peace: with which the King was greatly offended, and said that then he should be under the law, which was treason to affirm, as he said: to which I said that Bracton saith *quod rex non debet esse sub homine, sed sub Deo—et lege.*

In defiance of the unanimous opinion of his judges—for his colleagues followed Coke—James did not again allow himself to be allured by the vision of an English King Solomon sitting upon the lion throne to judge causes in person.

I have been saying a good deal about Chief Justice Coke and the judges; and it is convenient at this point to refer to certain other decisions in the courts of law during the reign of James which raise and settle constitutional questions of the utmost importance, and at the same time exhibit Coke and his colleagues as pursuing a definite policy, the object of which was to establish the Bench as an independent authority arbitrating between the Crown and the subject.

Take (1) the extra-judicial opinion of 1610 by which Coke defined the legal limits of the use of *Proclamations.* The repeal of Henry VIII's statute giving proclamations the force of law[1] had not done away with proclamations; it had only deprived them of statutory authority, leaving them such weight as they possessed at common law. During the early part of the reign of James I proclamations had, as a matter of fact, been issued far more frequently than under Elizabeth, and the matter attracted the attention of Parliament. In their petition of July 7, 1610,[2] the Commons complained that proclamations had been issued creating new offences unknown to the law; imposing penalties for known offences greater than those authorised by law; and requiring accused persons to be brought before

[1] 3 Henr. VIII, c. 8.   [2] Prothero, pp. 302–7.

tribunals which were not legally authorised to try their offence. In his answer to the petition the King undertook to consult the judges, and he submitted to Coke and his colleagues test questions which covered the whole ground in dispute. The reply of the judges[1] is one of the minor charters of English liberty.

That the King by his proclamation cannot create any offence which was not an offence before, for then he may alter the law of the land by his proclamation in a high point, for if he may create an offence where none is, upon that ensues fine and imprisonment...; That the King hath no prerogative but that which the law of the land allows him...; But the King, for prevention of offences, may by proclamation admonish his subjects that they keep the laws and do not offend them, upon punishment to be inflicted by the law...; If the offence be not punishable in the Star Chamber, the prohibition of it by proclamation cannot make it punishable there.

"Here are set forth in a few words", says Sir William Anson,[2] "some salient features of our constitution, and this at a time when a clear statement of the points at issue between Crown and Parliament was greatly needed, and when the first step to be taken towards a settlement of constitutional difficulties was that the nature of those difficulties should be understood".

(2) A case of 1615, known as *Peacham's Case*, is constitutionally important as an instance of an attempt on the part of the Crown to influence the judges privately. Edmond Peacham, the Rector of Hinton St George in Somerset, having written some intemperate accusations against his bishop, was tried for libel in the High Commission Court in 1614 and sentenced to be deprived of his orders.[3] During his imprisonment his house was searched, and notes for a treasonable sermon were discovered which brought him under the eye of the Council. He hinted that the King would one day be smitten with a death as sudden as that which overtook Ananias or Nabal, and James, we are told, was so impressed that he slept every night behind a barricade of featherbeds; so the Council was more anxious than usual to procure a conviction. Yet as the sermon had not been printed or published, it was uncertain whether it could be

---

[1] Coke, *12th Report*, p. 76.
[2] *The Law and Custom of the Constitution* (4th edition), i. 323.
[3] Gardiner, *History of England* 1603–1642, ii. 272.

regarded as an "overt act" proving the traitorous imagination of compassing the King's death. In this difficulty the Council according to custom consulted the judges, and enquired of them whether the course proposed was legally unassailable, and if the evidence was sufficient to procure a conviction. Hallam's suggestion that the judges were being "tampered with"[1] is entirely without foundation. It was not an innovation to consult the judges in such a case; the innovation came when the King, fearing lest in debate among themselves the hostile Coke should carry his colleagues with him, gave instructions that the judges should not, as heretofore, be consulted collectively, but separately and individually. To this course of action Coke offered an uncompromising resistance. His chief idea in politics was the maintenance of the independence and authority of the judicial bench, and he saw quite clearly that the Crown might apply pressure successfully to individuals which would have been resisted by the judges acting collectively. "Such particular and auricular taking of opinions", he told Bacon, "is not according to the custom of this realm",[2] and at first he refused to answer. In the end he surrendered and gave his opinion, but it was hostile to the Crown.

(3) The case of *Commendams*[3] in 1616 raised a similar question. The interest of it lies in Coke's determined but unsuccessful resistance to an attempt on the part of the Crown to delay proceedings in a case where the royal prerogative was concerned. While Bishop Neile held the see of Lichfield, he had received from the King the grant of a living to be held *in commendam*—with his bishopric; but two other persons claimed that the presentation was theirs and not the King's, and in the course of the proceedings before the Exchequer Chamber they questioned the King's right to make presentations *in commendam* at all. At this point the King intervened in defence of his prerogative, and directed Attorney-General Bacon to write to Chief Justice Coke requesting that the judges would delay their

---

[1] *The Constitutional History of England* (edition of 1876), i. 343.
[2] Bacon, *Letters* (ed. Spedding), v. 100.
[3] A full account of the case is given in Gardiner, iii. 13–19.

decision until the King had spoken with them. But in this also, Coke saw impending an attack upon the independence of the judicial office. If the judges were to be called into the King's presence to debate with him the merits of a pending action, would not the courtier displace the judge and the independence of the Bench be gone? At first he carried his colleagues with him, and a joint letter was sent to the King saying that their oath forbade them to delay justice, and Bacon's letter was against law. But the King called the judges into his presence, and a scene took place in which comedy and tragedy were combined in something like equal proportions.[1] After hearing in respectful silence a lecture from James in which he pointed out with some reason that in cases which concerned his prerogative he was virtually a party, and therefore entitled to be heard, all the twelve judges threw themselves simultaneously upon their knees and implored pardon, Coke alone venturing while in that posture to argue with the King. They were then asked one by one "whether if at any time in a case depending before the judges which his Majesty conceived to concern him either in power or profit, and thereupon required to consult with them, and that they should stay proceedings in the meantime—they ought not to stay accordingly?" Eleven of the judges answered in the affirmative; Coke alone replied that "when that case should be, he would do that should be fit for a judge to do". The case of *Commendams* was fatal to Coke, and he was soon afterwards deprived for his "perpetual turbulent carriage" towards the Church, the prerogative, and the courts of law.[2] "The common speech is", wrote Chamberlain to Carleton on November 14, 1616, "that four P's have overthrown and put him down—that is, pride, prohibitions, praemunire, and prerogative".[3] The first dismissal of a judge for reasons that were in the main political, is a landmark in constitutional history.

A word should be said here about the remarkable and lifelong antagonism between Coke and Bacon. As early as

----

[1] See the account of the proceedings printed in Bacon, *Letters*, v. 357–69.
[2] *Ib.* vi. 95.   [3] *D.N.B.* xi. 235.

1593 they had both been candidates for the post of Attorney-General, and Coke had been appointed; while in 1598 Coke had made the wealthy Lady Elizabeth Hatton his second wife, to whom Bacon had been paying assiduous court. And now Coke's disgrace coincided with Bacon's rise; and in the long conflict between King James and his Chief Justice it was Bacon who had had the planning of the King's campaign. But the antagonism between the two men was not accidental or personal only; they represent opposing tendencies in thought and action. Bacon was by far the greater man, for in him the philosopher included both the lawyer and the statesman; and thinking after the manner of a philosopher he advocated a large reform of English law. Coke on the other hand, with a mind fanatically narrow, was possessed with a profound veneration for the law as it stood—for its technicalities as well as its substance—and he was convinced that it was not by change and reform but by the following of precedents that the liberties of England were to be defended. Thus upon one of the great test questions in the politics of the time—the nature and limits of the royal prerogative—Bacon half suggested, half accepted the mystical views of James; while Coke resolutely opposed the inferences which the King drew from the principles which he laid down, and entrenched himself in precedents, and verbal interpretations of statute law. Coke's idea was that the Bench should be independent of the Crown and should act as arbiter of the Constitution to decide all disputed questions. Bacon, on the other hand, referred all disputed questions to the King, saying, with his mind running upon the ivory throne on which King Solomon sat to give judgment, that the judges "should be lions, but yet lions *under* the throne".[1] Thus Coke represented a rigid conservatism—the conservatism of constitutional

---

[1] "And therefore it is proper for you by all means with your wisdom and fortitude to maintain the laws of the realm. Wherein, nevertheless, I would not have you head-strong, but heart-strong; and to weigh and remember with yourself that the twelve Judges of the realm are as the twelve lions under Salomon's throne: they must be lions, but yet lions under the throne: they must shew their stoutness in elevating and bearing up the throne" (Speech to Justice Hutton, *Letters and Life,* ed. J. Spedding, vi. 201).

liberties as they were; Bacon represented reform—but reform carried out by a philosopher-king wielding a sovereignty unlimited and half-divine. We shall come upon the same antagonism again, a generation later, in the persons of Pym and Strafford.

But that State is rare in which the kings are philosophers or the philosophers kings. Bacon was not a king, and James was not really a philosopher. The philosopher had fallen on evil days, for the kings were Stuarts; and what was really needed was the conservation of existing liberties against encroachment, and not the efficient paternal government which Bacon and Strafford dreamed of but which James and Charles could never hope to attain.

In the eyes of his contemporaries Coke's legal fame overtopped his other claims to greatness. In 1631, when his death was expected, Charles I gave orders that his papers should be secured, lest anything against the prerogative should be found among them and published, "for he is held too great an oracle among the people, and they may be misled by anything that carries such an authority as all things do which he either speaks or writes". 'His parts", says Fuller, "were admirable; he had a deep judgment, faithful memory, active fancy; and the jewel of his mind was put into a fair case.... His learned and laborious works on the laws will last to be admired by the judicious posterity whilst Fame has a trumpet left her and any breath to blow therein".[1]

Another fruitful source of controversy between James I and his Parliaments is to be found in the region of finance.

"The only disease and consumption which I can ever apprehend as likeliest to endanger me", wrote James to his Council in 1607, "is this eating canker of want, which being removed, I could think myself as happy in all other respects as any other king or monarch that ever was since the birth of Christ".[2]

At this time his financial position seemed almost hopeless. The expenses connected with colonization in Ireland had been very heavy and, unlike Elizabeth, James had a family to provide for. Thus in 1606 there was an annual deficit

[1] *Worthies* (ed. Nuttall), 1840, ii. 452.
[2] Strype, *Annals of the Reformation* (edition of 1824), iv. 560.

of some £50,000 on a revenue of about £315,000, and the debt of £400,000 left by Elizabeth had risen to £735,000;[1] while a parliamentary grant of £375,000 spread over four years had done little to relieve the situation. Robert Cecil, Earl of Salisbury, the son of the great Lord Burghley, who in 1608 had been appointed Lord Treasurer, suggested that the royal revenue derived from impositions might be increased. Historically, impositions were additional customs, over and above tonnage and poundage, levied at the ports for the purpose of protecting native trade from the competition of alien merchants, and this regulating power had always been regarded as vested in the Crown. Moreover, the decision in Bate's case in 1605[2] had provided a firm legal foundation for Cecil's new policy. "No exportation or importation", said Chief Baron Fleming in the judgment given in the Court of Exchequer, "can be but at the King's ports. They are the gates of the King, and he hath absolute power by them to include or exclude whom he shall please".[3] Thus in 1608 a revised Book of Rates was issued, by which the rates were slightly and cautiously increased so as to bring in a revenue of about £70,000 more than heretofore. But not content with getting the money, James could not resist the temptation to philosophise about the authority by which he obtained it.

"This special power and prerogative", he said, "hath both by men of understanding in all ages, and by the laws of all nations, been yielded and acknowledged to be proper and inherent in the persons of princes, that they may, according to their several occasions, raise to themselves... fit and competent means by levying of customs and impositions".

[1] F. C. Montague, *The Political History of England* 1603–1660, p. 33.

[2] See Prothero, pp. 340–53. From the legal point of view Bate had no case, and even the Parliamentarian Hakewill admitted afterwards that at the time, when he was listening to the judgments which the Exchequer Barons gave in favour of the Crown, he had been perfectly satisfied with their arguments. Hallam's attack upon the impartiality of the judges, "some corrupt with the hope of promotion, many more fearful of removal or awestruck by the frowns of power" (*Const. Hist.* i. 318) is singularly devoid of foundation in respect of a case which preceded by ten years the dismissal of Chief Justice Coke.

[3] *State Trials*, ii. 389.

The discontent of the merchants and the language used by the King brought the new policy under the consideration of Parliament, which was called to the session of 1610 mainly in order to deal with the King's necessities, now represented, in spite of the increase in impositions, by a deficit of about £300,000.[1] The Commons were not disposed to accept the decision in Bate's case, but as the revenue from impositions was not part of the King's parliamentary revenue, James had a case when on May 11 he sent a message through the Speaker "to command the House not to dispute of the King's power and prerogative in imposing upon merchandises exported or imported".[2] Against this prohibition the Commons pleaded their ancient privilege of freedom of speech, which was now beginning to take a new shape. In a petition of May 23[3] they claimed it as

an ancient, general, and undoubted right of Parliament to debate freely all matters which do properly concern the subject and his right or state; which freedom of debate being once foreclosed, the essence of the liberty of Parliament is withal dissolved.

The King did not persist, and a great debate on impositions took place which marks a stage in the progress of constitutional ideas. Hakewill's speech[4] comes very near to being an anticipation of the modern doctrine of supply. Indefinite taxes, like indefinite penalties, are alien to the whole spirit of the law of England.[5] There are only two ways in which impositions can be legally levied: either under statute law or under common law. A survey of the King's functions shews that from these two sources is drawn a revenue certain in amount and sufficient to meet all necessary expenses of government. Each liability is met by a corresponding source of revenue, and the object of this is, to secure certainty for the subject as to the

[1] Gardiner, ii. 65.   [2] Prothero, p. 296 *n.*
[3] Printed, with omissions, in *ib*. pp. 296–8.
[4] *Ib*. pp. 342–51.
[5] "The common law of England, as also all other wise laws in the world, delight in certainty and abandon uncertainty, as the mother of debate and confusion, than which nothing is more odious in law" (*ib*. p. 344).

amount of his burdens. If the moneys thus provided are insufficient, let the King come to Parliament for more. This neat and logical account of the sources of the royal revenue left no room for supreme sovereignty or absolute power; and if Hakewill thus eliminated it by implication, White-locke, in a scarcely less important speech,[1] openly attacked it. The supreme and ultimate power in the State, he says in effect, rests not in the King alone but in Parliament.

It will not be denied that the power of imposing hath so great a trust in it...that it hath ever been ranked among those rights of sovereign power. Then is there no further question to be made but to examine where the sovereign power is in this kingdom, for there is the right of imposition. The sovereign power is agreed to be in the King; but in the King is a twofold power—the one in Parliament, as he is assisted with the consent of the whole State; the other out of Parliament, as he is sole and singular, guided merely by his own will. And if of these two powers in the King, one is greater than the other and can direct and control the other, that is *suprema potestas*, the sovereign power, and the other is *subordinata*. It will then be easily proved that the power of the King in Parliament is greater than his power out of Parliament, and doth rule and control it.

Such arguments as these are remote from the facts and ideas of the Tudor past, but they shew how the future was beginning to shape.

The outcome of the debate of 1610 was an arrangement with the King. James undertook to remit the most burdensome of the impositions, and the Commons agreed to grant him the remainder on condition that it should be declared illegal by statute to levy impositions in the future without consent of Parliament; but before the bargain was completed fresh disputes arose over other matters, and on February 9, 1611, James dissolved his first Parliament, after it had sat, although with long intervals between the sessions, for nearly seven years.[2]

---

[1] Prothero, pp. 351-3.

[2] The "Great Contract" of this session was another proposed arrangement with the King which was never carried into effect. As a form of taxation, the feudal dues payable to the Crown had long been obsolete. As fiefs were no longer spheres of government but only landed estates, there was now no reason why the King should take over the property of a minor under the name of wardship. As the monarchy was no longer itinerant, but had

During the interval between his first and second Parliament James fell into bad hands. In 1612 his wise adviser Cecil died, and his place in the King's confidence was taken—not by the wiser Bacon, who was in favour of calling another Parliament, but by the Scottish upstart Carr, a man without experience and without ideas. Under his influence James postponed Parliament for three years, in the meantime trying to meet his financial necessities by every wasteful and irritating expedient that the ingenuity of his officials could suggest. But the task was an impossible one. The expenditure had come to exceed the revenue by something like £200,000 a year; and the King's debts, which Cecil had succeeded in reducing to £300,000, stood in 1613 at £680,000. Thus in 1614 James was compelled to summon his second Parliament.

Before it met, Bacon urged the King to adopt a programme of conciliation, making such concessions as would serve to bring in supplies without endangering the more important parts of the prerogative. But James preferred the alternative policy of procuring a submissive Parliament by influencing the elections.[1] He entered into communication with influential persons in every district, who "undertook" to secure the election in their own localities of members pledged to supply the King's needs. But the scheme leaked out; it could be represented as a conspiracy against the independence of Parliament; and the candidates of the "undertakers", as they were nicknamed, were everywhere rejected. Of the members elected, we are told, three parts "were such as had never been of any former Parliament, and many of them young men and

---

"a fixed seat and constant access to fair markets", the reason for purveyance had disappeared (Goldwin Smith, i. 446). It was therefore proposed to convert all military tenures into free socage, and to compound for wardship and other feudal dues by granting £200,000 a year to the King as part of his permanent revenue. The dissolution of Parliament in 1611 prevented the bargain from being completed, and military tenures were not abolished until the Restoration.

[1] About this there was, of course, nothing new. Elections had long been influenced by great persons, and of these the Crown was in some ways the most influential. The novelty lies in the systematic character of the King's proceedings.

not of any great estate or qualities".[1] "Many sat there", wrote one of Sir Dudley Carleton's correspondents, "who were more fit to have been among roaring boys than in that assembly". Thus the King's policy only had the effect of replacing the country gentlemen of position by new men, with whom compromises and bargains would be more difficult, and who would be less susceptible to the influence of the Court. Nevertheless, the great names of the next reign were not altogether absent, for Wentworth sat for Yorkshire, Eliot for St Germans in Cornwall, and John Pym for the borough of Calne in Wiltshire.

With this Parliament the King attempted to resume Cecil's policy of financial bargaining; but the Commons replied by raising the question of impositions, and demanding the reinstatement of the clergy who had been deprived of their livings in 1604. James pressed them in vain to proceed to supply; they insisted on dealing first with grievances—and after a two months' session he dissolved them. As this Parliament passed no Act and granted no supplies, it came to be known as the "Addled Parliament".

By various desperate expedients, James succeeded for a time in doing without a Parliament, but his financial difficulties were now drawing to an end, for in 1619 he was fortunate enough to discover a financier in the person of Lionel Cranfield, a merchant of the City of London, who took over the task of financial reform. He was so successful in reducing expenditure and making the most of revenue, that by the time James met his third Parliament in 1621, although he was not solvent, he was in a much better position than in 1614.

The attitude of the Parliament of 1621 was profoundly affected by considerations of foreign policy. In 1618 the Thirty Years' War had broken out on the Continent, and the success which was everywhere attending the arms of the Catholic League had already caused in England a revival of that panic fear for Protestantism which had been so frequent a political phenomenon in the days of Elizabeth. On the recovery of the Palatinate both King and people

[1] Forster, *Sir John Eliot*, i. 13.

were in accord, for James's daughter Elizabeth, like his son Henry who died in 1612, was greatly beloved, and her husband Frederick, Elector Palatine, was a Calvinist. It was for slighting words about the Elector Palatine and his wife that the Parliament of 1621 laid upon Floyd the most ferocious series of punishments ever inflicted in England for a political offence.[1] But James's plan for recovering the Palatinate by diplomatic representations at the Court of Spain, supported by a scheme for a Spanish marriage for his heir, appeared to Parliament dangerous in the highest degree; and under the pressure of this sense of danger the Commons were provoked to the annexation of a new province. They drew up a petition to the King on matters of foreign policy.

The attitude of James towards this innovation was precisely the attitude of Elizabeth.

"Mr Speaker", he wrote, on December 3, 1621,[2] "we have heard by divers reports, to our great grief, that our distance from the Houses of Parliament caused by our indisposition of health" (he was at Newmarket), "hath emboldened some fiery and popular spirits of some of the House of Commons to argue and debate publicly of matters far above their reach and capacity, tending to our high dishonour and breach of prerogative royal. These are therefore to command you to make known in our name unto the House, that none therein shall presume henceforth to meddle with anything concerning our Government or deep matters of State, and namely, not to deal with our dearest son's match with the daughter of Spain".

In Elizabeth's reign such a royal message would have led to the offender's being clapped up in the Tower by order of the House itself. Now, the Commons persisted in their petition, with an added protest against the King's attempt "to abridge us of the ancient liberty of Parliament for

[1] The Commons condemned him "to pay a fine of £1000, to stand in the pillory in three different places for two hours each time, and to be carried from place to place upon a horse without a saddle, with his face towards the horse's tail, and holding the tail in his hand". This sentence was increased in severity by the Lords, who condemned Floyd "to be degraded from the estate of a gentleman; his testimony not to be received; he was to be branded, whipped at the cart's tail, to pay £5000, and to be imprisoned in Newgate for life" (D.N.B. xix. 343).

[2] Prothero, p. 310.

freedom of speech, jurisdiction, and just censure of the House".[1]

The King's rejoinder to this profoundly stirred the Commons. After exhorting them "to remember that we are an old and experienced King, needing no such lessons",[2] he proceeded to take the ground which they could never allow him to occupy without a protest—that their privileges were not, as the House had called them, an "ancient and undoubted right and inheritance",[3] but only "derived from the grace and permission of our ancestors and us".[4] The result was that the whole House concurred in the famous Protestation of December 18, 1621, which was subsequently torn from the Journals by the King's own hand:

That the liberties, franchises, privileges, and jurisdictions of Parliament are the ancient and undoubted birthright and inheritance of the subjects of England; and that the arduous and urgent affairs concerning the King, State, and defence of the realm, and of the Church of England, and the maintenance and making of laws, and redress of mischiefs and grievances which daily happen within this realm, are proper subjects and matter of counsel and debate in Parliament; and that in the handling and proceeding of those businesses every member of the House of Parliament hath, and of right ought to have, freedom of speech to propound, treat, reason, and bring to conclusion the same....[5]

The King might tear the page from the Journals after the dissolution, but he could not alter the fact that the Commons, here the real revolutionaries, had now thrown over all the Tudor limitations which warned them off matters of State or the forbidden ground of the Royal Supremacy in matters of religion, and had brought within the scope of their survey all "arduous and urgent affairs concerning the King, State, and defence of the realm, and of the Church of England".

The supplies granted by the Parliament of 1621 were not much worth considering, but the King's fourth Parliament met in 1624 under different auspices. In October, 1623, Charles and Buckingham had returned

---

[1] Prothero, p. 311.   [2] *Ib.* p. 312.
[3] *Ib.* p. 312.   [4] *Ib.* p. 313.   [5] *Ib.* p. 314.

from Madrid without the Infanta—an event which was celebrated by bonfires in the streets of London and a special anthem in St Paul's: "When I shall come out of Egypt, and the house of Jacob (*Jacobi*) from amongst the barbarous people".¹ When Parliament met it was to hear with joy that the treaties with Spain were dissolved, and to grant large supplies for the impending war. The Commons were ready to pay liberally if they could be sure that the money would really go to a war with Spain, and in order to secure this they took the novel constitutional step of settling upon the war the money they voted, by means of unprecedented clauses introduced into the Subsidy Bill.² The experiment was not at once repeated, but we may regard it as the first tentative step towards the appropriation of supply.

The Parliaments of 1621 and 1624 also revived impeachment, after a long disuse of more than a century and a half; and the impeachment of Mompesson for monopolies and of Bacon for bribery in 1621 was followed in 1624 by that of the financier Cranfield, now Earl of Middlesex. Bacon's case is of special constitutional importance, for James proposed that he should be tried by a commission of the King's selection, consisting of six Lords and twelve members of the House of Commons, but the Lower House resisted the temptation, and supported the claim of the Lords to act as judges of an impeachment.³ The impeachment of a monopolist was without political importance, but in the cases of Bacon and Cranfield a great official was overthrown. And, moreover, "impeachment was an assertion of the responsibility of ministers to Parliament, whereas Tudor autocracy rested on the principle that ministers were responsible to the Sovereign alone".⁴ Thus was refurbished the rusty constitutional weapon which was to be used hereafter with fatal effect against Strafford and Laud.

¹ John Nichols, *The Progresses of King James I*, iv. 928–9.
² On these clauses see note on "The Subsidy Act of 1624", Appendix, p. 269 below.
³ C. H. Firth, *The House of Lords during the Civil War*, p. 38.
⁴ Goldwin Smith, i. 466.

The Earlier Parliaments of Charles I

PROFESSOR GWATKIN was no admirer of James I,[1] but he admits that although he had "a genius for getting into difficulties", he was "not without a certain shrewdness in stopping just short of a catastrophe. If he steered the ship straight for the rocks, he left his son to wreck it".[2] As later events were to shew, Charles I was conscientious; but he was obstinate in adhering to any line of conduct which he had once chosen, and was at the same time an easy victim to the advice of others upon all matters of detail. And for an adviser he had inherited Buckingham, who "seemed as an unhappy exhalation, drawn up from the earth not only to cloud the setting but the rising sun".[3] The key to the history of the first four years of the reign is to be found in the intimate personal friendship between the King and Buckingham, which had the effect of making Charles "a mere cipher to give effect to Buckingham's views".[4]

The King's first Parliament sat from June to August, 1625, and from the beginning there was trouble over religious questions. The Arminian movement had been gathering strength among the educated clergy, and the tide of reaction against Calvinism was flowing fast. The movement was associated with a revival of reverence and devotion in both public and private worship. Lancelot Andrewes, whose saintly life was now drawing to a close, was circulating among his intimate friends a book of private prayers which was to become famous in the next generation; and the nobler side of Arminianism was soon to find other expression in the life of George Herbert at Bemerton and of Nicholas Ferrar and his household at Little Gidding.

[1] "If James...was never drunk, he was seldom quite sober" (H. M. Gwatkin, *Church and State to the Death of Queen Anne*, p. 283).
[2] *Ib.* p. 276.
[3] *Memoirs of Colonel Hutchinson* (ed. C. H. Firth), i. 119. *Cf.* Thomas May, "Like an unhappy vapour exhaled from the earth to so great a height as to cloud not only the rising but the setting sun" (i. 6). [4] *D.N.B.* x. 71.

The weakness of Arminianism on the political side, however, lay in the fact that it was not, and could not be, a movement likely to command either parliamentary or popular support. A position "half-way between two infallibilities"—the infallibility of Geneva and the infallibility of Rome—appealed only to an educated minority; and the artistic and ceremonial revival with which it was associated, created in the popular mind an inevitable confusion between Arminianism and Rome. The Arminian clergy adopted, either from the practices of the early Church or from the customs of the East, what historians writing from the Laudian standpoint describe as "ceremonial enrichments",[1] and these visibly affected public worship. The country gentlemen who filled the benches of the House of Commons were not Puritan in the sense in which Thomas Cartwright and some of his contemporaries had been Puritan: they did not wish to set aside the Prayer Book, or to abolish bishops, or to destroy the organisation of the Church; but they were profoundly suspicious of Roman Catholicism and were disposed to regard Arminianism as a peculiarly subtle and dangerous form of the Romish poison. If we allow for the progress made towards independence, self-consciousness, and a sense of power, by the Parliaments of the reign of James, it is not surprising to find the Parliaments of the reign of Charles seeking to extinguish this unpopular variation in religion, and to vindicate the unity of the national belief, without caring how much they encroached upon the ecclesiastical supremacy of the Crown. And in this conflict there was no room for compromise, for the desire for liberty of conscience was at that time "hopelessly involved with the right to persecute",[2] and neither side contemplated for its opponents either comprehension within or toleration outside the Church.

Arminianism found its only ally in the monarchy, and in 1625 the religious position of the new King was disclosed to his Parliament by the famous case of Dr Montagu. In a pamphlet called *A Gag of the Reformed Gospel*, Matthew

[1] W. H. Frere, p. 386.
[2] G. M. Trevelyan, *England under the Stuarts*, p. 154.

Kellison, the President of the College at Douay, had attacked Calvinism in the Church of England, and to this Montagu had replied, although his point of view was not Calvinist but Arminian, and he began his personalities with his title, *A new Gag for an old Goose*. It was complained to the Commons that Montagu's book was Popish in tendency, and after some consideration the matter was referred to Archbishop Abbot, who addressed to the author the following advice:

Mr Montagu,...you see what disturbance is grown in the Church and the Parliament House by the book by you lately put forth. Be occasion of no scandal or offence; and therefore this is my advice unto you. Go home, review over your book. It may be divers things have slipped you which upon better advice you will reform. If anything be said too much, take it away; if anything be too little, add unto it; if anything be obscure, explain it; but do not wed yourself to your own opinion; and remember we must give account of our ministry unto Christ.[1]

Dr Montagu did "go home", but it was to prepare another book called *Appello Caesarem*, in which he set forth with greater precision the same views as he had expressed in his first book. The result was that the House of Commons summoned him to its Bar, but the King, who had made him a royal chaplain to have an excuse for protecting him, sent a message to say that "the things determined concerning Montagu without his privity did not please him, for that he was his servant and Chaplain in Ordinary, and he had taken the business into his own hands".[2] The immediate result was Montagu's liberation, although not until he had given bail in £2000; but the matter did not end there. The King's second Parliament pursued the subject, and brought to bear upon affairs ecclesiastical the revived constitutional process which had hitherto been limited in its operation to other spheres. On the ground that his books disturbed the peace of the Church, set the King against his subjects, and tended to draw the people to Popery, they prepared to impeach Montagu

[1] Quoted in S. R. Gardiner, *History of England* 1603–1642, v. 354.
[2] John Rushworth, *Historical Collections* (edition of 1682), i. 174.

before the Lords.[1] The impeachment was not proceeded with, as more important matters absorbed the attention of the House; but the King, taking sides, as it were, with the rebels against the unity of national worship and belief, gave Dr Montagu in 1628 the see of Chichester. Thus the alliance between the Crown and the Arminians which had been first formed in the reign of James, was firmly cemented in the reign of his son.

The King's Arminianism appeared more significant than it might otherwise have done, by reason of his marriage with a Roman Catholic princess, that "deadly mischief",[2] Henrietta Maria. When the marriage was under consideration in 1624, Charles had made a solemn declaration to Parliament that "whensoever it should please God to bestow on him any lady that were popish, she should have no further liberty but for her own family, and no advantage to the recusants at home".[3] Yet in defiance of this pledge, the marriage treaty contained a secret article undertaking that the penal laws should not be enforced; and thus, even before his reign began, Charles had exposed himself to the suspicion that in the interests of Popery he had been guilty of a breach of faith. By this he sacrificed the right to have the most favourable construction placed on his religious policy by his Parliaments, and this counted for a great deal in the present state of the English mind.

The religious policy of Charles I may perhaps be regarded as his own, but his foreign policy was undoubtedly Buckingham's, and in this period foreign policy affects constitutional history—especially through finance. Buckingham's policy was war with Spain, but the Parliament of 1625 was opposed to war with Spain by land, and the Commons would only vote two subsidies—about £140,000 —a sum quite inadequate for serious war. There were also difficulties upon another important point of finance. Ever since the reign of Edward IV it had been usual for Parliament to grant the King tonnage and poundage for

---

[1] The articles exhibited against him are printed in Rushworth, i. 209 ff.
[2] Gwatkin, p. 265.
[3] *D.N.B.* x. 70.

life at the beginning of his reign. So entirely had this grant been a matter of form, that the preambles of the Tonnage and Poundage Acts of the Tudor period always describe it as having been enjoyed by the Kings of England "time out of mind".[1] But when the usual grant was proposed in Charles I's first Parliament, the question of the legality of those other impositions, not included in tonnage and poundage, which James I had increased by means of the Book of Rates, was raised afresh; and the Commons decided to limit the grant of tonnage and poundage to one year only, in order to enable them to consider the whole system of indirect taxation. In this revolutionary step they were not supported by the Lords, who refused to pass a bill with limitations, and the grant fell through altogether; although the King, relying on the long prescription of the Crown, continued to levy tonnage and poundage without a parliamentary grant.

Supplies having thus failed them, the King and Buckingham adjourned the Parliament for three weeks, and as the plague was raging in London, it met next at Oxford, where they hoped to find it in a more generous mood. But during the recess, the terms of the French marriage treaty came to light, and it was now certain, what before had only been suspected, that the King had broken his pledge about the penal laws, and that Buckingham had undertaken to lend ships to Richelieu for use against the Huguenots of Rochelle. When Parliament met again at Oxford, the effect of this news was, as Rushworth tells us,[2] "to exasperate the spirit of that great assembly against the Duke of Buckingham". "In the government", said one member, "there hath wanted good advice: counsels and power have been monopolised".[3] Even Sir Robert Cotton, one of the most moderate of the members, in notes for a speech which was never delivered,[4] urged that the King should advise with "wise, religious, and worthy servants", and not be led by "young and simple counsel".[5]

---

[1] E.g. 1 Eliz. c. 20.   [2] i. 176.
[3] Quoted in Gardiner, v. 410.
[4] On this speech see Gardiner, v. 425 n.   [5] Forster, i. 249 n.

As the Commons refused to vote money except to be
spent by ministers in whom they had confidence, and as
the King refused to have his counsellors forced upon him
by Parliament, there was nothing for it but a dissolution:
this took place on August 12, 1625. From this time
onward it is easy to see in Parliament a growing opposition
to Buckingham, the "monopolist of counsels"—the man
whom Sir John Eliot called "the Aeolus of the time",[1]
whose function it was to "let loose discordant winds".
Henceforth, we are told, "against this prodigious greatness, which, like a comet, was suspected to threaten great
disasters to the kingdom, the general intention of" the
House of Commons, "began then to be inflamed".[2]

With a war upon his hands, the King could not go
very long without a Parliament, and the second Parliament
of the reign was summoned to meet in February, 1626.
But in the interval between the two Parliaments had
occurred the disastrous failure of the expedition to Cadiz.
This was due to defects of administration—the incom-
petence of the commander, the want of discipline amongst
the men, and the liability to disease engendered by the
want of a proper equipment—and for these Buckingham
as Lord High Admiral was responsible. The Commons
were as yet scarcely competent to intervene in the higher
politics or to criticise Buckingham's diplomatic dealings
with the powers of Europe, but they were excellent critics
of business deficiencies, and they would certainly have a
word to say about the Cadiz expedition. Moreover, it
came into their proper department, for the forces had
been equipped by means of loans on privy seals, and it
was a parliamentary question how these loans were to be
met.

Before Parliament came together, the King and Buckingham made a tactical blunder which served still further to
prejudice them in the eyes of the Commons. A futile
attempt was made to deprive Parliament of its leaders by
pricking as sheriffs in their respective counties those
members who had been most active against the Crown in
the Parliament of 1625. As Rudyerd put it, "The rank

---

[1] Forster, i. 170.   [2] Ib. i. 217.

weeds of Parliament are rooted up, so that we may expect a plentiful harvest the next".[1] The attempt only recoiled upon its authors.

"So shallow are these rivulets of the Court", wrote Sir John Eliot,[2] "that they think all wisdom like their murmur...but in this they deceive themselves....Great is the variety in a kingdom, both of knowledge and ability....The forms of wisdom are as various as are men's...and in all these some are excellent, yet appear not while their works are done by others, but are content and happy to be shadowed in themselves....Yet against all, when necessity shall require, they are ready and willing to stand forth".

Thus, as the King found to his cost, the resources of ability in Parliament were not exhausted when the old leaders were withdrawn, and their places were at once taken by new men who were even more bitter against the counsellor by whose advice he was guided. Of these new leaders, the greatest was Eliot himself, one of Buckingham's friends and adherents, who less than a year before had written to assure him that he hoped to become "wholly devoted to the contemplation of" his "excellence".[3] But Eliot was no mere courtier; he was a country gentleman of Cornwall, of singular independence of mind and character, and he had himself seen the miserable, half-starved men from the Cadiz expedition crowding the streets of Plymouth the winter before.[4] He jumped rather hastily to the conclusion that Buckingham, who was really nothing worse than incapable and vain, had betrayed England, and was dragging her into war solely in order to pocket the tenths of prize goods which were the perquisite of the Lord High Admiral.[5] This readiness to rush to extremes was a weakness of the oratorical temperament, but it was Eliot's extraordinary genius as an orator that gave him his power in the House of Commons. Nothing like it had ever been heard in Parliament before. He threw himself upon Buckingham much as Burke in a later generation threw himself upon Warren Hastings; and Burke's own weapon lay ready to his hand. The House presented a remon-

---

[1] Gardiner, vi. 34.
[2] John Forster, *Sir John Eliot*, i. 261.
[3] *Ib.* i. 112.
[4] Gardiner, vi. 61.
[5] *D.N.B.* xvii. 188.

strance to the King asserting its right to question the
highest subjects of the Crown,[1] and when he gave them
no satisfaction, the Commons impeached Buckingham
before the Lords, as their predecessors had impeached
Mompesson, Cranfield, and Bacon.

As he was not on good terms with the Commons, it
would have been to the King's interest to cultivate the
good will of the House of Lords; but he had begun the
session with a provocative attack upon the privileges of
the House. The Earl of Arundel had been committed to
the Tower, ostensibly because of his son's clandestine
marriage, which Charles described as "a misdemeanour
which was personal to his Majesty, and had no relation
to affairs in Parliament";[2] but everybody knew that if he
had not opposed Buckingham he would not have been
imprisoned. The Lords voted that no peer ought to be
imprisoned while Parliament was sitting, except for treason,
felony, or breach of the peace, and petitioned the King for
his release; and when they failed to obtain satisfaction,
declined to proceed with any business until Charles gave
way. Another opponent, the Earl of Bristol, had been
confined to his house at Sherborne by James I, and
although he had received a summons to the Parliament of
1625, he had been commanded not to obey it. To the
Parliament of 1626 he had received no summons at all,
and when the Lords insisted that the summons should be
sent, he was accused by the King of high treason; but his
defence contained damaging revelations about Buckingham's proceedings at Madrid.

The real charge against Buckingham was one of
incapacity, but impeachment requires a crime, and he was
therefore accused of neglect in guarding the Narrow Seas
against pirates, with causing the failure at Cadiz by
appointing unfit officers, with engrossing Crown lands,
and with selling offices for money. Speaking on the
impeachment, Eliot compared him to Sejanus. "In
reference to the King", he said, "he must be styled the
canker in his treasure; in reference to the State, the moth

---

[1] *D.N.B.* vi. 84.
[2] C. H. Firth, *The House of Lords during the Civil War*, p. 44.

of all goodness".[1] Supplies were asked for in vain. The
Commons agreed to vote four subsidies, but they insisted
that redress of grievances must precede supply, and
refused to take the final steps until the King abandoned
Buckingham. Charles attempted to stop the impeachment
by sending two of the managers, Sir Dudley Digges and
Sir John Eliot, to the Tower for words used in their
speeches, but the Commons, like the Lords, claimed that
they could not be arrested while Parliament was sitting
except for treason, felony, or breach of the peace, and
refused to proceed with any business until their members
were restored to them. Charles then took the only step
that remained open to him if he was to save his minister,
and dissolved what Whitelocke[2] calls this "great, warm,
and ruffling Parliament" before it had made him any
grant.

The King was now entirely without funds, and it was
necessary for him to take desperate measures. At first he
tried the expedient of calling upon the counties and
boroughs for the voluntary payment of the four subsidies
which Parliament had offered him; "resolving in a common danger to rely upon a common care and affection",[3]
but from all parts of the country the answer came that
money could not be granted "save in a parliamentary way".
Some clever person[4] then suggested to Charles that although
the Statute of Benevolences prevented him from compelling
his subjects to give him money, there was nothing to
prevent him compelling them to lend it. He therefore
took refuge in a "forced loan". In many places, however,
there was general resistance, and this the Privy Council
made an ill-advised attempt to break down. Poor men
were forced to serve under martial law as soldiers, or had
soldiers billeted upon them; while rich men were arrested
upon warrants from the Privy Council, and were lodged

---

[1] Rushworth, i. 355: cf. also Forster, *Sir John Eliot*, i. 329, where the
sentence occurs, "Ambition has no bounds, but like a violent flame breaks
still beyond; snatches at all, assumes more boldness, gives itself more scope"
(p. 328).

[2] *Memorials*, p. 7.   [3] Gardiner, vi. 125 *n.*

[4] Probably Sir Allen Apsley (*ib.* vi. 143).

in prison until they consented to pay. By these means the King raised the large sum of £236,000,[1] but in the course of his operations he found himself confronted by the opposition of the judges, and he went so far as to dismiss Chief Justice Crew for refusing to admit the legality of the loan. This is another landmark upon the Stuart road to ruin. Charles was now striking at the moral authority of the judicial bench, and this was destined to tell heavily against him when he claimed, later on, that he had the courts of law upon his side.

In connexion with the Forced Loan of 1626 there occurred a case of high constitutional importance which did more than anything else to concentrate public attention and public odium upon the King's methods—Darnel's Case, or "The Trial of the Five Knights".[2] Five gentlemen committed to prison by the Privy Council for refusing to contribute to the Forced Loan sued out a writ of *habeas corpus*, to which a return was made that they were imprisoned by special command of the King. The Court of King's Bench held that this return was sufficient in law, and it was not necessary for the cause of the imprisonment to be stated in the return. They therefore refused to bail the prisoners.

Meanwhile Buckingham had embarked on a fresh scheme for making war support war. The declaration of war with France appeared as if it might open up fresh sources of supply in the confiscation of French ships and goods as prize, and at the same time enable him to recover his lost popularity by assisting the Huguenots of Rochelle. But the expedition to the Island of Rhé was even more disastrous than the ill-fated attack upon Cadiz. There was no money to provide reinforcements; and there were no prizes, as the French merchant ships refused to come out of harbour to be captured. Buckingham was obliged to retreat with the loss of half his force. This, as someone said, was "the greatest and shamefullest overthrow since the loss of Normandy".[3] "Since England was England", said

[1] Gardiner, vi. 219.
[2] See also note on "Darnel's Case, 1626", Appendix, p. 270 below.
[3] Gardiner, vi. 202.

another, "it received not so dishonourable a blow".[1] It was thus with his minister discredited beyond all recovery that Charles had to meet his third Parliament—the Parliament of 1628.

Just before Parliament met, it was thought expedient to release seventy-six persons who were in prison for refusing to pay the Forced Loan, and of these twenty-seven, including Wentworth, were returned as members to the new Parliament. These men, who had suffered both in their liberties and their purses, turned at once to attack arbitrary taxation and arbitrary imprisonment, appealing in Parliament to the "fundamental laws" which the King's Bench had refused to take into account. "For mine own part", said Rudyerd, "I shall be very glad to see that good old decrepit law of Magna Charta, which hath been kept so long and lien bedrid, as it were—I shall be glad to see it walk abroad again, with new vigour and lustre, attended and followed with the other six statutes".[2] Eliot protested against the power which the King claimed "to antiquate the laws".[3]

"I can live", said Phelips, "although I pay excises and impositions more than I do; but to have my liberty, which is the soul of my life, taken from me by power, and to have my body pent up in a gaol without remedy by law, and to be so adjudged. O improvident ancestors! O unwise forefathers! to be so curious in providing for the quiet possession of our laws, and the liberties of Parliament, and to neglect our persons and bodies, and to let them lie in prison, and that *durante bene placito*, remediless".[4]

The Commons passed resolutions against arbitrary imprisonment and arbitrary taxation, and then asked the Lords for a conference about "some ancient fundamental liberties of the Kingdom",[5] at which Coke and Selden and two other representatives of the Lower House argued their case against the Attorney-General and other lawyers speaking on behalf of the Crown. This development of the system of conferences to secure an agreement between the two Houses is a constitutional fact of considerable

---

[1] Gardiner, vi. 202.   [2] Rushworth, i. 552.   [3] Forster, ii. 10.
[4] Thomas Fuller, *Ephemeris Parliamentaria*, p. 29.
[5] Firth, *Lords*, p. 48.

importance; and it plays its part again when out of these discussions a practical policy emerged. "Let us have a conference with the Lords", said Coke, "and join in a Petition of Right to the King for our particular grievances".[1]

The Petition of Right[2] dealt first with the two main grievances of arbitrary taxation and arbitrary imprisonment, providing (1) "That no man hereafter be compelled to make or yield any gift, loan, benevolence, tax, or suchlike charge, without common consent by Act of Parliament", and (2) That no free man be detained in prison without cause shewn. But to these were added two other grievances which had been felt bitterly by the humbler classes: the billeting upon them of Buckingham's disorderly levies, and the attempt which had been made, not so much to enforce discipline among the soldiers as to punish ordinary crimes committed by soldiers by the application of martial law instead of the ordinary law of the land. It was therefore further provided, (3) that soldiers and mariners should not be billeted upon inhabitants against their wills, thus recognising the ancient custom, "no man is forced to take soldiers but inns, and they to be paid by them";[3] and (4) that commissions for proceeding by martial law "against soldiers and mariners or other dissolute persons joining with them" be revoked, and no fresh commissions be granted in time to come.

The King fought hard to save his emergency power of imprisoning without shewing cause. The Petition, he said, involved "the very intermitting of that constant rule of government practised for so many ages within this Kingdom", and it would soon "dissolve the foundation and frame of our monarchy".[4] The middle party in the Lords tried to save the situation for him by proposing the addition of a saving clause,

We humbly present this Petition to your Majesty, not only with a care of preserving our liberties but with a due regard to leave

[1] Firth, *Lords*, p. 51.
[2] Gardiner, *Documents*, p. 69. See also the elaborate study by Frances Helen Relf, *The Petition of Right*, published by the University of Minnesota in 1917. This argues that the Petition was never a public statute, but was modelled rather upon the private bill.
[3] Rushworth, i. 504.   [4] Gardiner, vi. 277.

entire that sovereign power wherewith your Majesty is entrusted for the protection, safety, and happiness of your people.[1]

But the Commons would accept no saving clause. "No saving in this kind", said Eliot, "with what subtlety so ever worded, can be other than destructive to our work".[2] "We cannot", said Hakewill, "admit of these words with safety; they are applicable to all the parts of our Petition".[3]

"This is *magnum in parvo*", said Coke. "It is a matter of great weight, and, to speak plainly, will overthrow all our Petition. It trenches to all parts of it; it flies at loans, and at the oath, and at imprisonment, and at billeting of soldiers; this turns all about again. Look into all the petitions of former times: they never petitioned wherein there was a saving of the King's sovereignty. I know that prerogative is part of the law, but 'sovereign power' is no parliamentary word. In my opinion it weakens Magna Charta and all our statutes, for they are absolute, without any saving of 'sovereign power'; and shall we now add to it, we shall weaken the foundation of law, and then the building must needs fall. Take heed what we yield unto: Magna Charta is such a fellow that he will have no 'sovereign'."[4]

The Lords then proposed to substitute in their amendment the word "prerogative" for "sovereign power", but this found little favour, and, after further conferences, they agreed to join with the Commons in the Petition in the form in which they had proposed it.

When the Petition reached him, Charles, relying on the fact that there was no regular form of assent to a public petition of right, gave as his answer, "The King willeth that right be done according to the laws and customs of the realm...", but this appeared to the Commons to be too vague, and they pressed for *Soit droit fait come est desiré*, the regular form of assent to a private bill.[5] Meanwhile they proceeded to prepare a remonstrance against the counsellors who had advised the King. The King interrupted them by a message forbidding them to "lay any scandal or aspersion upon the State, Government, or ministers thereof".[6] But the Elizabethan tone was now

[1] Firth, *Lords*, p. 51.
[2] Gardiner, vi. 285.
[3] *Parliamentary History*, ii. 357.
[4] Rushworth, i. 562.
[5] Relf, pp. 48–58.
[6] Gardiner, vi. 302.

out of date, and in place of submission came fierce revolt. After a pause of passion and despair, during which, we are told, the whole House was in tears, the Commons proceeded to name the Duke of Buckingham as the author and first cause of all their miseries.

"What shall we do?", said the veteran Coke; "Let us palliate no longer. If we do, God will not prosper us. I think the Duke of Buckingham is the cause of all our miseries, and till the King be informed thereof, we shall never go out with honour or sit with honour here. That man is the grievance of grievances. Let us set down the causes of all our disasters, and all will reflect upon him".[1]

Then, says a contemporary observer,[2] "as when one good hound recovers the scent, the rest come in with a full cry, so they pursued it, and everyone came on home, and laid the blame where they thought the fault was".

If the King could have commanded the support of the Upper House, he might have made a stand against the Lower; and this was recognised by Sir Thomas Wentworth.

"We are now fallen", he said, "from a new statute and a new law to a Petition of Right, and unless the Lords co-operate with us, the stamp is out of that which gives a value to the action. If they join with us it is a record to posterity. If we sever from them it is like the grass upon the housetop, that is of no long continuance".[3]

But the Lords remained firm, and on June 7, 1628, the Petition of Right received the royal assent in the usual statutory form of a private bill.[4] The Commons voted the King five subsidies, and prepared a bill to grant him tonnage and poundage for life; but they were not prepared to forgive Buckingham. A remonstrance was prepared and presented, praying for his dismissal from his offices, but Charles replied by a sudden prorogation. During the

---

[1] Rushworth, i. 607.
[2] Thomas Alured, M.P. for Malton: Rushworth, i. 610.
[3] Firth, *Lords*, p. 53.
[4] " It was the practice for public bills to receive the royal assent at the end of the session. The fact that in the case of the Petition of Right it was given in the middle, is another reason for regarding the procedure, although in several ways exceptional, as analogous to that of the private bill" (Relf, pp. 47–8).

recess Buckingham was stabbed at Portsmouth by Felton, and thus one of the principal causes of the misunderstanding between King and Parliament was removed by death.

The political career of Buckingham may perhaps be regarded as the first chapter in the history of ministerial responsibility. The constitutional doctrine prevailing at the beginning of the seventeenth century was that the King chose his own advisers, who were responsible to him alone. It was not essential that they should have seats in Parliament, and although as a matter of fact they were generally in the House of Lords if not in the House of Commons, yet in their capacity of advisers of the Crown they had not—as the modern minister has—special parliamentary functions. It is true that the official channel of communication between the Crown and the Lords was a great minister—the Lord Chancellor—but although the Lord Chancellor discharged important functions both ministerial and parliamentary, he had not necessarily the King's ear and was not often the framer of his policy. And the official channel of communication between the Crown and the Commons was not a great minister at all, but the Speaker—although the duty of explaining and defending the King's policy also fell upon those privy councillors who happened to be members of the House. Thus there was no "ministry", in the modern sense of the word. The policy of the Government was the policy of a power outside the House of Commons, and it was only by a kind of accident that there were ministers there to defend it. On the other hand it was quite a new thing for the Commons to be effectively criticising it.

It has been usual to lay many sins against the Constitution at the door of Charles I, but his view of the constitutional position of Buckingham was the correct view, for it had a century of precedents behind it. He was within his rights when he said to his second Parliament, "I must let you know that I will not allow any of my servants to be questioned amongst you, much less such as are of eminent place, and near unto me".[1] Parliament had no power to punish the King's ministers for carrying out a

[1] Forster, i. 297.

policy which their master approved, except in one way—
a way that almost amounted to an act of violence. It was
arguable that Mompesson and Bacon were criminals, but
Buckingham was not a criminal; he was only an unpopular
and incompetent minister. In his case impeachment is
ceasing to be a judicial proceeding and is becoming a
process of the Constitution. But as a process of the Constitution it was, at the best, but a clumsy piece of machinery.
From its very nature it required a crime, and we find the
action of the Commons so entirely governed by this
necessity that they tried to prove in the course of the
impeachment that Buckingham had poisoned King James.
Buckingham had not poisoned King James, but it was at
any rate constitutionally desirable that he should have
done so.

It has been said that Buckingham was in a sense the
first prime minister, because in his day the real responsibility for the policy of the Government was visibly
concentrated in a single adviser of the Crown; but this is
a premature use of a much later constitutional term. To the
Commons, at any rate, this concentration of power
appeared anything but desirable. One of the charges
against Buckingham in the impeachment of 1626 was his
engrossing of offices,[1] and complaints are frequent of his
"monopoly of counsels" and appropriation of power and
patronage. It is strange that both what the Commons
desired in respect of Buckingham and also what they hated
in him are characteristics of the modern prime minister.
When the Commons were trying to obtain his dismissal
in 1628, an unknown writer made this remarkable comment
upon the politics of his day:

It behoveth without doubt his Majesty to uphold the Duke against
them, who if he be decourted it will be the corner-stone upon
which the demolishing of his monarchy will be builded: for if they

---

[1] "He the said Duke, being young and unexperienced, hath of late
years with exorbitant ambition and for his own profit and advantage
procured and ingrossed into his own hands the said several offices, both
to the danger of the State, the prejudice of that service which should have
been performed in them, and to the great discouragement of others"
(Rushworth, i. 306).

prevail with this, they have hatched a thousand other demands to pull the feathers of royalty. They will appoint him counsellors, servants, alliances, limits of expenses, and account of his revenues.[1]

This is exactly what has been done. Every modern prime minister is a kind of Buckingham—a "monopolist of counsels", with prodigious power and patronage. We may say of him as his enemies said of Buckingham, that he is "a blazing star, in course so exorbitant in the affairs of this commonwealth".[2] But there is a fundamental difference, due to the establishment of ministerial responsibility in its modern sense. At any moment the "blazing star" may be quenched in obscurity—without impeachment and without attainder—by the withdrawal of the confidence of the House of Commons.

[1] In Rushworth, i. 356.   [2] Rushworth, i. 304.

The Eleven Years of Non-Parliamentary Government

WITH Buckingham dead and the royal assent given to the Petition of Right, it might have been expected that the relations between Charles I and his third Parliament would begin to improve. But for this there were too many unsettled questions. The consent of Parliament had not yet been given to the levying of tonnage and poundage, and, moreover, the religious question was once more coming to the front. Dr Montagu's appointment to the Bishopric of Chichester in 1628; pardons granted to divines who had fallen under the displeasure of Parliament; the indulgence shewn to Roman Catholic priests; the revival of Arminian ceremonies in the churches: all contributed to the creation of a dangerous atmosphere. Thus when Parliament met again on January 20, 1629, it was "in an irritable humour". The Commons prepared resolutions on religion declaring that Popery and Arminianism were spreading,[1] and demanding that those who attacked the orthodox doctrine should be punished, their books suppressed, and preferment in the Church given only to "learned, pious, and orthodox men".[2] Merchants were refusing to pay tonnage and poundage, and the seizure of their goods was debated in the House. The King refused to allow his officers to be questioned, and sent an order to the Speaker to adjourn the House.

As soon as prayers were ended the Speaker went into the chair and delivered the King's command for the adjournment of the House till Tuesday sevennight following. The House returned him answer, that it was not the office of the Speaker to deliver any such command

[1] "For an Arminian is the spawn of a Papist...and if you mark it well, you shall see an Arminian reaching out his hand to a Papist, a Papist to a Jesuit, a Jesuit gives one hand to the Pope and the other to the King of Spain" (Speech of Mr Rouse concerning Religion: Wallace Notestein, *Commons' Debates for* 1629, p. 13).

[2] Gardiner, *Documents*, pp. 77–82.

unto them, but for the adjournment of the House it did properly belong unto themselves; and after they had settled some things they thought convenient to be spoken of, they would satisfy the King.[1]

Thereupon Speaker Finch, true to the traditional character of his office as the King's agent and not the Commons' servant, attempted to leave the chair, but two strong young members, Holles and Valentine, held him down, while other members denounced him with so much energy that he shed "abundance of tears".

Yet notwithstanding the Speaker's extremity of weeping and supplicatory oration quaintly eloquent, Sir Peter Heyman (a gentleman of his own country), bitterly inveighed against him, and told him he was sorry he was a Kentish man, and that he was a disgrace to his country, and a blot to a noble family.[2]

The sobbing Speaker still declined to act in defiance of the King's order, and when Eliot produced a protestation, he refused to put it to the vote, and its author threw it in the fire. The King sent for the Serjeant to bring away the mace, but the House despatched him without it. Soon after, Black Rod was heard knocking at the door with a message from the King, who had sent for his guard to break into the House.[3] Thereupon Holles, delivering from memory the terms of the protestation which Eliot had destroyed, put it to the vote in the form of three resolutions, which were carried by acclamation:

(1) Whosoever shall bring in innovation of religion, or by favour or countenance seem to extend or introduce Popery or Arminianism or other opinion disagreeing from the true and orthodox Church, shall be reputed a capital enemy to this kingdom and commonwealth. (2) Whosoever shall counsel or advise the taking and levying of the subsidies of tonnage and poundage, not being granted by Parliament, or shall be an actor or instrument therein, shall be likewise reputed an innovator in the government and a capital enemy to the kingdom and commonwealth. (3) If any merchant or person whatsoever shall voluntarily yield or pay the said subsidies of tonnage and poundage, not being granted by Parliament, he shall likewise be reputed a betrayer of the liberties of England, and an enemy to the same.[4]

[1] Wallace Notestein, *Commons' Debates for* 1629, p. 103.
[2] *Ib.* pp. 104–5.   [3] *Ib.* p. 106.
[4] Gardiner, *Documents*, p. 82.

On March 10[1] an abrupt dissolution followed, "the most gloomy, sad, miserable day for England that happened in five hundred years last past".[2] But for the present the victory was with the King, for it was only in Parliament that he could be fought. Sir Benjamin Rudyerd, the reasonable Parliamentarian, who had said in the House on April 28, 1628, that "moderation is the virtue of virtues and the wisdom of wisdoms", recognises this.

"Let it be our masterpiece", he said, "so to carry our business as we may keep Parliaments on foot; for as long as they are frequent there will be no irregular power; which, though it cannot be broken at once, yet in short time it will fade and moulder away. There can be no total and final loss of liberty but by loss of Parliaments; as long as they last, what we cannot get at one time we may have at another".[3]

The King took quite a different view of Parliaments. "They are of the nature of cats", he wrote to Wentworth later,[4] "they ever grow cursed with age". He now inflicted on the nation the "loss of Parliaments" for a period of eleven years.[5] This opened the way for him to take vengeance on his enemies, and his prosecution of Eliot and other leaders of the Commons was to illustrate the truth of Wentworth's own observation, that it was ill contending with the King outside of Parliament.[6]

Associated with what is sometimes called the "Eleven Years' Tyranny" of 1629 to 1640, are the famous names of Wentworth and Laud.

[1] The Houses had adjourned on March 2, 1629.

[2] Firth, *Lords*, p. 54.

[3] Thomas Fuller, *Ephemeris Parliamentaria*, p. 155.

[4] January 22, 1635; Masson, *Life of John Milton*, i. 644: *cf.* Cottington to Wentworth, October 29, 1633: "The King hath so rattled my Lord Keeper that he is now the most pliable man in England, and all thoughts of Parliaments are quite out of his pate" (Masson, i. 620).

[5] The loss of Parliaments meant a great diminution in the opportunities of appeal to public opinion outside Parliament. In the Introduction to his *Commons' Debates of* 1629, Professor Wallace Notestein has shewn how this was already taking shape and being moulded by the speeches of members circulating in the country, in violation of the old rule of the secrecy of parliamentary proceedings, which was now breaking down.

[6] "My rule, which I will never transgress, is never to contend with the prerogative out of Parliament, nor yet to contest with a king but when I am constrained thereto or else make shipwreck of my peace of conscience" (quoted in Gardiner, vi. 128).

In the earlier years of the reign Wentworth had appeared among the opponents of Buckingham. It has been said with truth that the kind of government he desired was a reforming government that should also be a strong government; and his main principle of policy was the avoidance of external complications with a view to internal reforms. This threw him into opposition to Buckingham's policy of foreign adventure, and engendered in his proud, unyielding spirit a personal hostility to Buckingham himself. He opposed the Forced Loan in 1627, suffering imprisonment for refusing to pay, and contributed some weighty phrases to the support in debate of the Petition of Right; but he did not follow his colleagues in the line they took over tonnage and poundage. Although he believed in a strong State, seeking in all ways the public good, he differed from them in thinking that initiative belonged to the Crown and not to the Commons. "The authority of a king is the keystone which closeth up the arch of order and government."[1] Moreover, on religious matters Wentworth was separated from the majority in the Lower House by a widening gulf, for he was not a Puritan, and as time went on, this fact drew him nearer to the King, from whom alone, in his view, effective opposition to Puritanism could come. Thus in 1628—not long before the death of Buckingham—he accepted a peerage and the Presidency of the Council of the North. In this capacity he displayed a remarkable genius for government, and a high sense of the importance of efficiency in administration. In 1633, without resigning this office, he added to it the heavier burden of the government of Ireland.

Wentworth was bred at St John's College, Cambridge, and Laud was an *alumnus* of St John's College, Oxford; but while Wentworth had nothing in common with St John the Evangelist, there are to be found in Laud some traces of St John the Baptist's spirit. Burnet calls him "a zealous man", and Whitelocke's father, who knew him well, says that he was "too full of fire".[2] In questions of morals, in particular, he had much in common

---

[1] Gardiner, vii. 25.   [2] Morley, *Cromwell*, p. 36.

with the Puritans, for he called on all men everywhere to repent. Part of the reputation for harshness acquired by the Court of High Commission was due to Laud's conscientious and courageous attempts to enforce the discipline of the Church upon individuals. He intended, says Clarendon,[1] "...that it should be applied to the greatest and most splendid transgressors, as well as to the punishment of smaller offences and meaner offenders". But men of sincerity and courage are not always wise, and Laud failed in his handling of questions of doctrine and worship. In this sphere he carried on the tradition of Cranmer and Hooker, accepting as the basis of belief, not the Bible alone, but the Bible as interpreted by the practice of the Early Church. The Puritans with whom he had to deal followed Calvin, who had attempted to extract a definite system of doctrine from the Bible alone, and this view was in the ascendant, both among the clergy and in the Parliament House. It is this that leads a hostile contemporary[2] to say of him that he was "a man not altogether so bad, as unfit for the state of England".

From the correspondence between Wentworth and Laud comes the familiar name which has been given to the system of government with which they are associated; for they often use the word "thorough" to describe the spirit of their policy. In the seventeenth century the words "thorough" and "through" were interchangeable.

"Thorough," says Gardiner, "is the resolute determination of going through with it,...of disregarding and overriding the interested delays and evasions of those who made the public service an excuse for enriching themselves at the public expense, or the dry, technical arguments of the lawyers which would hinder the accomplishment of schemes for the public good".[3]

"For the State indeed, my Lord", writes Laud on September 9, 1633,[4] "I am for Thorough; but I see that both thick and thin stays somebody where I conceive it should not, and it is impossible for me to go thorough alone".

"I am confident", wrote Wentworth in the following December,[5]

---

[1] *History of the Rebellion* (ed. W. D. Macray, 1888), i. 125.
[2] Thomas May, *History of the Long Parliament* (edition of 1647), i. 28.   [3] viii. 67.
[4] Strafford, *Letters and Dispatches*, i. 111.   [5] *Ib.* i. 173.

"that the King being pleased to set himself in the business, is able by his wisdom and ministers to carry any just and honourable action thorough all imaginary opposition, for real there can be none; that to start aside for such panick fears, phantastick apparitions, as a Pym or an Eliot shall set up, were the meanest folly in the whole world; that the debts of the Crown taken off, you may govern as you please".

This is Wentworth's idea of a strong government which should also be beneficent coming to the front again; but statesmen inspired by this spirit, and chafing under the restraints imposed by the delays and technicalities of the lawyers, would be likely to draw largely on absolute power in order to reach their goal of a strong, orderly, and reforming government. "Thorough" might be good government, but it would certainly be prerogative government, and it might come perilously near to arbitrary government. Yet this much, at any rate, can be said in defence of its authors, that in days when politicians were bent only on self-aggrandisement, they set before themselves great public objects and pursued them with energy and devotion. The King's measures were planned by them, and the whole frame of government was permeated by their spirit. As a contemporary writer remarks, "They struck a league like sun and moon to govern day and night, Religion and State".[1]

The system of the "Eleven Years' Tyranny" has two aspects, financial and ecclesiastical. While Laud alienated all those who cared for Calvinism, the measures of Finch, Noy, and the Lord Treasurer Weston threw into opposition to the Government all those who feared and hated arbitrary taxation.

The financial measures of the Crown gave all classes a common grievance. (1) Tonnage and poundage continued to be levied upon the royal authority alone, and those who refused to pay were imprisoned either by the Council or by the Star Chamber. Nevertheless there was general resistance. "The obstinacy lies not only in the merchant's breast, but moves in every small vein through the kingdom."[2] One Richard Chambers not only refused to pay, but in the very presence of the Council "did then and

---

[1] Leighton, *Epitome*, p. 68.   [2] Gardiner, vii. 84.

there in an insolent manner...utter these undutiful, seditious, and false words—'That the merchants are in no part of the world so screwed and wrung as in England; that in Turkey they have more encouragement'".[1] The Star Chamber held "that the words spoken were a comparing of his Majesty's government with the government of the Turks, intending thereby to make the people believe that his Majesty's happy government may be termed Turkish tyranny". They therefore fined Chambers £2000, and committed him to the Fleet prison under order to make public submission "both at the Council Board, in Court of Star Chamber, and at the Royal Exchange"—the centre of London's mercantile life. Chambers endorsed the submission prepared for him to sign with a number of texts, referring to "them that devise iniquity" and seek "the oppression of the poor and violent perverting of judgment and justice", and ended by refusing to sign upon any terms. He remained in prison for six years.

Tonnage and poundage was nothing new, but the King's financial advisers devised other expedients of a novel kind which constituted, not so much a breach of the law as a systematic attempt to take advantage of the law's technicalities. Thus (2) in 1630 the law relating to compulsory knighthood, which required the owners of an estate worth £40 a year to receive knighthood, was revived and enforced, those who had neglected it being required to compound by heavy payments. By this expedient, "which", says Clarendon,[2] "though it had a foundation in right, yet in the circumstances of proceeding was very grievous", the King "received a vast sum of money from all persons of quality or indeed of any reasonable condition throughout the kingdom".

(3) In 1634 and subsequent years large sums were raised by the revival of the Forest Laws, and especially of claims to land which had been disafforested. Under cover of the rule of law that no prescription could bar the title of the Crown, an attempt was made to revive the King's rights over all land that had once been forest. It

<hr />

[1] *State Trials*, iii. 374.   [2] i. 85.

was said that the Earl of Southampton would lose £2000
a year by the extension of the New Forest; and the Earl
of Salisbury was fined £20,000 and the Earl of West-
morland £19,000 for alleged encroachments on Rocking-
ham Forest.[1] Proclamations against the extension of
London were also enforced, and the Earl of Bedford had
to pay a composition to avoid a suit in the Star Chamber
for his buildings in Covent Garden. Peers were summoned
for breach of the proclamations against living in London
instead of upon their estates in the country; and the laws
against the conversion of arable to pasture were enforced
under the name of "depopulation". "Everyone who
could be fined for anything was fined. A landowner was
fined for depopulation if he had pulled down a cottage."[2]
This burden, says Clarendon, speaking of the Forest
Laws, "lighted most upon people of quality and honour,
who thought themselves above ordinary oppressions, and
therefore like to remember it with more sharpness".[3]

If the King struck at the merchants by tonnage and
poundage, at the gentry by compositions for knighthood,
and at the peerage by the Forest Laws, he attacked the
ordinary consumer through (4) monopolies. The Act of
1624[4] against them had contained a special exception in
favour of the City of London or any other corporate town,
and also "any corporations, companies, or fellowships of
any art, trade, occupation, or mystery, or to any companies
or societies of merchants within this realm erected for the
maintenance, enlargement, or ordering of any trade of
merchandise". This clause was probably intended to save
the rights of the great London Companies, but the
ingenious Weston conceived the idea of using it to legalise
a new kind of monopoly. In 1632 he formed a corporation
of soap boilers, which undertook to pay the King a royalty
of £4 a ton on all the soap manufactured by it. The
Company was allowed to test and condemn the soap
produced by manufacturers who did not join it and thus,
under cover of maintaining the quality of England's soap,
the King was able to tax the whole soap manufacture in a

---

[1] Firth, *Lords*, p. 57.   [2] Goldwin Smith, i. 492.
[3] i. 85.   [4] 21 Jac. I, c. 3.

perfectly legal way. It was said that the new Company was largely controlled by Roman Catholics, and there was a general outcry against "Popish soap",[1] the use of which, as someone remarked, would certainly corrupt the body and might not improbably also corrupt the soul.[2] The principle on which the Soap Company was founded was capable of indefinite extension, and monopolies were granted to chartered companies on every side—so that Colepeper was able to say of the monopolists, in a speech delivered in the Long Parliament,

These, like the frogs of Egypt, have got possession of our dwellings, and we have scarce a room free from them: they sup in our cup, they dip in our dish, they sit by our fire; we find them in the dye-vat, wash-bowl, and powdering-tub; they share with the butler in his box, they have marked and sealed us from head to foot.[3]

The most famous of all the devices was (5) that of ship-money. It had long been the practice in time of war to issue writs requiring the seaports to provide ships for the King's use. As late as 1619, for the war against Algiers, James I had raised nearly £50,000 from the great seaport towns in lieu of ships, the greater part of it being paid by the Port of London.[4] Thus ship-money was nothing new: the innovation lay in the methods and frequency of the charge, and the wide range of its application.

The first writ, issued in 1634,[5] kept fairly well within the precedents. It applied only to the seaport towns; it asked for ships and not for money, although landholders not having a ship were to be assessed for the cost of equipment; and it alleged the necessity of getting together a naval force for punishing the depredations of pirates.[6]

---

[1] Gardiner, viii. 74.　　　　　　　[2] Trevelyan, *Stuarts*, p. 161.

[3] *Parliamentary History*, ii. 656.

[4] Gardiner, iii. 288.

[5] Gardiner, *Documents*, p. 105.

[6] "Because we are given to understand that certain thieves, pirates, and robbers of the sea, as well Turks, enemies of the Christian name, as others, being gathered together, wickedly taking by force and spoiling the ships and goods and merchandises, not only of our subjects but also the subjects of our friends in the sea, which hath been accustomed anciently to be defended by the English nation, and the same at their pleasure have carried away, delivering the men in the same into miserable captivity" (*ib.*).

But the writ of 1634 was only intended to pave the way for the bolder experiment of 1635. The writ of 1635 extended ship writs to the inland counties as well as the maritime counties and seaport towns; and although in the writ itself the ancient form of asking for a ship was carefully maintained, instructions were sent to the sheriff with the writ, requiring him to levy on his county—instead of a ship—a specified sum of money. Finally in 1636 a third writ of ship-money was issued. This followed the second in form, but it is specially important for two reasons: (1) because it was no longer possible to pretend that the writs were being issued to meet a war-emergency. It now became obvious, even to the most charitable critics of the King's policy, that ship-money was fast becoming a permanent tax—or, as Clarendon puts it, "for a spring and magazine that should have no bottom, and for an everlasting supply of all occasions".[1] (2) Because the legality of the writs was now generally questioned, and it came to be tested in the Law Courts in 1637 in John Hampden's famous case.[2]

Of the twelve judges who heard the case, five gave judgment in favour of Hampden and seven in favour of the Crown. This decision marks the beginning of the collapse of the system of arbitrary government which had been established after the dissolution of Charles I's third Parliament in 1629. From the purely financial point of view, the "Eleven Years' Tyranny" was proving a success. In 1635, for the first time in the history of his reign, the King's revenue nearly met his expenditure; and by 1638 the finances were in a more flourishing state than they had been at any time since the Stuarts had succeeded to the throne. The money raised by taxation was not more than the financial needs of the State required, and it was all honestly applied to the purposes for which it was raised. It is now known that ship-money was really used to build a fleet of great ships which was to serve as the nucleus of the naval power of the Commonwealth in the First Dutch War. The grievance was that the money was raised without

[1] i. 85.
[2] See also note on "Hampden's Case (1637)", Appendix, p. 273 below.

Parliament, and upon a system which could be applied year after year to make the Crown permanently independent of Parliament. And the decision of the judges by so narrow a majority carried no conviction on the legal questions raised. The respect for law and reverence for Parliament which the Tudors had "so thoroughly drilled into the English people"[1] were now turned against the Stuarts. The claim made by Charles I in Hampden's case to override the law on a fancied emergency, gave him the reputation of a breaker of the law.

And if there should be resistance, the King had at his disposal no adequate means of breaking it down, for he had no local bureaucracy of paid officials to enforce the new taxation. The only officials in the English system of local government were the sheriffs and the justices of the peace, and it was through them that everything had to be done. But the sheriffs and the justices of the peace were appointed from that very class of country gentry with whom the King had quarrelled in Parliament. Again and again he dismissed his county officials for opposing him, but he was obliged to replace them from the same social class. The government of his shire was the hereditary right of the country gentleman, and it would have been a desperate and revolutionary measure indeed, if the King had appointed tradesmen or yeomen to the vacant posts. The justices of the peace were not dependent on the royal favour and they did not support themselves upon official salaries. Thus they looked, not to the Court but to the county, and their first deference was to the opinion of their own class. The system of the "Eleven Years' Tyranny" was destined to be "wrecked on the rock of the county organisation".

The decision in Hampden's case also caused a general loss of confidence in the courts of law. As Clarendon points out,[2] ship-money had been declared lawful "upon such grounds and reasons as every stander-by was able to swear was not law". The reasoning of the judges "left no man anything which he might call his own", and all men "found their own interest, by the unnecessary logic of that

[1] J. Macy, *The English Constitution*, p. 272.   [2] i. 87, 90.

argument, no less concluded than Mr Hampden's". It is not necessary to go so far as Hallam, and to say, "Those who had trusted in the faith of the judges...looked with indignation on so prostituted a crew";[1] but the parliamentary leaders now perceived that the majority of the judges was likely to be always against them, even if the minority was not dismissed. This knowledge made Parliament a necessity for them. They had nothing to hope for from the judges, who were leaving them to work out their own salvation independently of the courts of law; and the only other place where salvation was to be found was in Parliament.

Another result of the decision was an increase in the reluctance with which ship-money was paid. "The King's moneys", wrote Laud to Wentworth on May 14, 1638,[2] "come in a great deal more slowly than they did in former years, and that to a very considerable sum". But the case brought Hampden himself decisively to the front.

"He was rather of reputation in his own country", says Clarendon,[3] "than of public discourse or fame in the kingdom before the business of ship-money; but then he grew the argument of all tongues, every man enquiring who and what he was, that durst at his own charge support the liberty and property of the kingdom and rescue his country from being made a prey to the Court. His carriage throughout that agitation was with that rare temper and modesty, that they who watched him narrowly, to find some advantage against his person to make him less resolute in his cause, were compelled to give him a just testimony. And the judgment that was given against him infinitely more advanced him than the service for which it was given".

While the King's financial policy was uniting all classes against him, the ecclesiastical policy of Laud was making trouble in a different direction.

One of the special characteristics of Laud as a thinker was his belief in the power of outward ceremonial upon the minds and consciences of men. He called it "the

---

[1] *Constitutional History*, ii. 23.
[2] Strafford, *Letters*, ii. 171.
[3] iii. 62.

beauty of holiness",[1] and repudiated the Puritan view that
ceremonial tended to superstition. "But this is the
misery", he complained, "'tis superstition now-a-days for
any man to come with more reverence into a church than
a tinker and his bitch come into an ale-house".[2]

"Of all diseases", he writes in another place,[3] "I have ever hated
a palsy in religion, well knowing that too often a dead palsy ends
that disease in the fearful forgetfulness of God and His judgments.
Ever since I came in place, I laboured nothing more than that the
external worship of God, too much slighted in most parts of this
kingdom, might be preserved, and that with as much decency and
uniformity as might be; being still of opinion that unity cannot long
continue in the Church where uniformity is shut out at the church
door. And I evidently saw that the public neglect of God's service
in the outward face of it, and the nasty lying of many places dedicated
to that service, had almost cast a damp upon the true and inward
worship of God, which, while we live in the body, needs external
helps, and all little enough to keep it in any vigour".

If a churchman of the seventeenth century, and an
Archbishop, thus believed sincerely in the necessity for
outward ceremonial to inward spiritual life, it went without
saying that he would use the power of the law to enforce
it. Arminians and Puritans alike were unable to conceive
of a national religious system in which there should be
room for more than one Church. It is true that the Puritans
cared little for ceremonies. Their position on these matters
was to receive expression later on in Milton's splendid prose,
when he described the ancient ceremonial of the Church as

"deformed and fantastic dresses,...fetched from Aaron's old
wardrobe or the flamens' vestry", by means of which "the soul,...
given up justly to fleshly delights, bated her wing apace downward,
and finding the ease she had from her visible and sensuous colleague,
the body, in performance of religious duties, her pinions now broken
and flagging, shifted off from herself the labour of high-soaring any
more, forgot her heavenly flight, and left the dull and droiling carcase
to plod on in the old road and drudging trade of outward conformity".[4]

[1] "But all that I laboured for in this particular was, that the external
worship of God in this Church might be kept up in uniformity and decency
and some beauty of holiness. And this the rather, because I found that with
the contempt of the outward worship of God the inward fell away apace"
(*Works*, iii. 407).   [2] *Ib.* vi. 57.   [3] *Ib.* iv. 60.
[4] "Of Reformation in England" (1641) in *Prose Works*, ii. 365.

But if the Puritans cared little about uniformity of worship, they cared greatly about unity of belief. Thus where Laud used the power he had, and employed the King's ecclesiastical supremacy to enforce uniform ceremonial, the Puritans in Parliament sought to obtain power which they did not yet possess, to compel by means of statutes a doctrinal unity.

Laud's first steps towards the enforcement of uniformity were taken in the University of Oxford and in his own diocese of Canterbury; but in the years 1634 to 1637 he widened his range of action and conducted a visitation as metropolitan over the whole of the Southern Province, arranging for a similar and simultaneous visitation of the Province of York by the northern Archbishop. Clergymen who refused to conform to the Prayer Book, or who resisted the removal of the Communion Table to the east end of the church, or who objected to bow at the name of Jesus when it occurred in the service, were questioned and remonstrated with; and if they remained obstinate, were summoned before the High Commission Court to answer for their disobedience. The aid of the court was also invoked to maintain a censorship of theological writings, and to prevent the importation of Calvinist literature from abroad.[1]

One of the results of the Laudian policy was the promotion of emigration to America. Anglican divines complained that men "flew out of England as out of Babylon", and in 1634 one of Laud's agents, reporting that 600 pilgrims were about to start from Suffolk, remarked that "even bankrupts" were "able to earn a reputation for holiness by flight".[2] Mr Trevelyan goes so far as to call Laud "the founder of the Anglo-Saxon supremacy in the New World".[3]

Another result was to lead men, most unjustly, to regard the Archbishop as a Roman Catholic in disguise. We know from his own diary that in 1633 he was twice sounded

[1] *Cases in the Star Chamber and High Commission Court*, ed. S. R. Gardiner (Camden Society, 1886), p. 274.

[2] Gooch, p. 92.

[3] *England under the Stuarts*, p. 173.

with regard to his willingness to accept a Cardinal's hat, "but my answer was", he writes, "that somewhat dwelt within me which would not suffer that till Rome were other than it is".[1] And after all, he was the friend and patron of the latitudinarian Chillingworth, who said of the Civil War, with rare impartiality, that "all the scribes and Pharisees were on one side and all the publicans and sinners on the other".

[1] *Works*, iii. 219.

The Long Parliament and Reform

"HOWEVER annoying may be the difficulties of a government exposed to general ill-will", says Gardiner,[1] "they are not likely at once to endanger its existence. It is when dangers threaten it from abroad, and when it becomes necessary to rouse the national spirit in its defence, that the weakness of an unpopular government stands clearly revealed."

The danger which was to bring about the collapse of the system of arbitrary government came from the side of Scotland.

The Church of Scotland had inherited from Knox the Calvinistic system of doctrine and a Presbyterian organisation. James I had little sympathy with a Church which produced clergy who publicly lectured him, plucking him by the sleeve and calling him "God's sillie vassall",[2] and the reintroduction of episcopacy into Scotland had been part of his policy; but he had been careful to leave the Presbyterian form of Church government locally untouched. And before he died he had warned Williams of the danger of the course which Laud was afterwards to take. He told him that if Laud hoped "to make that stubborn Kirk stoop more to the English pattern" he "knows not the stomach of that people".[3] But in 1633 Laud embarked upon an attempt to plant "the beauty of holiness" in Scotland and to Anglicanise the Scottish Church. In 1633 arrangements were made for an Anglican service in

---

[1] *Documents*, p. xxvii.

[2] "Mr Andrew...brake off upon the King in so zealous, powerful, and unresistible a manner, that howbeit the King used his authority in most crabbed and choleric manner, Mr Andrew bore him down, and uttered the commission as from the mighty God, calling the King but 'God's sillie vassall', and, taking him by the sleeve, says this in effect, through mickle hot reasoning and many interruptions..." (James Melvill's *Diary*, p. 370).

[3] G. M. Trevelyan, *England under the Stuarts*, p. 186. *Cf.* John Hacket, *Life of Archbishop Williams*, Pt. i. p. 64. "The plain truth is", said James, "that I keep Laud back from all place of rule and authority because I find he hath a restless spirit, and cannot see when matters are well, but loves to toss and change, and to bring things to a pitch of reformation floating in his own brain, which may endanger the steadfastness of that which is in a good pass, God be praised".

Holyrood Chapel; and a little later the clergy were required
to wear gowns in all public places and (as the Scotch term
for the surplice ran) to perform Divine Service "in whites".[1]
In 1634 the two High Commission Courts for Glasgow
and St Andrews, established in 1610, were amalgamated
into a single Court for Scotland, with wider powers; and
the bishops were brought to the front in the Government,
nine of them being introduced into the Scottish Privy
Council. In 1636 a Book of Canons was issued, requiring
the clergy to use a liturgy not yet published; and these
Canons were imposed by a mere letter missive from the
Scottish Privy Council, as if Scotland were "but a pendicle
of the diocese of York".[2] Finally, when in 1637 the new
liturgy appeared, it contained one or two significant
variations from the English Prayer Book. The new book
was at once pronounced "Popish in its frame and forms",[3]
and Baillie tells us[4] that "almost all our nobility and gentry
of both sexes counts that Book little better than the Mass".
On July 23, 1637, a riot took place in St Giles's, Edinburgh, when a woman threw her stool at the head of the
clergyman who was reading the new service: "so that",
says Fuller,[5] "the same book had occasioned his death,
and prescribed the form of his burial". The rioters were
everywhere supported by popular feeling, and the organisation of the "Tables" was established, to petition
the Council that the Service Book and Canons might be
withdrawn. Out of this grew the National Covenant of
February 27, 1638,[6] which pledged its signatories "to
labour by all means lawful to recover the purity and liberty
of the Gospel as it was established and professed" before
the recent innovations, since these "have no warrant of
the Word of God", and "do sensibly tend to the re-
establishing of the Popish religion and tyranny, and to
the subversion and ruin of the true reformed religion, and
of our liberties, laws, and estates". The document was
subscribed by the "noblemen, barons, gentlemen, bur-

---

[1] Cf. Laud, Works, iii. 301.
[2] Robert Baillie, Letters and Journals, i. 2.
[3] Masson, i. 673.   [4] i. 4.
[5] Church History, iii. 400.   [6] Gardiner, Documents, pp. 124–134.

gesses, ministers, and commons" of the realm, and was the protest of an entire nation.

A national movement organising itself on so great a scale threatened trouble for the government of "Thorough", for the system of the Eleven Years' Tyranny was not calculated to stand the strain of war.

"In the Exchequer, being examined upon this occasion", wrote Northumberland to Strafford on July 23, 1638,[1] "there is found but two hundred pounds....The King's magazines are totally unfurnished of arms and all sorts of ammunition, and commanders we have none, either for advice or execution. The people thorough all England are generally so discontented by reason of the multitude of projects daily imposed upon them, as I think there is reason to fear that a great part of them will be readier to join with the Scots than to draw their swords in the King's service....God send us a good end of this troublesome business, for to my apprehension no foreign enemies could threaten so much danger to this kingdom as doth now this beggarly nation."

And the fears of Northumberland were fully shared by the statesman to whom his letter was addressed. "The business...indeed gathers fearfully and apace", he wrote to Windebank from Ireland on August 10,[2] "and sits wondrous dark upon the public peace: may God be pleased in his mercy to disperse and clear up all again". Then, foreseeing, perhaps, the possibility of his own recall, and the collapse of his Irish administration, he adds: "The skirts of the great rain, if not part of the thundering and lightning, I confess is probable enough will fall upon this kingdom".

The rest of the year 1638 was spent in trying to come to terms with the Scots; and eventually it was agreed that the Service Book and Canons should be dropped, and that a General Assembly of the Church of Scotland should meet at Glasgow to settle matters of religion. The King hoped that by these concessions he had solved his difficulties, but popular assemblies sometimes do unexpected things. The Assembly at Glasgow turned at once upon Episcopacy, and the bishops were summoned before it as culprits. This was to touch the King in his tenderest

[1] Strafford, *Letters*, ii. 186. [2] *Ib.* ii. 202.

point, and he dissolved the Assembly rather than allow it to usurp the functions of the Royal Supremacy. But in Scotland the Presbyterian discipline had educated men to believe that a General Assembly of the Church was a higher authority than the civil power. The teaching of the Scottish divines was theocratic and the people "appealed from Saul the king to Samuel the prophet". The Assembly refused to dissolve. Hamilton, the King's Commissioner, withdrew, but business proceeded as if nothing had happened. They condemned the Service Book and Canons, denounced the High Commission Court, abolished the episcopal office, and excommunicated the "some time pretended bishops".

This was a declaration of war, and the organisation of the "Tables" was converted into a provisional government for carrying it on. Scotland was still feudal, and the nobles and gentry could dispose of military force. They had come up armed to the Glasgow Assembly, and its proceedings had the support of the Earl of Argyle, "the head of the Campbells, the most powerful fighting clan in the Highlands".[1] Scots were serving as professional soldiers abroad, and many of these came home to enlist under General Leslie, one of the officers of Gustavus Adolphus, who was summoned to take the chief command. Men were also armed and drilled in every shire, and Leslie soon had under him a force of 22,000 foot and 500 horse, with a nucleus in it of professional soldiers who had seen service.

"Such was the wisdom and authority of that old little crooked soldier", writes Baillie,[2] "that all, with an incredible submission from the beginning to the end, gave over themselves to be guided by him as if he had been Great Solyman."

And the war which Leslie waged was of the nature of a crusade.

Everyone encouraged another. The sight of the nobles and their beloved pastors daily raised their hearts; the good sermons and prayers, morning and even, under the roof of heaven, to which their

[1] G. M. Trevelyan, *History of England*, p. 399.
[2] i. 213. Leslie was of small stature and almost deformed.

drums did call them for bells; the remonstrances very frequent of the goodness of their cause; of their conduct hitherto by a Hand clearly Divine.[1]

Against this formidable force Charles could only raise about 14,000 men,[2] for he could not obtain sufficient money, and men did not respond readily to his call. A large number of peers came with their followers to his camp at York, but they heartily disliked the service upon which they were summoned. They probably sympathised with the view expressed by Lord Saye and Sele, who is reported to have said that he was ready to defend England against any invader, "but to go and kill a man in Scotland, he was not satisfied thereof".[3] The King's money ran out before the armies met, and the bloodless episode sometimes known as the "First Bishops' War" was closed on June 18, 1639, by the Treaty of Berwick. By this Charles undertook to submit all controversies, both civil and ecclesiastical, to a new Scottish Parliament and a fresh Assembly of the Church. We are told that the disbanding of the English army was like the "break-up of a school"; but Secretary Windebank's son wrote from Berwick in disgust:

We have had a most cold, wet, and long time of it; but we kept our soldiers warm with the hopes of rubbing, fubbing, and scrubbing those scurvy, filthy, dirty, nasty, lousy,...slovenly,...loggerheaded, foolish, insolent, proud, beggarly, impertinent, absurd, grout-headed, villainous, barbarous, bestial, false, lying, roguish, devilish, long-eared, short-haired, damnable, atheistical, Puritanical crew of the Scotch Covenant. But now there is peace in Israel.[4]

The "peace in Israel" was not destined to last long, for the Assembly at Edinburgh confirmed all the acts of the earlier one at Glasgow, and thus Charles was again faced with the abolition of episcopacy in Scotland—the one thing which he was determined not to allow, and the Covenanters not to relinquish. But before renewing the conflict, he acted on the advice of Wentworth, who in 1639 visited England and was made Earl of Strafford, and summoned an English Parliament to meet on April 13,

---

[1] i. 213.   [2] Firth, *Lords*, p. 64.   [3] *Ib.* p. 64 *n.*
[4] Quoted in Masson, ii. 70.

1640, in the hope that he would obtain supplies for another attempt to defend episcopacy and coerce the Scots.

This policy did not seem at the time so futile or so dangerous as historians have made it appear since. The traditional attitude of England towards Scotland was one of hostility, and Strafford may very well have thought that the patriotism of Parliament could be counted upon for supplies to protect the northern counties from invasion. He himself took care to speak of the First Bishops' War as "a border incursion"; and the King, in his speech through the Lord Keeper at the opening of the Short Parliament, emphasised the ultimate danger to England which a rebellion in Scotland involved, especially when it was associated with the overtures which the Scottish leaders had made to the King of France.

"Some men of Belial", he said, "some Zeba, hath blown the trumpet there;...they have addressed themselves unto foreign states;... than which nothing could be of more dangerous consequence to this and his Majesty's other kingdoms. Whosoever they be that do or shall wish England ill, they may know it to be of too tough a complexion and courage to be assailed in the face, or to be set upon at the fore-door; and therefore it is not unlikely but they may, as in former times, find out a postern gate".[1]

But events were to shew that Strafford had made a great miscalculation. The man who read rightly the difficult signs of this stormy time was not Strafford but Pym, who in the Short Parliament began for the first time "to play that part of unacknowledged leader of the House of Commons which was all that the ideas of that age permitted".[2] Pym saw, what Strafford did not see, that the ancient hatred between the nations, laid asleep for scarcely a generation; the fear lest Scotland should become again a "postern gate" for foreign enemies—these things now seemed less than a common hatred of Anglicanism and common grievances against the Crown. Thus, although the King offered to abandon ship-money if the Commons would grant him twelve subsidies, Pym succeeded in convincing the House on April 27 that redress of grievances must precede supply. At a private meeting of leading

[1] *Parliamentary History*, ii. 530, 531.　　[2] *D.N.B.* xlvii. 77.

members held on May 4 it was agreed that on the following
morning Pym should move that the King be asked to
come to terms with his northern subjects,[1] and to avert
this catastrophe Charles dissolved the Short Parliament
on the following day, after a session of scarcely more than
three weeks. "There could not a greater damp have
seized upon the spirits of the whole nation", writes
Clarendon,[2] "than this dissolution caused, and men had
much of the misery in view which shortly after fell out".

Since Parliament had failed them, the King and
Strafford fell back once more upon force. On May 5, the
day of the dissolution, a meeting of a committee of the
Council took place at which Strafford was present. Vane
and others wished the King to content himself with
protecting England from invasion; but Strafford pressed
for a vigorous offensive war—the money being found by
a loan from the City of London, and the troops by the
employment of the army which he had organised in Ireland.

"Go on vigorously", he said, if we may trust Vane's hurried notes
of his speech, "or let them alone....The quiet of England will
hold out long....Go on with a vigorous war, as you first designed,
loose and absolved from all rules of government; being reduced to
extreme necessity, everything is to be done that power might admit.
...They refusing, you are acquitted before God and man. You
have an army in Ireland you may employ here to reduce this
kingdom".[3]

Strafford's intention no doubt was to use the Irish army
against Scotland—or if in England at all, only to put
down rebellion against the King. But two days after, it
was rumoured everywhere that the King had decided to
employ his Irish army against his English subjects.[4]

The policy of "Thorough" in relation to Scotland was
doomed to failure. The City of London refused a loan;
the English forces marching north were almost mutinous;
the Irish army was not yet ready to cross the sea. Thus,
although on August 3 Strafford was appointed "Captain-
general over the army in Ireland, and of such in England
as the King by his sign manual shall add thereunto",[5]

---

[1] D.N.B. xlvii. 77. [2] i. 183.
[3] Quoted in Gardiner, ix. 122. [4] D.N.B. lx. 278. [5] Ib. lx. 279.

he had no military force at his disposal sufficient to make head against the Scots. Meanwhile Leslie took the initiative, crossed the Tweed, and routed the forces opposed to him at Newburn on the Tyne. On the same day a petition was adopted, drawn up by Pym and signed by twelve leading peers, praying that Parliament might be summoned and grievances redressed. Thus pressure from within combined with disaster without to force the King to recognise the hopelessness of his position. He summoned a Great Council of Peers to meet at York on September 24, and seventy or eighty peers responded to the summons;[1] but they could only advise the raising of a loan from the City, guaranteed by the whole body of the peers, to tide things over until a new Parliament could meet, and the reopening of negotiations with the Scots. These began on October 2, and by the Treaty of Ripon, which ended the "Second Bishops' War", it was agreed that they should receive £850 a day until a permanent settlement was concluded, and meanwhile they were to occupy the counties of Northumberland and Durham as security that payment would be made. Thus, by the irresistible march of events, the unwilling King was forced to summon the Long Parliament, which would require at his hands an account for the dealings of eleven years of non-parliamentary government.

The Long Parliament which met on November 3, 1640, was a different organisation from Parliaments under the Tudors. The numbers of the House of Lords had been greatly increased by the creations and sales of James and Charles; for the fifty-nine lay peers of 1603 had risen by 1640 to 124.[2] The House of Commons was numerically the same as in 1603, but its wealth had increased relatively to that of the peers, for the growth of trade had affected the distribution of property in land. A news-letter of 1628 estimates that the Lower House could buy the Upper House thrice over;[3] and Lord Morley once pointed out[4] that "it is hardly an exaggeration to say that the House of Lords now contains a smaller proportion of ancient

---

[1] Firth, *Lords*, p. 70.   [2] *Ib.* pp. 1, 74.
[3] *Ib.* p. 31.   [4] *Oliver Cromwell*, p. 72.

blood than the famous lineages that figure in the roll" of the Lower House of the Long Parliament. By the development of conferences between the Houses and of Committees within either House, Parliament had changed "from a comparatively simple to a highly complex machine",[1] competent to examine subjects and work out policies without being any longer dependent on the peers and privy councillors who represented the Government. Sir Charles Firth suggests also[2] that the colonising enterprises undertaken by adventurer companies in the reign of Charles I brought together "the future leaders of the popular party in the two Houses of the Long Parliament" and taught them "to cooperate in the attempt to build up Puritan commonwealths beyond the seas". Thus the Earl of Warwick, Lord Saye, Pym, and St John were all members of "The Providence Company", and the same two peers met Sir Arthur Haslerig and John Hampden as members of the company of twelve which was associated with the foundation of the colony of Connecticut.

The Long Parliament, thus structurally different from earlier assemblies, was animated by a new spirit of hostility to the Court and the Government.[3] Pym told Hyde that "they must be of another temper than they were in the last Parliament; that they must not only sweep the House clean below, but must pull down all the cobwebs which hung in the top and corners"; and from this Hyde inferred that "the warmest and boldest counsels and

---

[1] Wallace Notestein, *The Winning of the Initiative by the House of Commons* (the Raleigh Lecture for 1924), p. 41. Professor Notestein here points out also that under the Tudors "the course of Parliament was under the general direction of privy councillors"; and procedure by way of small Committees, which it was easy for them to dominate, increased their influence. But after the end of Elizabeth's reign, the further development of the Committee system in the direction of Committees of the Whole House searching for grievances and initiating bills to remedy them, placed the privy councillors in a secondary position, and they are on occasion "hemmed down" or even hissed. Meanwhile the real leadership was passing to men of a different type. Pym and Hampden were not privy councillors.

[2] *Lords*, pp. 59–60.

[3] On the failure of the attempts made by the Court to influence the elections, see Mr R. N. Kershaw's article on "The Elections for the Long Parliament, 1640" in *E.H.R.* xxxviii. 496–508.

overtures would find a much better reception than those of a more temperate allay".[1] Yet in the hands of this hostile Parliament the King was powerless, for without it he could not pay the Scots a penny, and if he failed to keep his engagements and they elected to march on London, there was no armed force strong enough to stop them anywhere between Ripon and Whitehall. "No fear yet of raising the Parliament", wrote Baillie to his countrymen,[2] "so long as the lads about Newcastle sits still." The Long Parliament itself recognised how much it owed to the Scottish army of occupation, when it voted a lump sum of £300,000 under the name of a "Brotherly Assistance".[3]

In the first instance the Long Parliament set before itself three principal objects: (1) to release the sufferers from arbitrary government; (2) to punish the men by whose advice arbitrary government had been established; and (3) to make it impossible for arbitrary government ever to be established again.

The first of these purposes was attained by the release and compensation of the chief victims of the Star Chamber and the High Commission Court. Leighton, Prynne, Burton, and Bastwick had never spared the feelings of those whom they attacked. Leighton had called the bishops "bloody beasts"[4] and "knobs and wens and bunchy Popish flesh",[5] and had "most audaciously and wickedly" called the Queen "the daughter of Heth".[6] Prynne had referred to playhouses as "devils' chapels"[7] and to the frequenters of plays as "voluptuous, carnal persons";[8] and his attitude towards the bishops was so hostile that it was said of him, "So great is his antipathy against episcopacy, that if a seraphim himself should be a bishop, he would either find or make some sick feathers

---

[1] Goldwin Smith, i. 513.   [2] i. 283.
[3] Gardiner, ix. 272.   [4] *Sion's Plea against Prelacy*, p. 39.
[5] *Ib.* p. 7.   [6] *State Trials*, iii. 383.
[7] *Histriomastix* (edition of 1633), First Epistle Dedicatory.
[8] *Ib.* Epistle to the Christian Reader. *Cf.* also his statement of the purpose of his book as "the restraint and diminution both of plays and common actors, and all those several mischievous and pestiferous fruits of Hellish wickednesses that issue from them" (p. 6).

in his wings". Burton wrote much in Prynne's style, and the *Litany of John Bastwick* is one of the most violent Puritan pamphlets that was ever penned. The writer refers to "the Egyptian darkness of Popery and error,...the papal tyranny and servile bondage of the Beast"; he calls bishops, priests, and deacons "those little toes of Antichrist"; the clergy are "a generation of vipers, of proud, ungrateful, idle, wicked, and illiterate asses"; the churchwardens are described as "the servants and attendants of the Devil and Antichrist, so damnable an office this is"; and the officers of the ecclesiastical courts are "filthy locusts that came out of the bottomless pit". Bastwick accordingly invites the "Courteous Reader" to join in his "daily litany": "From plague, pestilence, and famine —from bishops,[1] priests, and deacons—Good Lord, deliver us". But the punishments inflicted on these men —degradation, whipping, the pillory, mutilation, enormous fines, and imprisonment for life—were incredibly cruel, and they served to fan the flame of the popular hatred against Laud. The time had now come when these victims of the system of arbitrary government could find redress. Leighton was released by the Long Parliament, and £6000 was voted him as compensation.[2] The two sentences upon Prynne were declared illegal; he was restored to his membership of Lincoln's Inn; and he also received pecuniary compensation.[3] To Burton and Bastwick similar reparation was made.

Nor was the business of vengeance upon evil counsellors long delayed. There took place "a general doomsday".[4] Strafford was impeached and sent to the Tower on November 11, Laud on December 19. On December 10 Secretary Windebank and on December 22 Lord Keeper Finch fled beyond seas.

The fall of Strafford is one of the most tragic stories of

---

[1] *Cf.* The Second Part: "The prelates are the most wicked, profane, and unconscionable men that live upon the earth, and inferior to the Pope in no impiety" (p. 9); and cathedrals "are so many dens of thieves and cages of filthiness and idolatry" (p. 18).

[2] *D.N.B.* xxxiii. 2.   [3] *Ib.* xlvi. 433.

[4] Firth, *Cromwell*, p. 51.

English history. On the eve of the meeting of Parliament, the King had sent for him from Ireland, assuring him that if he came, he "should not suffer in his person, honour, or fortune".[1] As soon as he arrived, he advised Charles to prefer a charge of high treason against those members of Parliament who had invited the Scottish army into England. The King hesitated, and Pym, who had a genius for prompt and intrepid action, anticipated Strafford, and within locked doors, moved for a committee to prepare an impeachment against the Earl. Strafford at once went down to the House of Lords. "I will go", he said, "and look my accusers in the face." The scene which followed is described by the Scottish Presbyterian Baillie.

With speed he comes to the House; he calls rudely at the door, James Maxwell, Keeper of the Black Rod, opens; his Lordship, with a proud, glooming countenance, makes towards his place at the board head, but at once many bid him void the House; so he is forced in confusion to go to [the] door till he was called. After consultation, being called in, he stands, but is commanded to kneel, and on his knees to hear the sentence. Being on his knees, he is delivered to the Keeper of the Black Rod to be prisoner, till he was cleared of these crimes the House of Commons did charge him with. He offered to speak, but was commanded to be gone without a word. In the outer room James Maxwell required him as prisoner to deliver his sword; when he had gotten it, he cries with a loud voice for his man to carry my Lord Lieutenant's sword. This done, he makes through a number of people towards his coach, all gazing, no man capping to him before whom that morning the greatest in England would have stood dis-covered: all crying, "What is the matter?" He said, "A small matter, I warrant you!" They replied: "Yes, indeed, high treason is a small matter!" Coming to the place where he expected his coach, it was not there; so he behoved to return that same way through a world of gazing people. When at last he had found his coach and was entering, James Maxwell told him: "Your Lordship is my prisoner, and must go in my coach"; so he behoved to do.[2]

"Thus he whose greatness in the morning owned a power over two kingdoms, in the evening straitened his person betwixt two walls".[3]

"To the Lords", says Sir Charles Firth,[4] "the question of Strafford's guilt or innocence was a judicial question, which must be legally proved, and the accused was entitled to certain definite

[1] *D.N.B.* lx. 279.   [2] Baillie, i. 272.
[3] Quoted in Morley, *Cromwell*, p. 79.   [4] *Lords*, p. 80.

rights. To the Commons the question was a political one. Strafford was a danger to the nation, and his capital punishment necessary to its safety".

Thus when the impeachment failed,[1] and it became clear that the Lords would acquit the prisoner, the Commons fell back upon a different procedure.

"Without question they will acquit him", wrote Sir John Coke on April 17, 1641,[2] "there being no law extant whereupon to condemn him of treason. Wherefore the Commons are determined to desert the Lords' judicature, and to proceed against him by bill of attainder, whereby he shall be adjudged to death upon a treason now to be declared".

On April 21 the Attainder Bill passed its third reading in the Commons by 204 to 59, and was sent up to the Lords. During its passage there, on May 3, crowds of citizens and apprentices beset Westminster, and "cried to every Lord as they went out and in, in a loud and hideous voice, for justice against Strafford and all traitors";[3] and this gave a good excuse for absentees. During the impeachment, the attendance of peers had been about eighty, but at the final vote on the Attainder Bill there were only forty-five present, twenty-six being for and nineteen against the Bill. This change is not really to be accounted for by fear of violence. It is chiefly due to a change in the political situation.[4] The King still talked of appealing to force against the Parliament, and neither Lords nor Commons could forget that there was an English army undisbanded in the north and an Irish army over sea. Fear of mob violence may have played a small part in reducing the opposition to the Attainder Bill, but far more important was the fear of military violence at the hands of the King.

Strafford was executed on May 12, 1641; it was not until January 10, 1645, that Laud, the other representative of absolutism, followed him to the block. As in Strafford's case, an impeachment which could not be sustained gave place to an Act of Attainder. The record of his end in the

---

[1] See note, "The Trial of the Earl of Strafford, 1640", Appendix, p. 277 below.

[2] Firth, *Lords*, p. 83.   [3] *Ib.* p. 86.   [4] *Ib.* p. 91.

inscription upon his coffin is a model of concise Latinity.
Securi percussus, immortalitatem adiit.[1]

In order to prevent the re-establishment of arbitrary
government in the future, the Long Parliament passed
eight statutes.

(1) To prevent the recurrence of the long intermission
of Parliament which had made the "Eleven Years'
Tyranny" possible, the Triennial Act of February 15,
1641,[2] was passed to ensure that not more than three
years should elapse without a Parliament being summoned. This Act does not, however, provide that no
Parliament should sit for more than three years; and thus
although it guards against the actually experienced danger
of too few Parliaments, it does nothing to protect the
country against too long Parliaments, of which it had as
yet had no experience. There was nothing in the Triennial
Act of 1641 to interfere with Charles II's Pension
Parliament. The Act also contains some constitutional
machinery of a curious and novel kind, devised to meet the
general distrust of the King's good faith. (*a*) In order to
guard against the danger of his summoning Parliament
as a matter of form only, and then dissolving it again
immediately, it is provided that Parliament shall not be
prorogued or dissolved, or either House adjourned without
its own consent, until it had sat for fifty days at least.
(*b*) In order to compel the compliance of the executive
with the conditions now laid down by the legislature, it
is provided that if the King fails to summon Parliament
when it is due to meet under the Act, the Chancellor shall
under penalties issue the writs without the King's authority;
failing the Chancellor, the peers are to assemble and issue
the writs; failing the peers, the sheriffs are to hold elections
without writs; and failing the sheriffs, the electors are to
assemble and elect representatives without being summoned
to an election. This legislation was welcomed by men of

---

[1] The full inscription runs thus: "In hac cistulâ conduntur exuviae
Guilelmi Laud Archiepiscopi Cantuariensis qui securi percussus immor-
talitatem adiit die x Januarii aetatis suae LXXII Archiepiscopatus XII"
(*Works*, iv. 40).

[2] 16 Car. I, c. 1, printed in Gardiner, *Documents*, p. 144.

all parties, because it was the best guarantee of Parliaments that the statesmen of the age could invent.

"I take this", said the Royalist Lord Digby,[1] "to be the *unum necessarium*; let us procure this, and all our other desires will effect themselves. If this bill miscarry, I shall have left me no public hopes; and once passed, I shall be freed of all public fears".

(2) The Act of May 10, 1641, against the Dissolution of the Long Parliament without its own consent,[2] came about almost by an accident. The main reason for the Act was not constitutional but financial. The Commons wanted to raise a loan on the security of the customs, in order to anticipate taxation and pay promptly what was due to the Scottish army in the North. But the objection was taken by the lawyers that any security which the House might offer to the financiers would become worthless as soon as the assembly which offered it ceased to exist. If Parliament should be dissolved, the King could legally repudiate the loan, for his revenue could not be made liable for an indefinite period for debts which Parliament had contracted. If Parliament were to raise a loan to which the King was not a party, there must be some guarantee for its continued existence independently of the King. It may well be believed that Pym and his supporters had no objection to seeing their legal position against the King thus strengthened, and that there were other arguments for the Bill besides those which were urged in debate. But this did not appear, and Hyde and Falkland voted for it as readily as Hampden and Pym.[3] It had, however, one result which was probably unforeseen; it prevented Charles, at a later stage of the controversy, from appealing to the nation by a dissolution against the violence of the Long Parliament. Henceforth the life of Parliament was

[1] *Parliamentary History*, ii. 702.
[2] 17 Car. I, c. 7, printed in Gardiner, *Documents*, p. 158. The Act provided that "this present Parliament now assembled shall not be dissolved" nor shall it be prorogued or adjourned "unless it be by Act of Parliament to be passed for that purpose"; and that neither the House of Peers nor the House of Commons shall be adjourned "unless it be by themselves or their own order".
[3] Gardiner, ix. 360.

protected against the King, who could do nothing unless he proceeded by way of military violence.

(3) The Tonnage and Poundage Act of June 22, 1641,[1] settled the controversy concerning impositions finally in favour of Parliament. It legalised impositions in the past but prohibited them for the future, and in granting tonnage and poundage to the King, the grant was limited to two months, instead of being, as heretofore, a grant for life.

(4) The Act of July 5, 1641, "for the abolition of the Court of Star Chamber",[2] abolished the Star Chamber, the Courts of the North and of Wales, the special Court of the Duchy of Lancaster, and the Court of Exchequer of the County Palatine of Chester. It also deprived the Council Table of its power to give judgment in civil and criminal cases, although not of its power to examine and commit accused persons; but the exercise of this power to commit was, by a special clause in the Act, clearly brought under the review of the King's Bench or Common Pleas, either court being required, on application, to issue a writ of *habeas corpus*, to demand and obtain the cause of the commitment, and to decide within three days whether to bail or to remand.

(5) An Act of July 5, 1641, "for the abolition of the Court of High Commission",[3] abolished that Court by repealing the clause of Elizabeth's Act of Supremacy under which it had been constituted; and at the same time deprived the ecclesiastical courts in general of power to inflict fine, imprisonment, or corporal punishment, or to tender the *ex officio* oath. It was further provided that "no new Court shall be erected, ordained, or appointed... which shall have...the like power, authority, or jurisdiction as the said High Commission Court now hath or pretendeth to have".

(6) An Act was passed on August 7, 1641, "for the declaring unlawful and void the late proceedings touching

---

[1] 17 Car. I, c. 8, printed in Gardiner, *Documents*, p. 159.
[2] 17 Car. I, c. 10, printed in *ib*. p. 179.
[3] 17 Car. I, c. 11, printed in *ib*. p. 186.

ship-money, and for the vacating of all records and process concerning the same".[1]

(7) Another Act of the same date[2] restored the boundaries of the royal forests to their limits in the twentieth year of King James; and (8) an Act of August 10, 1641,[3] was passed "for the prevention of vexatious proceedings touching the Order of Knighthood".

The practical effect of these statutes taken as a whole was to deprive the Crown of all the extraordinary powers which it had possessed under the Tudor sovereigns.[4] The "Eleven Years' Tyranny" had shewn that it was technically possible for the King, without any direct violation of the Tudor precedents, to dispense with Parliament altogether for a long period of time. The history of the Courts of Star Chamber and High Commission had shewn that he possessed powers which enabled him to punish men for offences against the Government as if they had been offences against the law of the land. The history of Stuart finance had shewn that it was possible for the King to extort large sums of money from his subjects without common consent given in a parliamentary way. The Long Parliament had now succeeded in preventing him from obtaining any more money without common consent; it had made it impossible for him to punish his opponents without the goodwill of juries; and, most important of all, it had succeeded in making itself indispensable in the State. Having accomplished all this, it had achieved all that was immediately necessary in the way of constitutional reform.

[1] 17 Car. I, c. 14, printed in Gardiner, *Documents*, p. 189.
[2] 17 Car. I, c. 16, printed in *ib*. p. 192.
[3] 17 Car. I, c. 20, printed in *ib*. p. 196.
[4] It "destroyed the Tudors' expanded executive" (Keith Feiling, *A History of the Tory Party* 1640–1714, p. 38).

The Long Parliament and Revolution

DOWN to the end of August, 1641, the Long Parliament had been unanimous. The reforms which had been accomplished were within the lines of the ancient constitution, and they were all destined to be permanently accepted in 1660 by the government of the Restoration. But after August, questions came up for discussion upon which opinion, in Parliament and in the country alike, was irreconcilably divided. In trying to solve the insoluble religious problem, the two great parties fell asunder which were destined later on to measure swords upon the battlefields of Marston Moor and Naseby as Roundheads and Cavaliers.

The imprisonment of Laud and the abolition of the High Commission Court had not settled ecclesiastical controversies or determined the future destinies of the Church. It was, indeed, generally agreed that the drift towards Arminianism must be stopped, for the nation was, at any rate, one in its Puritanism; and in order to stop it, many thought it desirable that the control of the Church should be taken out of the hands of the Crown governing through bishops, and that it should be placed instead under statutes formulated and passed by Parliament. If things were left as they were, a new Archbishop might at any time revert to the policy of Laud, and make Arminian innovations in public worship; it was therefore necessary that the details of worship should be prescribed by Parliament for all time, and a system established which the private caprices of those in authority could not change. Thus it came about that the Long Parliament was quite as anxious to make a new Church settlement as it had been to strike at Strafford or to destroy the Star Chamber and the High Commission Court. Unanimity in a policy of destruction was easy to secure, but when it came to construction—and ecclesiastical construction—the rift soon shewed itself, and a process began which before long broke up the Long Parliament into two hostile camps.

The first signs of the division appear about February, 1641. Neglecting an unimportant minority which defended the Laudian order as it stood, it may be said that the main current of opinion upon the Church question was beginning to separate into two streams. (1) An important body in the Commons, particularly those who had been maintaining close relations with Scotland,[1] were in favour of abolishing the bishops and transferring their functions to popular assemblies elected after the Presbyterian model.

"To speak plain English", said Fiennes,[2] "these bishops, deans, and chapters do little good themselves, by preaching or otherwise, and if they were felled, a great deal of good timber might be cut out of them for the use of the Church and kingdom at this time".

This party also desired a complete change in the Prayer Book, if not its entire abandonment. Their policy came to be described as "Root and Branch", and it was supported in debate by Nathaniel Fiennes, Oliver St John, and Denzil Holles. It was also occasionally countenanced by Pym and Hampden, although in 1641 they were not yet reckoned "root and branch men". (2) In opposition to these extremists was the great body of moderate men, who wished to see the bishops retained, but their functions modified in such a way as to share their authority with the clergy of their dioceses. These viewed with favour Archbishop Ussher's scheme for limited episcopacy, and they were ready to content themselves with a few alterations in the Book of Common Prayer. The leaders of this party were Hyde and Falkland, and their best orator was the brilliant and versatile Lord Digby, who has been described as "possessed of every quality which lifts a man to success—except discretion".[3] Colepeper, Selden, Hopton, and Waller were also upon the same side. The moderate party had strong support outside Parliament, for the House of Commons was more Puritan than the country.

The views of the moderate party are illustrated by a

---

[1] Heylyn, Laud's biographer, calls them "the Scotizing English", on the analogy of the "Medizing Greeks" of the Persian War (*Life of Laud*, edition of 1668, p. 398).

[2] Rushworth, iv. 182.   [3] Gardiner, ix. 276.

speech delivered by Lord Digby in the great debate on ecclesiastical questions which took place February 8–11, 1641.

There is no man within these walls more sensible of the heavy grievance of Church government than myself, nor whose affections are keener to the clipping of these wings of the prelates whereby they have mounted to such insolencies; nor whose zeal is more ardent to the searing them so as they may never spring again. But having reason to believe that some aim at a total extirpation of bishops, which is against my heart,... I cannot restrain myself from labouring to divert it—or at least to set such notes upon it as may make it ineffectual to that end.[1]

*   *   *   *

If we hearken to those that would quite extirpate episcopacy, I am confident that instead of every bishop we put down in a diocese we shall set up a pope in every parish.... For my part,... I do not think a king can put down bishops totally, with safety to monarchy, ...from this reason, that upon the putting down of bishops, the government of assemblies is like to succeed it; that (to be effectual) must draw to itself the supremacy of ecclesiastical jurisdiction, that (consequently) the power of excommunicating kings as well as any other brother in Christ; and if a king chance to be delivered over unto Satan, judge whether men are likely to care much what becomes of him next.... Let us not destroy bishops, but make bishops such as they were in the primitive times. Do their large territories, their large revenues offend? Let them be retrenched. The good Bishop of Hippo had but a narrow diocese. Do their courts and subordinates offend? Let them be brought to govern as in the primitive times—by assemblies of their clergy. Doth their intermeddling in secular affairs offend? Exclude them from the capacity. It is no more than what reason and all antiquity hath interdicted them.[2]

Unrealised aspirations are often as interesting historically as achieved results; and it is worth while to notice that the views of Digby and his party took shape in an abortive Bill for Church Reform,[3] which got so far as a second reading in the House of Lords on July 3, and then disappeared into the limbo of uncompleted legislation. If it had survived, this scheme would have effected three important changes. (1) It would have deprived the clergy

---

[1] Rushworth, iv. 170.   [2] *Ib.* iv. 173–4.
[3] Printed in Gardiner, *Documents*, p. 167.

of all power to "intermeddle" in secular affairs; (2) it proposed to associate with each bishop in the government of his diocese "twelve ministers being in Holy Orders, and being fit both in respect of their life and doctrine to be assistants"—four of them being chosen by the King, four by the House of Lords, and four by the House of Commons; and (3) it provided that the appointment of bishops should in future be taken out of the absolute discretion of the King, who should only have the right of selecting one of three persons to be nominated by the Dean, Chapter, and "assistants" of the vacant diocese. Thus this bill made large inroads upon the Royal Supremacy —first in favour of Parliament, and then in favour of the semi-popular diocesan administration which Parliament was to set up.

It is curious that the projects of the Root and Branch party can also be studied in an abortive Bill. Sir Harry Vane the younger, and some of those who worked with him, notably Cromwell and St John, were prepared to go faster and farther than Hampden and Pym. Vane, who is described by Clarendon[1] as "a man above ordinances", who had "swallowed some of the fancies and extravagances of every sect or faction", was the chief expounder of the principles of Root and Branch. In a speech delivered on June 12, 1641, he asserted that the whole fabric of episcopal government was "rotten and corrupt from the very foundation of it to the top", and must be pulled down in the interest both of religion and of the civil State.[2] There is therefore nothing surprising in the terms of a Bill of May, 1641, of which he was the chief promoter, although it stood in the name of Sir Edward Dering. This in its final form would have provided (1) that archbishops, bishops, deans, and chapters should be abolished, and all Church property vested in trustees; (2) that all ecclesiastical jurisdiction should be assigned to joint commissions of clergy and laity for every shire, these county commissions being under the supervision of two central commissions for the Provinces of Canterbury and York; and (3) that

---

[1] vi. 148.
[2] W. A. Shaw, *A History of the English Church* 1640–1660, i. 86.

ordination should in future be by five divines acting under warrant from the commissioners of the county in which the ordination was to take place. Dering's Bill never got further than a second reading, but it shews us that Root and Branch differs from the moderate policy in two main points: (1) the one scheme does and the other does not contemplate the association of the laity with the clergy in ecclesiastical administration; and (2) the one scheme does not and the other does retain through episcopal ordination "an organic relation with Catholic antiquity". It was in support of the principles of Root and Branch, thus taking shape in what was practically Presbyterianism by counties, that Milton now for the first time entered the arena as a controversialist with his pamphlet *Of Reformation touching Church Discipline*.[1]

Events might have shaped themselves otherwise than they did but for the want of statesmanship displayed by the King. The weak point in the plan of the moderate party was that it offered no satisfactory guarantee for the supremacy of Puritanism in the future. It assumed a cordial co-operation between the bishop and his clergy in the administration of every diocese; and yet the existing bishops were for the most part Arminian, and to expect Puritan clergy to work harmoniously with an Arminian bishop in that age was "to constitute anarchy and to call it government". The success of the scheme in the present was doubtful, and if men took the long view and were willing to wait, its success in the future depended upon the kind of bishop who was henceforth to be appointed. In these appointments the King was still to have great influence, and the important question was—could he be trusted to assist in the recruiting of the Bench from among those divines whose views were in harmony with the clergy in their dioceses and with the House of Commons outside? If men could only have believed that Charles would frankly accept the new order of things, recognise the strength of Puritanism, and co-operate with the dioceses in appointing bishops whose views were congenial to

[1] Published May–June, 1641 (*D.N.B.* xxxviii. 28).

them, everything would have been in favour of the moderate party; for there were many who profoundly distrusted the extremists and their plans for establishing a Presbyterian organisation, thinking, with Milton, that "new presbyter was but old priest writ large". But the King held aloof, and the conviction gained ground among those who were hesitating, that unless bishops were entirely abolished, he would restore them to their full authority, in spite of any limitations which the Long Parliament might succeed in setting up for a time. Thus Charles, although in obedience to personal convictions that were at once strong and sincere, played directly into the hands of the advocates of Root and Branch.

In 1641 the King was trying to increase the House of Lords and the Commons were trying to diminish it.[1] The former sought to make his majority there permanent by the creation of additional peers—among them Lord Digby, "who had made the Lower House too hot to hold him". The latter aimed at a diminution of the majority against them by the exclusion of the bishops and the Roman Catholic peers. The first Bishops' Exclusion Bill was rejected by the Lords on June 8, 1641, and a second Bill, sent up to them in October, was held up in the House. "The Bill for the removing the bishops out of our House sticks there", wrote Northumberland on November 12,[2] "and whether we shall get it passed or not is very doubtful, unless some assurance be given that the rooting out of the function is not intended". The Upper House also flatly refused to deprive the Roman Catholic peers of their votes. Thus in November, 1641, the Commons were finding that they could get no further in relation to questions of religion. Their ecclesiastical policy was blocked —mainly by the resistance of the House of Lords.

On the secular side a different series of problems had been raised for the Long Parliament by the outbreak of the Irish Rebellion on October 23. The policy of plantation carried out during the last sixty years had embittered and impoverished the native Irish, whose rights and customs

---

[1] Firth, *Lords*, pp. 92–3.   [2] *Ib.* p. 97.

had been thought no more of by the colonists "than if they had been the Matabele or Zulu of a later time".[1] To their resentment for past injuries had been added fears for the future engendered by Strafford's plantation of Connaught; and just at the time when the danger of rebellion was greatest, the strong government which he had built up in Ireland had been fatally weakened by his impeachment and the disbanding of his army. At the same time, if the Irish had had little to hope for from Strafford, they had everything to fear from the Puritanism of the Long Parliament. Where he had only attempted conversion, the Parliament would be likely to aim at the complete suppression of the Roman Catholic religion.[2] Thus the motives for the Rebellion were strong and the opportunity was favourable; but to the men of the time it came like thunder from a clear sky. Both in this respect, and in regard to the barbarities associated with it, it has been compared to the Indian Mutiny, and the feeling in England when the news arrived was like that aroused by the tidings of the massacre at Cawnpore. The Long Parliament saw in it the natural result of Popery, and proceeded to pass two fatal votes: (1) that the Popish religion should no longer be tolerated in any part of the King's dominions; and (2) that funds for the repression of the Rebellion should be raised by fresh confiscations of Irish land. "One vote turned a local insurrection into a general rebellion; the other made the rebellion an internecine war."[3]

On the immediate situation the Irish Rebellion had results of incalculable importance. (1) It widened the breach between the King and the Parliamentary majority; (2) it precipitated the division between parties in Parliament; (3) it profoundly modified the financial position; and (4) it led the Long Parliament to take its first revolutionary step, and to grasp at the power of the sword.[4]

---

[1] Morley, *Cromwell*, p. 94.   [2] Firth, *Cromwell*, pp. 57–8.

[3] *Ib.* p. 59.

[4] Mr Feiling (p. 39) suggests that the first revolutionary step of the Commons was "to publish during September" (1641) "resolutions of their own touching ecclesiastical innovations", but this is to interpret "revolutionary" differently. These resolutions, dated September 1, 1641, are printed in Gardiner, *Documents*, pp. 197–8.

More than one event had occurred already to make the Parliamentary leaders suspicious of the King, and afraid of military violence. The Army Plot, a plan for bringing the army to London to overawe the Parliament, had been betrayed to Pym as early as April, 1641, and in May he disclosed it in the House of Commons, where it no doubt influenced Strafford's fate. The effect of this conspiracy, in which the Queen was supposed to have been concerned, had been to create a condition of the public mind in which every kind of wild report found credence. At a debate in May a board in the floor of the gallery of the House of Commons cracked under the weight of two very stout members. Someone at once cried out that he smelt gunpowder, and a panic ensued in the House. A report was carried into the City that the Parliament House was falling and the members were killed. The City train-bands turned out to march to the assistance of the living and to collect the remains of the dead, and they got as far as Covent Garden before they learned that their help was not required.[1] The Army Plot was represented as "a formidable and bloody design against the Parliament",[2] and reports were circulated of "great multitudes of Papists gathering together in Lancashire; then of secret meetings in caves and under ground in Surrey; letters from beyond sea of great provisions of arms making there for the Catholics of England".[3] In August the King went to Scotland on the futile expectation of making for himself a party there. Anyone but Charles would have realised the absurdity of "attempting to save the English bishops by an appeal to the Presbyterian Scots"; and he soon found that they would not surrender their own claims or lend him aid to recover the ground which he had lost in England.[4] But for Pym and the Parliamentary leaders the King's visit to Scotland called up in a more menacing form the spectre of military violence. Leslie's army was just on the point of evacuating the northern counties and returning home again; and to excited imaginations it appeared that Charles might find there the armed support which he needed. So real did the danger seem, that on

---

[1] Gardiner, ix. 359.
[2] Clarendon, i. 322.
[3] Ib. i. 327.
[4] D.N.B. x. 79.

August 14, 1641, a committee of defence was appointed, with Pym as a member, "to take into consideration what power will be fit to be placed, and in what persons, for commanding of the trained bands and ammunition of the kingdom";[1] and in this policy, at present only a suggestion to meet an eventuality, may be discerned the first sound and sign of coming war. It was while Pym and his colleagues were anxiously speculating upon the possible consequences of the King's visit to his northern kingdom, that on October 19 they received the news of the plot known as the "Incident"—a scheme for seizing and carrying off Argyle and Hamilton, the leaders of the party which was opposing the King in Scotland. It was rumoured that Charles had connived at the plot, and it appeared in England like a rehearsal of what the English Parliamentary leaders most feared for themselves. No doubt they exaggerated the danger, for the King was still keeping a tenacious and almost desperate hold upon legality, and was not yet prepared to use force, even if he could command it; but the Houses were sufficiently alarmed to ask for a guard of one hundred men to be stationed night and day in Palace Yard.[2] It was while the members were thinking on these lines that—a fortnight after the news of the "Incident"—they received on November 1 information of the outbreak of the Irish Rebellion, and rumour connected the name of the Queen with a great plot hatched in Rome for the suppression of Protestantism in the three kingdoms, of which the rising in Ireland was to be the opening scene. Thus it is not surprising to find Clarendon[3] saying of the Irish Rebellion that it "made a wonderful impression upon the minds of men, and proved of infinite disadvantage to the King's affairs, which were then recovering new life".

The Irish Rebellion raised an urgent practical question, and it was this which precipitated the division between the parties. For its suppression a military force would be needed; but was it safe to vote a great army to "a king who was at least as desirous to put down the Parliament

---

[1] *Commons' Journals*, ii. 257.
[2] Gardiner, x. 32.   [3] i. 397.

of England as to conquer the insurgents of Ireland"?[1]
Pym tried to meet the difficulty by proposing an amendment to the suggested arrangements for landing troops
in Ireland, asking Charles to "employ only such counsellors and ministers as shall be approved by his Parliament",[2] and declaring that if he should refuse, Parliament
would find some way of defending Ireland against the
rebels without him. We have here the first suggestion
that the control of the executive for certain purposes might
be transferred from the Crown to the two Houses. There
was now, however, in the House of Commons a large
minority which was not prepared to accept the revolutionary policy of Pym. On November 8 it was approved
on a division, but only by a majority of 41, the votes
being 151 to 110.[3] From this time forward the party
which was opposed to great ecclesiastical changes supported
the authority of the King, and the party which was in
favour of Root and Branch supported the authority of the
Commons. The parties already divided on religious
grounds were now divided on political grounds also; in
other words the Episcopalian party now becomes a Royalist
party, and the Puritan party a party of Parliamentarians.

The new division of parties is very clearly brought out
by an event which was always regarded by the older
historians as pre-eminently *the* turning-point in the history
of the Great Rebellion—the voting of the "Grand Remonstrance"[4] on November 22, 1641. This document
contains (1) a long recitation of the evils from which the
kingdom had suffered; a list of the reforms already
achieved by the Long Parliament; and a statement of the
grievances still to be redressed. It contains (2) a statement
of the religious policy of the party, which is practically
Root and Branch.

We confess our intention is...to reduce within bounds that
exorbitant power which the prelates have assumed unto themselves.
...And we do here declare that it is far from our purpose or desire

---

[1] Macaulay on Hallam: quoted in Gardiner, *Cromwell*, p. 18.
[2] Gardiner, *Documents*, pp. 199–201.
[3] *Commons' Journals*, ii. 307.
[4] Printed in Gardiner, *Documents*, pp. 202–32.

to let loose the golden reins of discipline and government in the Church, to leave private persons or particular congregations to take up what form of Divine Service they please; for we hold it requisite that there should be throughout the whole realm a conformity to that order which the laws enjoin according to the Word of God.... And the better to effect the intended Reformation, we desire there may be a general synod of the most grave, pious, learned, and judicious divines of this island, assisted with some from foreign parts professing the same religion with us—who may consider of all things necessary for the peace and good government of the Church, and represent the results of their consultations unto the Parliament, to be there allowed of and confirmed, and receive the stamp of authority, thereby to find passage and obedience throughout the kingdom.

It also contains (3) a statement of the political plans of the parliamentary party, which may be described as an amplification of the policy embodied in Pym's amendment to the instructions for suppressing the Irish Rebellion.

That his Majesty be humbly petitioned by both Houses to employ such councillors, ambassadors, and other ministers...as the Parliament may have cause to confide in.... It may often fall out that the Commons may have just cause to take exceptions at some men for being councillors, and yet not charge those men with crimes, for there be grounds of diffidence which lie not in proof. There are others, which though they may be proved, yet are not legally criminal....We may have great reason to be earnest with his Majesty not to put his great affairs into such hands, though we may be unwilling to proceed against them in any legal way of charge or impeachment.

The authors of the Grand Remonstrance here recognise the weak point of impeachment as a constitutional process for getting rid of the King's evil counsellors.

The Grand Remonstrance was designed as an appeal to the nation; and much of its importance lies in the fact that it was to be printed and circulated. It is an appeal primarily against the House of Lords, which was regarded by its authors as standing in the way of further reformation.

"But what can we the Commons, without the conjunction of the House of Lords", ran one of its clauses, "and what conjunction can we expect there, when the Bishops and recusant Lords are so

numerous and prevalent that they are able to cross and interrupt our
best endeavours for reformation, and by that means give advantage
to this malignant party to traduce our proceedings"?

The Remonstrance is also an appeal from one party
against the other—from Root and Branch against limited
episcopacy, and from those who wished to appoint the
King's ministers for him against those who wished him
still to choose them for himself. Thus it was fiercely
debated at every stage, and the critical division was not
taken until after midnight—in those days an unheard-of
thing. And when the votes were counted the Ayes were
159 and the Noes 148; it was only carried by a majority
of *eleven*! So high did party feeling run that after the
division, when Hyde and Colepeper on behalf of the
minority sought to enter a protest against the decision,
some members waved their hats wildly in the air, and others
"took their swords in their scabbards out of their belts
and held them by their pommels in their hands, setting
the lower part on the ground".[1] "I thought", wrote an
eye-witness, "we had all sat in the valley of the shadow of
death; for we, like Joab's and Abner's young men, had
catched at each other's locks, and sheathed our swords in
each other's bowels".[2] On the other hand Cromwell said
to Falkland "that if the Remonstrance had been rejected,
he would have sold all he had the next morning, and never
have seen England more; and he knew there were many
other honest men of the same resolution".[3] The earlier
historians did not fail to grasp the significance of the event.
"At this time", says May,[4] "began that fatal breach
between King and Parliament to appear visibly and wax
daily wider, never to be closed until the whole kingdom
was by sad degrees brought into a ruinous war".

At the time of the Remonstrance, the King's financial
position had changed for the worse. Before his return
from Scotland he had allowed himself to think that the
clouds were lifting. During September both the English
and Scottish armies had been disbanded, and they had

---

[1] D'Ewes's *Diary*, quoted in Gardiner, x. 77.
[2] Gardiner, x. 77.   [3] Clarendon, i. 42c.
[4] *History of the Long Parliament*, Lib. ii. p. 19.

been costing £80,000 a month;[1] while on the other hand
he had received from the Long Parliament altogether
about a million and a half in parliamentary grants. But
the Irish Rebellion of October, 1641, upset the whole
calculation. It required force for its suppression, and
force would cost money. Thus one of its results was to
place the King once more in the hands of the House of
Commons. Failing an appeal to force, they now had the
game in their hands, for they could starve the King into
surrender; and it was this knowledge that nothing but
force could resist them which made them so afraid of
force. Everything therefore turned on whether the policy
pursued by the King was such as to arouse or to allay their
fears. Unfortunately, Charles was capable of alternately
pursuing inconsistent policies; and at this time there
were two policies competing for his favour—either of
which needed time for its success—each of which, if
pursued at all, rendered the other not merely ineffective
but disastrous. (1) The first was the policy of the constitutional Royalists, which is indicated by Clarendon[2] in a
passage written with reference to the King's position after
he had retired to York, although it has an earlier application:

And the truth is (which I speak knowingly) at that time the King's
resolution was to shelter himself wholly under the law; to grant
anything that by the law he was obliged to grant, and to deny what
by the law was in his own power, and which he found inconvenient
to assent to; and to oppose and punish any extravagant attempt by
the force and power of the law, presuming that the King and the
law together would have been strong enough for any encounter that
could happen; and that the law was so sensible a thing, that the
people would easily perceive who endeavoured to preserve and who
to suppress it, and dispose themselves accordingly.

(2) The other policy was the policy of the Queen and the
courtiers, which appealed not to the law but to force.
Between the passing of the Remonstrance in November
and the end of the year, Hyde's policy was in the ascendant,
and the King aimed at a constitutional government founded
—not of course on a majority in the Commons, but on a

Royalist minority in the Commons and a majority in the
House of Lords. It was a step in this direction when on
January 2, 1642, he called to office Colepeper and Falkland, two leading members of the party which was
supporting him in the Lower House.[1] But all the while
he was coquetting with the other policy. Only a few days
earlier, on December 23, he had appointed the ruffian
Sir Thomas Lunsford Lieutenant of the Tower, an act
which was regarded as intended to prepare the way for
some violent proceedings against the persons of the
Parliamentary leaders. The Lord Mayor told the King
that he could not answer for the peace of the City unless
Lunsford were removed, and Charles yielded; but there
were three days of rioting, when apprentices and citizens
crowded to Westminster to support the Commons.[2] They
demonstrated loudly against certain "false, evil, and
rotten-hearted Lords", and "did not stick openly to
profess that they would pull the bishops in pieces".[3] On
December 29 twelve of the bishops signed a protest
against this interference, declaring that everything done
in the House of Lords in their absence was illegal. Their
conduct found no defenders, and when the Commons
impeached them, only one member spoke in their favour.
"He did not believe they were guilty of high treason,
but that they were stark mad—and therefore desired they
might be sent to Bedlam."[4]

The protest of the bishops would have had little effect
on the situation, for the loss of their votes did not place
the King's supporters in a minority in the Upper House,
had not Charles seized this moment to throw away all his
constitutional advantages by making an unprovoked
attack upon the leaders of Parliament. By his instructions
the Attorney-General, on January 3, 1642, charged with
high treason Lord Mandeville and five members of the
Lower House—Pym, Hampden, Holles, Haslerig, and
Strode—and asked the Lords to order their arrest. Charles
appears to have acted on the advice of the Queen, who
thought that the Commons were about to impeach her,[5]

[1] D.N.B. x. 80.   [2] Firth, Lords, p. 103.   [3] Ib. p. 104.
[4] Clarendon, i. 476.   [5] Gardiner, x. 128.

but the step had fatal consequences. Instead of ordering an arrest, the Lords, jealous for their privileges, appointed a committee to enquire into the Attorney-General's action. Thereupon the King himself sent the Serjeant-at-Arms to arrest the five members of the Commons, and when the House refused to give them up, he went down in person on the following day to take them, with 400 armed men at his back, only to find that "the birds had flown". The King was within his rights in accusing the Five Members, but he was guilty of a mere act of military violence when he came down in person to Parliament to arrest them at the head of an armed force. Such an event was entirely without precedent. It has been pointed out that the usual entry in the Journals of the House breaks off suddenly, "as if the excitement of the scene had paralysed the clerks at their work".[1] The House itself was stricken with amazement, fury, and shame. "Such a night of prayers, tears, and groans", wrote an eyewitness long afterwards, "I never was present at in all my life".[2] As one writer said at the time, "The obedience of his Majesty's subjects hath been poisoned".[3] The danger which had been dreaded had come at last, and it was now certain, what before had only been suspected, that the King was prepared, even in violation of his pledged word, to throw the sword into the scale. The House appealed to the City for protection, and adjourned its sittings to the Guildhall, and when it returned to Westminster it met under a guard of train-bands.

The attempted arrest of the Five Members had two other results of some constitutional interest. (1) Speaker Lenthall's famous answer, when, from the Speaker's chair which he had borrowed, the King asked him if he saw any of the Five Members present, marks a revolution in the character of the office. Lenthall fell on his knees and said,

May it please your Majesty, I have neither eyes to see nor tongue to speak in this place but as this House is pleased to direct me, whose servant I am here; and humbly beg your Majesty's pardon that

---

[1] Masson, ii. 341.   [2] Quoted in Morley, *Cromwell*, p. 104.
[3] Quoted in Forster, *Arrest of the Five Members*, p. 287.

I cannot give any other answer than this to what your Majesty is pleased to demand of me.[1]

Hitherto the King's agent in the House, charged with the duty of managing his business in the Commons as the Lord Chancellor managed it in the Lords, the Speaker now becomes, and henceforth remains, the servant of the House itself. (2) The reaction against the King in the Upper House caused by the *coup d'état*, contributed to, although it does not entirely account for, the passing into law of the Bishops' Exclusion Bill. On January 10, 1642, Charles left the City, in which he was scarcely safe any longer, just in time to miss the spectacle of the Five Members returning in triumph to Westminster in open defiance of his authority, escorted by the City train-bands in arms. He went first to Hampton Court and thence to Windsor, to begin preparations for reducing his rebellious subjects to their due obedience; and these preparations came to include an attempt to get possession of Hull and Portsmouth, a scheme for landing foreign troops in England, and other evidences of a design to appeal to force.[2] In the latter part of January all this became known, and the result was to break up the King's party in the House of Lords. "Some of the majority absented themselves; others changed sides";[3] and in February the two Houses were acting together. The Bishops' Exclusion Bill[4] passed the Lords on February 5, and on February 13 it received the royal assent, on the same day as the Impressment Bill[5] for raising troops for service in Ireland. The exclusion of the bishops made a visible change in the appearance of the House of Lords, and, as Clarendon points out, it weakened the King's position, "as it perpetually swept away so considerable a number out of the House of Peers which were constantly devoted to him";[6] but even those who had defended them were scarcely sorry. "They who hated bishops", Falkland was wont to say, "hated them worse than the Devil"; and "they who loved them did not love them so well as their dinner".[7]

[1] Rushworth, iv. 478.   [2] Firth, *Lords*, p. 111.   [3] *Ib.*
[4] Printed in Gardiner, *Documents*, p. 241.
[5] Printed in *ib.* p. 242.   [6] Clarendon, i. 567.   [7] *Ib.* i. 363.

The Long Parliament and the Civil War

DOWN to 1642 the proceedings of the Long Parliament had been constitutional in form, for all its measures had received the royal assent. But early in March the King refused his assent to the Militia Bill; and from this point the proceedings of Parliament are in form, as well as in substance, revolutionary.

The Militia Bill was a direct result of the Irish Rebellion. The Impressment Act was about to call an army into existence to suppress it, and an army constituted a danger to whichever side failed to control it. Thus in order to protect itself from military violence, the Long Parliament proceeded to grasp at the power of the sword. In February, 1642, both Houses had concurred in a demand that the fortresses and militia should be entrusted to those in whom they had confidence, and they drew up a list of persons to be nominated as lords-lieutenant in the room of those who at present held office by the King's appointment. The King's reply to this invitation to surrender his military power to his enemies was at first evasive,[1] and the Houses proceeded to their first act of open defiance of the Crown. In August, 1641, when the King was in Scotland, a good deal of inconvenience had arisen out of the fact that he had left no authority with the Chancellor for the use of the Great Seal; and the suggestion had been thrown out that the necessary powers could be conferred by an "Ordinance" of the two Houses. Sir Simon D'Ewes, the great authority of the day on constitutional law, looked up the history of the Ordinance, and reported that it had always been regarded as of very great weight—forgetting that the Ordinance of earlier constitutional history was a declaration of the King without the concurrence of the two Houses and not a declaration of the Houses without

[1] It was afterwards sufficiently decisive. On March 9, when Pembroke pressed him to surrender the militia, he replied, "By God! not for an hour. You have asked that of me in this was never asked of a king, and with which I will not trust my wife and children" (Gardiner, x. 172).

the concurrence of the King.[1] Nevertheless, on this authority the expedient of the Ordinance was employed more than once during the King's absence, and it was upon the same expedient, by this time grown familiar, that the Houses now fell back. The arrangements for the militia which Charles had practically refused to sanction were made in spite of him by the adoption on March 5, 1642, of the Militia Ordinance,[2] by which the new parliamentary lords-lieutenant were formally appointed, and empowered to "lead, conduct, and employ" the militia of the counties "according as they from time to time shall receive directions from the Lords and Commons assembled in Parliament".

The King, who had established himself at York early in March, replied on May 27 by a proclamation[3] forbidding the militia to act in obedience to the Ordinance, and thus the issue was fairly joined. The next four months were spent in what Clarendon[4] calls "paper skirmishes", while preparations for the real war were being steadily pushed on. Of these documents, the most important was the Nineteen Propositions[5] of June 1, 1642, which constitutes the ultimatum of Parliament. Hitherto the Houses had been driven by a real or imagined necessity to claim various parts of the royal authority; now they demanded all branches of sovereignty for themselves. Among other things the Propositions claim (1) that the King's Council, his officials, and even the educators of his children, shall henceforth be appointed by Parliament; (2) that the Militia Ordinance shall be made a statute, and Parliament thus receive the power of the sword; and (3) that the Church settlement shall be determined by the views of Parliament. In a word—the King is asked to surrender both his executive authority and his military power, and also to abandon the Church of England to her foes. Charles was sufficiently clearsighted to see all that the Nineteen Propositions meant to the monarchy.

"These being passed", he said, "we may be waited on bareheaded,

---

[1] Gardiner, x. 4.   [2] Printed in part in Gardiner, *Documents*, p. 245.
[3] Printed in *ib.* p. 248.   [4] ii. 206.
[5] Printed in Gardiner, *Documents*, p. 249.

we may have our hand kissed, the style of Majesty continued to us, and the King's authority declared by both Houses of Parliament may be still the style of your commands; we may have swords and maces carried before us, and please ourself with the sight of a crown and sceptre,...but as to true and real power, we should remain but the outside, but the picture, but the sign of a King".[1]

On the other hand, Parliament in thus attacking monarchy believed that it did so in its own defence, and to secure to posterity the ancient liberties.

"The question in dispute between the King's party and us", said Ludlow,[2] was, "as I apprehended, whether the King should govern as a god by his will, and the nation be governed by force like beasts; or whether the people should be governed by laws made by themselves, and live under a government derived from their own consent".

The questions at issue could only be decided on the field of battle. On July 4 the Houses appointed a Committee of Safety, consisting of five peers and ten commoners, who were to serve as a channel of communication between Parliament and the military authorities; and on July 12 it was voted "that an army shall be forthwith raised for the safety of the King's person, defence of both Houses of Parliament,...and preserving of the true religion, the laws, liberty, and peace of the kingdom"; the Commons declaring that they "will live and die with the Earl of Essex, whom they have nominated general in this cause".[3] On the other hand, the King had already issued commissions of array; and on August 22 his standard was raised at Nottingham, "in the evening of a very stormy and tempestuous day".

"The standard itself was blown down", says Clarendon,[4] "the same night it had been set up, by a very strong and unruly wind, and could not be fixed again in a day or two till the tempest was allayed. And this was the melancholic state of the King's affairs when the standard was set up".

It was a new thing for an English Parliament to be

---

[1] *His Majesty's Answer to the Nineteen Propositions* (Rushworth, iv. 728).
[2] *Memoirs*, i. 206.
[3] Votes printed in Gardiner, *Documents*, p. 261.   [4] ii. 291.

conducting a war; and it must not be forgotten that
Parliament itself was divided. Of the Peers, about half
actively supported the King and a quarter the Parliament,
the rest being minors or absentees; thus only about thirty
remained at Westminster, and the majority joined the
King at York.[1] Of the Commons, about 300 adhered to
the Parliament in London, and 175 followed the King.[2]
In the country at large also there was a similar division.
Roughly speaking, the north and west declared for the
King and the south and east for the Houses;[3] but in
many of the Parliamentary counties there were important
minorities of Royalists who would have rallied to the King
if he had ever succeeded in winning his Marston Moor
or Naseby—the brilliant and impressive victory which
would have been the signal for his supporters to declare
themselves openly. It was undoubtedly the case, however,
that "the portion of Lot had fallen to the Parliament",
for in the days before the development of minerals and
manufactures in the north, the wealth of England was
concentrated in the south and east, and the lion's share of
the customs was collected at the Port of London. It is
also roughly true that the nobility and gentry followed the
King and the townsmen and yeomen the Houses; but here
again qualifications have to be made. The Parliamentary
party, quite as much as the Royalists, was led by men of
good family. Hampden, Haslerig, Digges, and Vane
were landed gentry; Blake and Bradshaw were at any rate
of no mean origin; Cromwell was a country squire. The
military commanders appointed by the Houses were men of
distinguished birth and high position. Essex was the son of
Elizabeth's favourite Earl, and his mother was Sir Philip
Sidney's widow. Fairfax was a peer's son, the owner of a
great estate, a man of literary tastes and the writer of
meritorious verses. When he occupied Oxford with his

---

[1] Firth, *Lords*, p. 115.

[2] Firth, *Cromwell*, p. 69. On the part played by personal loyalty
to the King, see the excellent chapter on "The Cavaliers" in Feiling,
pp. 42 ff.

[3] Thorold Rogers draws the dividing line across the map from Scarborough
to Southampton (*History of Agriculture and Prices*, v. 11).

troops, his first act was to place a guard over the University Library.[1]

The comparatively simple geographical and social divisions were also complicated by local feeling,[2] for the Civil War of the seventeenth century still retains a curious affinity to the Wars of the Roses. As soon as Devonshire submitted to the Parliament, Cornwall went the other way, and Sir Ralph Hopton was able to form a party for the King there, and to dispossess the Parliamentarian gentlemen who had appropriated the control of the county militia.[3] On the other hand, the King's great scheme for an advance on London in 1643 was wrecked upon county patriotism.[4] The Yorkshiremen refused to leave their county so long as it was exposed to forays from the Parliamentary stronghold of Hull; the Welshmen would not cross the Severn while Gloucester remained untaken; and the Cornishmen went home again in order to protect their country from the men of Devon and the hostile garrison of Plymouth.[5] Thus Charles was compelled to postpone his advance until he had reduced the fortresses in his rear, and this lost him his opportunity.

At the beginning of the war both sides tried to make use of the existing military system of the country; and the first operation of all was the King's attempt to seize Hull, the place where the munitions collected for the war with the Scots had been stored. The counterpart of this occurred elsewhere also, in local attempts to obtain control of the county magazines in which the train-bands kept their arms and ammunition.[6] With the exception of those of London, the train-bands soon proved useless, for they had little training, less discipline, and were often immobilised in their own counties. Both sides then fell back on volunteers, and when by the middle of 1643 these began to be exhausted, both sides resorted to impressment.

---

[1] *D.N.B.* xviii. 148.

[2] A good account of the part played by local feeling in the Civil War will be found in the Introduction to Feiling, *History of the Tory Party*.

[3] S. R. Gardiner, *The History of the Great Civil War*, i. 79–80.

[4] *Ib.* i. 78.   [5] *Ib.* i. 229.

[6] Firth, *Cromwell's Army*, p. 15.

There were also permanent levies made by associated counties; of these the most important was Cromwell's Eastern Association. As there was at first no lack of trained officers who had seen something in the Thirty Years' War of Continental military methods, it seemed likely that they would be able to make armies if these methods could furnish them with the raw material.

On the King's side the mechanism of the State was of the simplest, for in theory he took all important decisions in consultation with his Privy Council. At the beginning of 1643 this consisted of eleven peers and five commoners, with Falkland as Secretary of State;[1] but "amongst them", as Clarendon complains, "there were not many who had been acquainted with the transaction of business".[2] This Council was always liable to be overridden by Prince Rupert and the soldiers, who thought "themselves the best judges of all counsels and designs, because they were for the most part to execute them"; although "they neither designed well nor executed". In January, 1644, however, a Royalist Parliament met at Oxford, and was attended by about fifty lords and 120 commoners. Of this "mongrel Parliament", as Charles called it, we know little, for its records were destroyed; but some of its members incurred the King's displeasure by advocating a compromise.[3]

On the Parliamentary side new machinery had to be devised in order to meet the situation created by the military alliance with the Scots. The Civil War in England had been watched by them from the beginning with the keenest interest. "We conceive", wrote Baillie, "through the burning of our neighbours' houses in England and Ireland, and the great reek that begins to smoak in our own, dangers cannot be small".[4] They saw in Root and Branch the first step towards the implanting in England of the methods of their own Church, and they were prepared to render military aid to the Parliament, provided that the establishment of Presbyterianism south of the Tweed was made a condition of the bargain. The necessity

[1] Firth, *Lords*, p. 128.   [2] ii. 536.
[3] Firth, *Lords*, p. 130.   [4] ii. 60.

for broadening the basis of resistance to the King had been
grasped by Pym as early as January, 1643, but at that
time he had failed to carry the Parliament with him.[1] In
the autumn of the year, however, the high tide mark of
Royalist success was reached, and military necessity
converted Parliament to Pym's policy. No one liked the
Scottish discipline—as Alexander Henderson said long
after, the disposition of England was "so generally
opposite", and the people "so naturally inclined to freedom
that they can hardly be induced to embrace any discipline
that may abridge it"[2]—but the payment of the Scotch
price seemed a lesser evil than the restoration of the King's
authority. Thus in September, 1643, the "Solemn League
and Covenant"[3] was signed and sworn to by the English
Parliament, by which it undertook "the reformation of
religion in the kingdoms of England and Ireland, in
doctrine, worship, discipline, and government, according
to the Word of God and the example of the best reformed
Churches", and to "endeavour to bring the Churches of
God in the three kingdoms to the nearest conjunction and
uniformity in religion, confession of faith, form of Church
government, directory for worship and catechising, that
we and our posterity after us may as brethren live in faith
and love, and the Lord may delight to dwell in the midst
of us". Another clause of the Covenant pledged the
Parliament to "endeavour the extirpation of Popery,
prelacy,...superstition, heresy, schism, profaneness, and
whatsoever shall be found to be contrary to sound doctrine
and the power of godliness". The Scots undertook, as
soon as the Covenant was signed, to raise an army under
the veteran Leslie for service in the north of England in
return for a monthly payment of £30,000. Out of com-
pliment to their new allies, both Houses appointed
Presbyterian chaplains, gave up the Prayer Book in their
daily services, and decided to sit upon Christmas Day.[4]

---

[1] *D.N.B.* xlvii. 82.
[2] Quoted in G. P. Gooch, *English Democratic Ideas in the Seventeenth Century*, p. 171.
[3] Printed in Gardiner, *Documents*, pp. 267–71.
[4] Firth, *Lords*, p. 137.

The Scots themselves laid stress upon the religious side of the Covenant, and regarded it in some sort as a declaration against the Pope. "Were that Covenant now painted upon the wall within the Pope's palace", said Alexander Henderson, "it would doubtless put him into Belshazzar's quaking condition". It may also be regarded as a kind of retaliation for the Service Book and Canons. Laud had tried to bring Scotland into ecclesiastical uniformity with England and had failed; the Scottish divines now succeeded in bringing England into ecclesiastical uniformity with Scotland. "By means of the League and Covenant", says Seeley,[1] "Scotland had, as it were, imposed a Service Book upon England". But the political and military consequences of the Covenant were no less important than its religious consequences. (1) It widened still further the breach between Royalists and Parliamentarians by making it impossible for the Parliament henceforth, in negotiating with the King, to accept anything less than the establishment of Presbyterianism; and (2) the arrival of Leslie's army in the north in January, 1644, was destined to lead up to the victory of Marston Moor on July 2 and to turn the scale in that part of England decisively against the King. And the Covenant also had a constitutional consequence. On February 16, 1644, soon after the Scots had crossed the border, Vane and St John proposed and carried an Ordinance[2] for appointing a "Committee of Both Kingdoms" to direct their armies. This was to consist of seven peers and fourteen commoners (of whom Oliver Cromwell was one) empowered to act as a joint committee with the four commissioners for Scotland resident in London, and "to advise, consult, order, and direct concerning the carrying on and managing of the war for the best advantage of the three kingdoms,...and likewise with power to hold good correspondence and intelligence with foreign States".

The appointment was in the first instance for three months only, but on May 22 it was renewed without

---

[1] *The Growth of British Policy*, i. 422.
[2] Printed in Gardiner, *Documents*, p. 271.

limitation of time and with more comprehensive authority.[1] In both cases, however, the Committee was "to observe such orders and directions as they from time to time shall receive from both Houses of Parliament". It ordered the disposition of troops with all the authority of Parliament itself, and for many years played the part of a War Office, at first under its original name and then as the "Committee at Derby House".[2] These large results following upon the alliance with Scotland, enable us to appreciate a significant remark made by Fuller, who recognised that the vigorous participation of the Scots in the war was the first step in the downfall of the King. "A Scottish mist", he said, "may wet an Englishman to the skin".[3]

For both sides the financing of the war constituted a difficult and perplexing problem. At the beginning, an important part was played by voluntary contributions of money and jewels, and especially plate, of which there was an enormous quantity in the country. The supporters of the King were on the whole richer in that kind of property and they were also more generous than the gentlemen on the other side;[4] although this was counterbalanced by

[1] This second Ordinance is printed in Gardiner, *Documents*, p. 273.

[2] *The Quarrel between Manchester and Cromwell* (Camden Society, New Series XII), p. xix.

[3] *Worthies*, ii. 543.

[4] This was not always the case. Clarendon tells what he calls "a pleasant story...which administered some mirth" concerning two great lords near Nottingham, the Earl of Kingston and Lord Dencourt, who were applied to on the King's behalf. His messenger was well received by the Earl of Kingston, who "expressed, with wonderful civil expressions of duty, the great trouble he sustained in not being able to comply with his Majesty's commands:...all men knew that he neither had nor could have money.... But, he said, he had a neighbour,...the Lord Dencourt, who was good for nothing and lived like a hog...and who could not have so little as twenty thousand pounds in the scurvy house in which he lived, and advised that he might be sent to, who could not deny the having of money". Another messenger who interviewed Lord Dencourt "got no more money, nor half so many good words", for that lord "with as cheerful a countenance as his could be (for he had a very unusual and unpleasant face) told him that though he had no money himself, but was in extreme want of it, he would tell him where he might have money enough; that he had a neighbour,... the Earl of Kingston, that never did good to anybody, and loved nobody but himself, who had a world of money, and could furnish the King with as much as he had need of" (ii. 332–3).

the great sacrifices made for the cause by the City of London, now entirely under Puritan control. A time came, however, when voluntary contributions were exhausted, and it became necessary for both sides to devise new expedients in taxation. It then became apparent that the real resources of the country were in the hands of the Parliament. In addition to the customs taken at the Port of London, for a time it held Bristol also, then the second commercial city in the kingdom, and its control of the navy gave it the customs revenue in other sea-ports. This last accession also enabled Parliament to stop the importation of arms from abroad by the King, and from the naval bases of the Thames and Portsmouth to supply and maintain the two vitally important fortresses of Hull and Plymouth. If sea-power had been on the other side, a Royalist blockade of London might have given the war a different issue, for, as Ranke remarks,[1] "the leaders of the Parliamentary majority derived their main strength from their alliance with the capital".

Parliamentary war-taxation is important because most of the expedients then adopted were incorporated into the permanent financial system of the country at the Restoration. (1) The subsidy was replaced by what were known as "monthly assessments", payments made by the counties on the basis of the subsidy books, but with two important differences from the subsidy. (a) Parliament did not undertake the assessment of individuals but only fixed the total amount which each county or borough was to pay for each month, leaving the assessment and collection of the tax to the local authorities. (b) The local authorities, much more keenly interested than the central authority had ever been in an equitable distribution of the burden among individual taxpayers, threw over the old conventional rates of the subsidy, and out of their local knowledge assessed the taxpayers at what they were really worth. Thus while the frequent monthly payments furnished the military authorities with a constant supply of ready money, the change in the system of assessment remedied a whole series of ancient grievances. (2) In 1643, Pym, copying

[1] *History of England*, ii. 358.

from a Dutch model, introduced the excise—a tax levied inland upon articles of consumption, as distinguished from customs, which were levied at the ports upon articles of external trade. (3) A part of the military expenses of the Parliament were met by the exaction of compositions from the Royalists. These were justified in the eyes of the men who levied them by the long series of precedents for the confiscation of the estates of traitors. They are the Parliamentary counterpart of forfeiture for treason, and as a rule the business was managed with a remarkable sense of equity and fair play.

By the Solemn League and Covenant the Long Parliament stood pledged to a Presbyterian Church settlement after the pattern of Scotland; and it had already equipped itself with an ecclesiastical advisory council to which the construction of such a settlement could be referred. The Westminster Assembly of Divines had been summoned in July, 1643, not long before the Covenant was signed. It consisted of thirty laymen, including men so eminent as Selden, Pym, and Vane, and 120 divines, mainly Presbyterians but with a small Episcopalian group and five "Dissenting Brethren".[1] Its business was to substitute for the Laudian idea of unity of ceremonial that unity of belief which was the idea of the English Puritans, and to superimpose upon this the Scottish conception of unity of discipline. The Assembly sat on five days in the week, from nine in the morning till one or two in the afternoon, and any member was fined sixpence who was late for prayers at half-past eight. The Scottish Presbyterian Baillie attended one of the meetings held on a special fast-day, and describes the proceedings thus:[2]

This day was the sweetest that I have seen in England.... We spent from nine to five very graciously. After Dr Twisse[3] had begun with a brief prayer, Mr Marshall prayed large two hours most divinely, confessing the sins of the members of the Assembly in a wonderfully pathetic and prudent way. After, Mr Arrowsmith preached one hour, then a psalm; thereafter, Mr Vines prayed near

---

[1] An annotated list of the members of the Assembly is printed in Masson, ii. 515–24.

[2] Baillie, ii. 184.   [3] He was the Prolocutor of the Assembly.

two hours, and Mr Palmer preached one hour, and Mr Seaman prayed near two hours; then a psalm. After, Mr Henderson brought them to a short, sweet conference of the heart confessed in the Assembly, and other seen faults to be remedied, and the conveniency to preach against all sects, especially Anabaptists and Antinomians.

The last phrase is significant, for the Assembly was not unanimous. The minority of five "Dissenting Brethren" was opposing the establishment of the Presbyterian discipline upon novel grounds.

"The shock of war", says Green,[1] "had broken the bonds of custom, and given a violent impulse to the freest thought". Milton in 1644[2] saw in London

a city of refuge, the mansion-house of Liberty, encompassed and surrounded with [God's] protection! The shop of war hath not there more anvils and hammers working to fashion out the plates and instruments of armed justice in defence of beleaguered truth than there be pens and heads there, sitting by their studious lamps, musing, searching, revolving new notions and ideas wherewith to present, as with their homage and fealty, the approaching reformation: others as fast reading, trying all things, assenting to the force of reason and convincement.

This stimulus to speculation involved the multiplication of sects,[3] and these came to be grouped together under the name of Independents. Their fundamental principle of thought finds its best and most eloquent expression in Pastor Robinson's memorable address to the Pilgrim Fathers in 1620, a paraphrase of which is still sung as a hymn in some Nonconformist churches.

I charge you before God and His blessed angels that...if God reveal anything to you by any other instrument of his, be as ready

---

[1] *History of the English People*, iii. 236.

[2] In *Areopagitica* (Prose Works, ii. 91).

[3] Thomas Edwards, one of the English Presbyterians, made a catalogue of 176 "errors, heresies, and blasphemies", but at the time when he wrote (August, 1644) the number of recognised sects was much smaller. Masson enumerates thirteen: Baptists or Anabaptists; Old Brownists; Antinomians; Famulists; Millenaries or Chiliasts; Seekers; Divorcers; Anti-Sabbatarians and Traskites; Soul-sleepers or Mortalists; Arians, Socinians, and other Anti-Trinitarians; Anti-Scripturists; Sceptics or Questionists; Atheists. Ten years later five new sects had sprung up: Fifth-Monarchy Men; Ranters; Muggletonians; Boehmenists; Quakers (Masson, iii. 143, 146–59; v. 16).

to receive it as ever you was to receive any truth by my ministry, for I am verily persuaded the Lord has more truth yet to break forth out of his Holy Word. For my part I cannot sufficiently bewail the condition of the Reformed Churches, who are come to a period in religion, and will go at present no farther than the instruments of their reformation. The Lutherans cannot be drawn to go beyond what Luther saw,...and the Calvinists...stick fast where they were left by that great man of God, who yet saw not all things....I beseech you remember it is an article of your Church covenant that you be ready to receive whatever truth shall be made known to you from the written Word of God.[1]

The application of this principle of progressive revelation to seventeenth-century conditions was bound to lead to diversity of doctrine, and each successive variation was likely to create for itself a new sect. But although Independency attracted the speculators in religion who were seeking something new, it also drew to itself men like Milton who desired a genuine liberty of thought. "The national importance of Independency", says Gardiner,[2] "dates from 1644, because it offered a home to all who in that year recoiled alike from the bonds of Presbyterianism and the bonds of episcopacy". Its principle of Church government, deriving from the earlier Brownists and Barrowists, was the autonomy of each separate congregation, and its independence of bishops, or presbyteries, or any other external authority. This was the principle put forward by the minority of five in the Westminster Assembly, for they held, as Fuller puts it,[3] "that the pressing of an exact concurrence to the Presbyterian government was but a kind of conscience-prison, whilst accurate conformity to the Scotch Church was the very dungeon thereof".

Their fight against the domination of Presbyterianism at first appeared hopeless; but outside the Westminster Assembly the cause of Independency was steadily gaining ground, and especially in the Parliamentary army, where it had in Cromwell a powerful ally. As a practical man he was chiefly concerned to get hold of the material out of which the best soldiers could be made, and he was

---

[1] Neal, *History of the Puritans* (edition of 1754), i. 490.
[2] *Cromwell's Place in History*, p. 31.   [3] *Church History*, iii. 466.

not disposed to reject a promising recruit because his religious views were eccentric. He therefore used the influence which his great position gave him against the Presbyterian officers and chaplains who were trying to exclude heresy from the army. In March, 1644, in thus defending a cashiered Anabaptist officer, he took occasion to lay down the principle of toleration.

"Ay, but the man is an Anabaptist", he wrote. "Are you sure of that? Admit he be, shall that render him incapable to serve the public?...Sir, the State, in choosing men to serve them, takes no notice of their opinions; if they be willing faithfully to serve them, that satisfies".[1]

Entirely modern as this statement of it sounds, the toleration of Cromwell's day was only a temporary expedient to meet special circumstances. The sects differed from each other upon innumerable points of doctrine, but they agreed upon two fundamental matters. (1) They all accepted the principle of Independency, the autonomy of each separate congregation—the only system of Church government that was possible for them; and (2) they were all united against a Presbyterian Church settlement which would leave no room for individual heresies, but would maintain by penance, excommunication, and even by temporal punishments, the unity of the Church. To religious bodies thus situated, the principle of toleration was essential, for it was the principle upon which the sects could federate against their foes. To the mind of Cromwell himself, toleration appeared as something more than an expedient, but here he rose above most of his contemporaries.

"All that believe", he wrote on September 14, 1645,[2] "have the real unity, which is most glorious because inward and spiritual.... As for being united in forms, commonly called uniformity, every Christian will for peace-sake study and do, as far as conscience will permit; and from brethren, in things of the mind we look for no compulsion but that of light and reason". "I profess to thee", he wrote much later, in November, 1648,[3] "I desire from my heart, I have prayed for it, I have waited for the day to see union and right

[1] Carlyle, *Cromwell's Letters and Speeches* (ed. Mrs S. C. Lomas), i. 171.
[2] *Ib*. i. 218.　　　　　　　　　　　[3] *Ib*. iii. 390.

understanding between the godly people—Scots, English, Jews, Gentiles, Presbyterians, Independents, Anabaptists, and all".

But even Cromwell had his limitations, for he never included Episcopalians among the "godly people", and still less Roman Catholics.

The position of Cromwell and the Independents with regard to toleration was immensely strengthened by Marston Moor, for it was an Independents' victory, as Cromwell and the Independent troops of the Eastern Association had come up just in time to save the Presbyterian Scots from being swept away. "It had all the evidence", he wrote on July 5, "of an absolute victory obtained by the Lord's blessing upon the godly party principally. We never charged but we routed the enemy, ...God made them as stubble to our swords".[1] The majorities in Parliament and the Assembly might still be against him, but Cromwell and his soldiers could no longer be ignored. The result was the acceptance by Parliament, without a division, of a "Toleration" or "Accommodation" Order, passed on September 13, 1644, instructing those bodies which were concerned with the settlement of Church government "to endeavour the finding out some way how far tender consciences, who cannot in all things submit to the common rule which shall be established, may be borne with according to the Word, and as may stand with the public peace". At the same sitting the Speaker, "by command of the House", gave thanks to Lieutenant-General Cromwell for "the faithful service performed by him in the late battle near York, where God made him a special instrument in obtaining that great victory".[2]

If Marston Moor led up to toleration, the indecisive battle of Newbury, when the King was allowed to escape to Oxford under cover of night, led to the Self-denying Ordinance. By the end of 1644 most of the Parliamentary peers, with the exception of the Earl of Warwick who commanded the fleet, had ceased to justify confidence in them as military leaders. The attack launched in Parliament

---

[1] *Letters and Speeches,* i. 176.   [2] Gardiner, *Civil War,* i. 483.

by Cromwell the Independent against Manchester the Presbyterian was partly a protest against the system under which generals were selected to serve in the field on account of their high family or great Parliamentary position,[1] and the Self-denying Ordinance was an attempt to remedy this by placing the conduct of the war in more competent hands. In the form in which it was ultimately passed on April 3, 1645,[2] it discharged every member of either House, at the end of forty days, "of and from all and every office or command, military or civil", granted by the Long Parliament, although nothing was said to prevent their reappointment.

Concurrently with the Self-denying Ordinance was pushed on the Ordinance for the reorganisation of the Parliamentary army under the form known as the "New Model". By the middle of 1644 the military authorities were beginning to find their way to the same conclusion as was to be arrived at by Washington more than a century later in an entirely different sphere of action.

"Short enlistments", he said to the American colonists in 1776,[3] "and a mistaken dependence on militia, have been the origin of all our misfortunes; the evils of a standing army are remote, but the consequence of wanting one is certain and irretrievable ruin. To carry on the war systematically, you must establish your army on a permanent and national footing".

The result was that at the end of the year the Committee of Both Kingdoms was instructed to report on the state of the Parliamentary armies, and especially "to consider

---

[1] "For what do the enemy say? Nay, what do many say that were friends at the beginning of the Parliament? Even this, that the members of both Houses have got great places and commands, and the sword into their hands; and, what by interest in the Parliament, what by power in the Army, will perpetually continue themselves in grandeur, and not permit the war speedily to end, lest their own power should determine with it" (Cromwell's Speech of December 9, 1644: *Letters and Speeches*, i. 186).

[2] Printed in Gardiner, *Documents*, p. 287. "This, done on a sudden, in one session, with great unanimity, is still more and more admired by some as a most wise, necessary, and heroic action; by others as the most rash, hazardous, and unjust action as ever Parliament did. Much may be said on both hands, but as yet it seems a dream, and the bottom of it is not understood" (Baillie, ii. 247).

[3] Quoted in Morley, *Cromwell*, p. 168.

of a frame or model of the whole militia".[1] The result of their labours was the New Model Ordinance, which passed the Lords on February 15, 1645, although it was not until April that the reorganisation was complete. This incorporated the three armies commanded by Essex, Waller, and Manchester into a single force, raising this to an establishment of about 22,000 men under the command of Sir Thomas Fairfax. As a military engine the New Model was far more efficient than the looser organisation which it displaced. (1) There was a great increase in the strength of the cavalry—the arm in which hitherto the Royalists had specially excelled, and the one which was more important than any other under seventeenth century conditions of war.[2] (2) When the New Model was organised, it was provided with a powerful train of artillery, which, although it did little service in battle, was destined to be quickly effective against the Royalist castles and garrisons.[3] (3) As the men were better paid than hitherto, it was much easier to maintain discipline;[4] and (4) Fairfax and Cromwell succeeded, in virtue of their great military reputation, in emancipating themselves from the hampering supervision and control which the amateur strategists of the Committee of Both Kingdoms had maintained over the earlier generals, although the commander-in-chief was still required to take the advice of professional councils of war.[5]

On June 14, 1645, the fruit of these measures of reorganisation was gathered in. The New Model met the King's whole army at Naseby, and overwhelmed it. Though the cavalry were saved, the infantry were slain or captured almost to a man; and nearly 500 officers were taken, with the King's whole train of artillery and a great store of arms. Thus, even if he could raise fresh regiments, he no longer had arms to equip them or competent officers to train them.[6] To all intents and purposes Naseby ended the war, for Charles was never in a position to fight a pitched battle again. He still had hopes of Montrose in

---

[1] Firth, *Cromwell's Army*, p. 32. [2] *Ib.* pp. 110–11.
[3] *Ib.* pp. 158, 169. [4] *Ib.* p. 285.
[5] *Ib.* pp. 56–7. [6] Gardiner, *Civil War*, ii. 216, 224.

Scotland, but that "meteoric career" came to an end at Philiphaugh on September 13; and with the fall of Bristol three days earlier, his last hope in England also disappeared. On April 27, 1646, he began his flight to the Scots at Newark, and on June 24 Oxford capitulated. "At Newark and Newcastle", as Ranke has remarked,[1] "he reminds us of his grandmother" Mary Stuart "at Fotheringay". He appears for a time as if he were a Scottish monarch in captivity in the hostile country of England.[2]

---

[1] *History of England*, ii. 478.   [2] Seeley, *British Policy*, i. 425.

The Long Parliament and the Army

WHEN Sir Jacob Astley surrendered in the West on March 21, 1646, with the King's last remaining force, he said to the victors, "You have now done your work and may go to play; unless you will fall out amongst yourselves".[1] The next chapter in the history of the Long Parliament is its quarrel with the army, which led up to military intervention in politics, and ended in what is sometimes called the "Second Civil War".

Even in the Presbyterian Parliament the Independents were gaining strength. During the greater part of the war the seats of the 200 members who had joined the King were left vacant; but after Naseby the Commons began to issue writs, and by the spring of 1646 nearly 150 new members had been chosen, while by the end of the year the number of these, who were commonly called "Recruiters",[2] had risen to 235. These fresh elections returned to the House of Commons some of the more famous names of the Commonwealth and the Protectorate—Blake, the Fleetwoods, Ludlow, Colonel Hutchinson, Henry Ireton, and Algernon Sidney. Thus Independency was not only strengthened numerically, but the intellectual energy of the party was powerfully reinforced. On the other hand, the numbers of the Lords had sunk very low, and they could not, like the Commons, recruit their House by means of fresh elections. In 1646 there were only twenty-eight peers qualified to vote in the House, and the attendance varied from seventeen to twenty-two.[3] Among these the division of opinion was very close, and more than once during 1646 the number of Presbyterians and Independents voting was exactly equal.[4] The Lords wanted to readmit some of the Royalist peers on payment of a fine, but under an Ordinance of June 29, 1644, no

---

[1] Rushworth, vi. 141.
[2] Gardiner, *Civil War*, ii. 449, and Firth, *Lords*, p. 153.
[3] Firth, *Lords*, p. 153.   [4] *Ib.* p. 154.

peer who had abandoned the Parliament could be readmitted without the approval of both Houses; and it was
practically certain that the consent of the Commons would
not be forthcoming.[1]

Far more important than the growth of Independency
in Parliament was its development in the Parliamentary
army. In its early days the army had not been specially
Puritan, or indeed specially religious. Writing of the
soldiers of 1560[2] Sir John Hayward observes, "For surely
if there be any behaviour that may be taxed with the note
of irreligious, it may be found amongst men of war", and
his view would not have been modified by association with
the army of Essex. A letter of September 13, 1642, from
one of its officers, usually quoted to illustrate the methods
of Prince Rupert, shews, however, that religious influences
were already at work.

Wednesday morning we had tidings that Prince Rupert, that
diabolical Cavalier, had surrounded Leicester and demanded £2000,
or else threatened to plunder the town; whereupon our soldiery
were even mad to be at them....Friday morning worthy Mr
Obadiah Sedgwick gave us a worthy sermon, and my company in
particular marched to hear him in rank and file. Mr John Sedgwick
was appointed to preach in the afternoon, but we had news that
Prince Rupert had plundered Marlborough and fired some adjacent
towns, and our regiment was immediately drawn into the field....
Sabbath-day morning Mr Marshall, that worthy champion of
Christ, preached unto us: afternoon, Mr Ash. These with their
sermons have already subdued and satisfied more malignant spirits
amongst us than a thousand armed men could have done.[3]

Occasional sermons are but the beginning of the
movement. It was to be reinforced by the successes of
Cromwell's "Ironsides", recruited from the freeholders
and farmers of the Eastern Counties, always the stronghold
of Puritanism. These "men of religion" proved more than
a match for Rupert's "men of honour", and Gainsborough
fight, on July 28, 1643, when they covered the retreat of
a Parliamentary force against the whole of Newcastle's
army,[4] suggested that the blessing of Heaven was visibly

[1] *Ib.* p. 154.   [2] *Annals of Queen Elizabeth*, p. 55.
[3] Quoted in Gardiner, *Civil War*, i. 32.
[4] Gardiner, *Civil War*, i. 223.

resting upon men "well equipped in the quiet of their consciences, and externally in good armour, standing firm as one man".[1] In the days before the introduction of bayonets or weapons of precision, footsoldiers were rarely a match for horse unless strongly posted, and superiority in cavalry was, other things being equal, superiority in war. Gainsborough fight proves that in the Ironsides the Parliament had at last succeeded in equipping itself with cavalry at least equal to the arm in which the Royalists specially excelled.

Later on, the effect of the Self-denying Ordinance had been to make a clean sweep of the higher Presbyterians who also sat in Parliament, and their places had been filled by men who, if not all declared Independents, were at any rate of the Independent type.[2] Moreover, since the Ordinance excluded members of both Houses from military command, Parliament had now lost its hold upon the generals, and the only link between Parliament and the army was Cromwell, who belonged to both, having been reappointed to military office because the best cavalry leader on the side of the Parliament could not be spared. Under the New Model Ordinance the army had now become a body of professionals, more easily moulded by its officers than the earlier fluctuating levies had been, and the new leaven of their influence soon began to work. In the summer of 1645 Richard Baxter became chaplain to a regiment of cavalry, and he found that every heresy was represented in its ranks.[3] But the error which he was called upon to controvert most often was that the civil magistrate had no authority in matters of religion, and every man had therefore a right to believe and to preach what he pleased.[4] "If I should worship the sun or moon like the Persians", said a soldier who may have been temporarily stationed in a public-house, "or that pewter pot on the table, no one has anything to do with it".[5]

The conversion of the New Model into a home of Independency was partly due to the labours of the army

---

[1] Gneist, *Constitutional History of England*, ii. 252.
[2] Gardiner, *Cromwell*, p. 33.   [3] Firth, *Cromwell*, p. 147.
[4] *Reliquiae Baxterianae*, p. 53.   [5] Masson, iii. 525.

chaplains. These had been at first Presbyterians, but after Edgehill most of the regular ministers went home, and so "lost all, by forsaking the army and betaking themselves to an easier and quieter way of life".[1] The more enthusiastic remained, and these were the more fanatical; thus religious instruction tended to pass into the hands of divines who were drawn together under the banner of Independency. This "intensive propaganda", which included the circulation of religious literature among the soldiers, led to an epidemic of unlicensed preaching in the army. An attempt had been made, when the New Model was first organised, to put down preaching by unordained persons, but little attention was paid to the order, and it soon became a dead letter. Things did not fall out quite as Macaulay imagined[2] when he drew his picture of "a corporal versed in Scripture" leading "the devotions of his less gifted colonel" and admonishing "a backsliding major"; but Baxter complains of the way in which the soldiers interrupted sermons, disputed with the ministers in public upon points of doctrine, and occupied the pulpits without being asked.[3]

From free speculation on matters religious, there ran a broad and easy road to free speculation on matters political. Baxter called Independency "Church democracy",[4] and it was bound to bring State democracy in its train. "Men who chose their pastors, naturally demanded the right to choose their magistrates too."[5] Thus where the Presbyterian party declared for the sovereignty of Parliament, the political thinkers of army Independency took their stand upon the sovereignty of the people. It was not at first the intention of the army to intervene either in politics or religion, but in 1647 the tide of events was beginning to carry it in that direction. In June Cromwell and the officers of the army had told the City of London that the men who had perilled their lives in the field "have as much right to demand and desire to see a happy settlement as we have to our money and the other common interest of soldiers";[6] and a pamphlet of July bore the significant

---

[1] *Reliquiae Baxterianae*, p. 51.   [2] i. 60   [3] Firth, *Army*, p. 334.
[4] *Reliquiae Baxterianae*, p. 53.   [5] Firth, *Lords*, p. 62.
[6] *Letters and Speeches*, i. 267.

title, *Vox Militaris*. From 1647 therefore, we may say, in
Seeley's Scripture phrase, that militant Independency
stands before the world "bright as the sun, clear as the
moon, terrible as an army with banners".[1]

As the army was becoming the stronghold of Independency, the Presbyterian majority in Parliament sought
to strengthen themselves against it by turning to the King.
The Presbyterian clergy were determined that no toleration should be allowed to the sects. "To let men serve
God according to the persuasion of their own consciences",
wrote one of them, "was to cast out one devil that seven
worse might enter". "I am confident of it upon serious
thoughts...", said another,[2] "that if the Devil had his
choice, whether the hierarchy, ceremonies, and liturgy
should be established in this kingdom or a toleration
granted, he would choose and prefer a toleration before
them". Yet a toleration was what the army agreed in
demanding, and the Parliament was beginning to fear
"that hydra-headed monster of accumulated heresies".

During the Civil War there had already been negotiations with the King. The Treaty of Oxford in 1643[3] had
reflected his earlier successes. The two Houses had
abandoned their claim to control the executive which they
had advanced in the Nineteen Propositions, and contented
themselves with finance and the power of the sword. On
the other hand, their ecclesiastical demands had become
more exacting, and they asked for the complete abolition
of Episcopacy and the settlement of the Church government of the future by Parliament, after consultation with
an Assembly of "godly, religious, and learned divines".
The Treaty of Uxbridge,[4] to all intents and purposes a
Scottish negotiation,[5] presented to the King on November
24, 1644, and discussed during the early months of
1645, reflected Marston Moor. Here the demand for

[1] *Growth of British Policy*, ii. 78.
[2] Thomas Edwards in *Antapologia*, August, 1644 (Masson, iii. 135).
[3] Printed in Gardiner, *Documents*, p. 262. In the seventeenth century
the word "treaty" was applied to diplomatic proceedings whether successful
or not, and was not reserved for the finished product of negotiation.
[4] Printed in Gardiner, *Documents*, p. 275.
[5] Gardiner, *Civil War*, ii. 66.

the control of the executive and the education of the King's children reappears from the Nineteen Propositions; and in addition to this (1) the control of the militia is to be vested in a permanent commission appointed by Parliament; (2) the ecclesiastical settlement is to be "according to the Covenant", which the King is to swear to and sign; and (3) the principle of the proscription of leading Royalists is introduced for the first time, the list being headed by the names of the King's own relatives—Rupert and Maurice of the Rhine. The Treaty also (4) transferred to Parliament the control of "the concluding of peace or war with foreign Princes and States", and it is therefore an episode in the long series of attempts on the part of Parliament, beginning with the reign of James I, to penetrate into the guarded area of foreign policy.[1] The surrender of Charles to the Scots was the occasion of another series of negotiations known as the Treaty of Newcastle,[2] sent to the King on July 13, 1646. This might have been expected to reflect Naseby, but in general it followed the lines of the Treaty of Uxbridge; the important difference being in the arrangements for the control of the militia. Instead of a permanent commission with extensive powers, Parliament itself was to hold the power of the sword for a period of twenty years—that is to say, during the probable life-time of Charles himself— but even after the twenty years had expired, bills for the raising and disposing of troops in all cases in which the Houses should declare that the safety of the kingdom was concerned, did not need the royal assent to become law. The King was also to take the Covenant himself and to consent to an Act imposing it on the three kingdoms. To these proposals Charles gave an evasive answer,[3] as his wife was afraid of the consequences of surrendering control over the militia, and he himself was determined not to sacrifice the bishops. The result was that the Scots, who now despaired of inducing him to accept Presbyterianism

[1] On these see Professor E. R. Turner's article on "Parliament and Foreign Affairs 1603–1760" in *E.H.R.* xxxiv. 172–97.
[2] Printed in Gardiner, *Documents*, p. 290.
[3] Printed in *ib.* p. 306.

and to take the Covenant, came to terms with the English Parliament, and on receipt of their arrears returned to Scotland, leaving the King behind them. In February, 1647, he was removed in the custody of the Parliament to Holmby House. His resolute and conscientious adherence to the bishops is a redeeming touch amid the King's intrigues.

"I confess", he wrote privately to Rupert after Naseby, "that speaking as to mere soldier or statesman, I must say that there is no probability but of my ruin; but as a Christian I must tell you that God will not suffer rebels to prosper or his cause to be overthrown, and whatsoever personal punishment it may please them to inflict upon me must not make me repine, much less to give over this quarrel, which by the grace of God I am resolved against, whatsoever it cost me; for I know my obligations to be both in conscience and honour neither to abandon God's cause, injure my successors, nor forsake my friends".[1]

"The King", Cromwell once said, "is a man of great parts and a great understanding", and when their fear of the army led the Presbyterians in Parliament to turn to him, he read the new situation well. In reply to secret proposals made by them,[2] he put forward on May 12, 1647, a third answer to the Propositions of Newcastle,[3] in which he offered concessions of the utmost importance. (1) He agreed to confirm a Presbyterian Church settlement for three years,

and also that a free consultation and debate be had with the divines at Westminster (twenty of his Majesty's nomination being added unto them) whereby it may be determined by his Majesty and the two Houses how the Church shall be governed after the said three years—or sooner, if differences may be agreed.

(2) He surrendered the power of the sword to the nominees of the Parliament for ten years, "and afterwards to return to the proper channel again, as it was in the times of Queen Elizabeth and King James of blessed memory".

"The historical importance" of this document, says Gardiner,[4] "can hardly be overrated". In it "the alliance was struck between the King and the Presbyterian party which led to the Second Civil

---

[1] Quoted in *D.N.B.* x. 81.   [2] See Gardiner, *Documents*, p. 309.
[3] Printed in *ib.* p. 311.   [4] *Ib.* p. xlv.

War in 1648, and ultimately to the Restoration in 1660. The Presbyterians with a majority in Parliament at their disposal gave up the attempt to coerce Charles which they had made in the Nineteen Propositions and in the Propositions of Oxford, of Uxbridge, and Newcastle, and fell back on the principle of re-establishing his authority",

subject to temporary concessions, as it was after the Long Parliament had carried its reforms but before the Civil War began.

Meanwhile these prospects of a settlement were being wrecked by the want of worldly wisdom displayed by the Presbyterian majority in Parliament. It was not un-reasonable that the army should be disbanded now that the war was over, and in February, 1647, a scheme for this purpose had been adopted by Parliament. Out of the 7000 horse and about 14,000 foot which constituted the New Model it was proposed to retain 6600 horse, foot-soldiers being assigned to garrison service only. Fairfax was still to keep the rank of general and was to be com-mander-in-chief of the new army, but all the other general officers were to be dismissed. No member of Parliament was to hold a commission in the army, and all the officers were to take the Covenant.[1] Of the remaining troops, 4200 horse and 8400 foot were to be sent to serve in Ireland, and of the rest about 6000 were to be disbanded. In this way Parliament struck at the higher organisation of the army, and made a clean sweep of the Independent officers of the New Model. The soldiers might have disbanded quietly, but for the method adopted in dealing with arrears of pay. In March, 1647, this was eighteen weeks for the infantry and forty-three weeks for the cavalry,[2] and the men naturally asked that before they disbanded or re-enlisted for Ireland, these arrears for past service should be paid in full. Parliament only offered six weeks in cash—afterwards raised under pressure to eight weeks; the rest was to be discharged by "debentures" issued "upon the public faith".[3] Thus the soldiers fell an easy prey to the arguments of the politicians among them, who

[1] Gardiner, *Civil War*, iii. 29–33. [2] *Ib*. iii. 39.
[3] Firth, *Army*, p 202.

saw that if the army were once disbanded "the sectaries would be broken". In April eight of the ten cavalry regiments each chose two representatives to explain their grievances to the generals, and the rest of the regiments soon after followed suit; to these representatives the name of "Agitators" or agents of the army was given. At the same time the officers began to meet in conclave to agree upon a common line of action with the men.

There is no doubt now, although at one time Royalist historians thought otherwise, that Cromwell did his best to accommodate the quarrel between the Parliament and the army. He sympathised with the grievances of the soldiers in the matter of pay, and he was certainly on the side of those among them who cared about toleration; but Cromwell was no fanatic. He had a clear and strong sense of the necessity for obedience to the civil power, and the evil that would ensue if the army should take upon itself to overthrow the institutions of the country by military violence. "Truly, gentlemen", he said to his officers, at a great meeting in Saffron Walden church on May 16, 1647,

it will be very fit for you to have a very great care in the making the best use and improvement that you can...of the interest which all of you or any of you may have in your respective regiments— namely, to work in them a good opinion of that authority that is over both us and them. If that authority falls to nothing, nothing can follow but confusion.[1]

But his task was extraordinarily difficult, because in the army he had to deal with two different kinds of enthusiast. On the one side was the political enthusiast like Rainborowe—or John Lilburne, whose writings were eagerly read by the soldiers, and were "quoted by them as statute law".[2] Lilburne violently attacked Cromwell as a traitor to army democracy, and said he must be bribed by the estate which Parliament had given him, or he would never have allowed himself to be "led by the nose by two covetous earthworms" like St John and Vane. On the other side was the religious fanatic, of whom Goffe may be taken as the type. In 1647, when the army was in

[1] *Letters and Speeches*, iii. 331.   [2] Firth, *Lords*, p. 167.

difficulties, Cromwell moved for a committee and Goffe proposed a prayer-meeting:[1] and this very well expresses the difference in their points of view. "I know a man may answer all difficulties with faith", Cromwell said to the Council of Officers in 1647, "and faith will answer all difficulties really where it is; but we are very apt all of us to call that faith that perhaps may be but carnal imagination".[2] Whether Cromwell and Ireton would have succeeded in the end in holding back Rainborowe and Goffe is uncertain, but their task was made impossible by the action of the Presbyterian majority in Parliament. While the army was wavering with regard to the use of force, the Parliamentary leaders, like the King arresting the Five Members, decided to appeal to it themselves. They began to remodel in the Presbyterian interest the City train-bands—a formidable force of 18,000 men; they discussed in secret with the Scottish commissioners in London a plan for bringing the army of Scotland into England to overawe the New Model; they sent orders to remove the artillery of the army from Oxford to the Tower; and they decided to bring the King from Holmby House to London. Their plans, which were known in the army as soon as they were made, were the signal for a general military revolt. Fairfax and Cromwell had now to choose between the military and the civil power, and they both elected to remain among their own people. The Agitators told Cromwell, "If he would not forthwith come and head them they would go their own way without him";[3] and he preferred to avoid military anarchy at the risk of civil war. "I am forced", said Fairfax, "to yield something out of order, to keep the army from disorder or worse inconveniences".[4] At the suggestion of the Agitators, afterwards approved by Cromwell, a party of horse secured the artillery at Oxford, and Cornet Joyce seized the person of the King at Holmby House and brought him to the headquarters of the army at Newmarket. This *coup d'état* was from the army point of view essential, for it cut Charles off from negotiations, and unless the

---

[1] Firth, in *Clarke Papers*, i. p. xlix. [2] *Letters and Speeches*, iii. 351.
[3] Firth, *Cromwell*, p. 164. [4] *D.N.B.* xviii. 144.

Parliament could complete with him the pending scheme for a three years' Presbyterian Church settlement, it was doubtful whether the Scots would come to the aid of the Parliament or the Presbyterian City of London support it in arms.[1] But the seizure of the King's person was regarded as a declaration of war. "It's now come to that", Sir Walter Erle said of the soldiers, "that they must sink us, or we sink them".[2]

The army next proceeded to equip itself with a political organisation, which appeared, "as if by magic, from a mutinous mass of troopers and musketeers".[3] The historical beginnings of this are to be found in the conspicuous part played in the campaigns of 1645 and 1646 by military councils of war, at which it was the custom for a large number of officers to be present.[4] As soon as the army began to intervene in politics, it became necessary for it to develop an organ for discussion, deliberation, and decision, through which the *vox militaris* might make itself heard. The appointment of the Agitators had brought the privates to bear upon affairs, and at one time it may have seemed possible that the Council of War, representing the officers, and the Council of Agitators, representing the privates, would travel by different roads; but by a master-stroke of statesmanship it was decided to fuse the two bodies into one Grand Council of the Army, consisting of the general officers, together with two commissioned officers and two soldiers to be chosen by each regiment; and thus all danger of independent action on the part of the privates was avoided. It was this Council which was destined a little later, acting on behalf of the whole army, to open negotiations with the King.

On June 15, 1647, the army put forward its demands in a document called *The Declaration of the Army*.[5] This passed lightly over the military grievances which had hitherto formed the staple of the soldiers' claims, and put forward a political programme containing some novel constitutional principles. (1) It claimed for the army the

---

[1] *D.N.B.* xviii. p. 165.   [2] Rushworth, vi. 515.
[3] Firth, *Lords*, p. 168.   [4] See Firth, *Army*, pp. 57–59.
[5] Printed in Rushworth, vi. 564–70.

right, hitherto lodged in the Parliament, or speaking on behalf of the people of England, inasmuch as it was not "a mere mercenary army, hired to serve any arbitrary power of a State, but called forth and conjured by the several declarations of Parliament to the defence of their own and the people's just rights and liberties". (2) Taking the modern democratic position that the people is the source of all power, it demanded an early dissolution to be followed by short Parliaments, as well as an Act of Oblivion and toleration for the sects. (3) It threw out a dangerous suggestion, which was to be acted upon later with fatal effect—that the Long Parliament should be purged of corrupt members, and especially of those who had defamed the army. A beginning was promptly made, for on the day on which the *Declaration* reached the Parliament at Westminster, the army accused eleven Presbyterian members of this offence among others, and on June 26 they withdrew from the House.

At the beginning of the month Parliament had been prepared to make concessions, even to paying the soldiers' arrears in full,[1] for the moderate party had obtained the ascendency in both Houses, but the Presbyterians of the City of London were roused to action by their ministers, and disorderly mobs assailed the Lords and then the Commons, and compelled them to rescind their conciliatory votes.[2] The army declared its intention of maintaining the independence of Parliament, and the Speakers of both Houses, accompanied by eight peers and fifty-seven of the Independents in the Commons, took refuge in the camp on Hounslow Heath. On August 6 Fairfax occupied London, the fugitive members returning with him, and the two Speakers were restored to their chairs. This was followed by steps on the part of the generals to press on the negotiations which only a few days before had been opened with the King. The willingness of Cromwell to negotiate with Charles is not so strange as it seems at first sight. The notion that he was already conspiring to remove the King from his path in order that he might mount the throne itself, is due only to the hostile imagination of

[1] Gardiner, *Civil War*, iii. 97.   [2] Firth, *Lords*, p. 170.

Royalist historians. The key to Cromwell's political position is to be found in a cryptic answer of his—made about this time—to one who sought to sound him about his ultimate aims. "No one rises so high", he said, "as he who knows not whither he is going."[1] He is one of the great opportunists of history, and the immediate object now before him was to return to the paths of constitutionalism, if only guarantees for the future could be found. It must not be forgotten that in his inner mind Cromwell profoundly distrusted the use of force. "What we... gain in a free way", he said to the Council of the Army, when the Agitators were pressing him to march on London, "is better than twice so much in a forced, and will be more truly ours and our posterities'.... That which you have by force I look upon it as nothing. I do not know that force is to be used, except we cannot get what is for the good of the kingdom without force".[2] Moreover he, like many of his contemporaries, was anxious for a final settlement, and weary of the inconclusiveness of the proceedings which seemed to bring peace no nearer. As someone said at the time: "Peace looks like St George on horseback—always in his saddle, but never the further in his journey".[3] It was becoming increasingly clear that no guarantees could be obtained from the Presbyterian majority in the Long Parliament—an oligarchy protected by statute from dissolution, and yet an oligarchy with which no terms could be made. It was at least conceivable that the political ideas of the army could be more easily realised, and toleration for the sects better secured, by means of an agreement with the monarchy. We may say that from the time of the quarrel with the Parliament and the occupation of London, the army began to rest its hopes mainly on the King.

The *Heads of the Proposals*,[4] put forward by the Council of the Army on August 1, 1647, proceeded from the indefatigable pen of Ireton. It is a sketch for a written constitution, differing widely from anything that had been

---

[1] Quoted in Gardiner, *Civil War*, iii. 143.
[2] *Letters and Speeches*, iii. 340, 342: *cf.* also p. 336.
[3] John Turberville, in the *Trevelyan Papers*, July 4, 1647.
[4] Printed in Gardiner, *Documents*, pp. 316–26.

hitherto proposed. Previous plans had been pervaded by suspicion of the King, and had sought to bring him under the control of Parliament. This was equally pervaded by suspicion of Parliament, and sought to bring it under the control of the constituencies. (1) The clauses intended to secure the subordination of the King to Parliament were for the most part borrowed from previous negotiations. The most important of them establishes the control of Parliament over the executive by providing "that an Act be passed for disposing the great offices for ten years by the Lords and Commons in Parliament,... and after ten years they to nominate three, and the King out of that number to appoint one for the succession upon any vacancy". The power of the sword was also vested in Parliament for the space of ten years, and the Lords and Commons were authorised during that time to raise money by ordinance "for what forces they shall from time to time find necessary". (2) The subordination of Parliament to the constituencies was secured by clauses that were novel and ingenious: that the existing Parliament shall be dissolved within a year; that future Parliaments shall be biennial, "each biennial Parliament to sit 120 days certain (unless adjourned or dissolved sooner by their own consent), afterwards to be adjournable or dissolvable by the King, and no Parliament to sit past 240 days from their first meeting"—an anticipation of the principle of the Triennial Act of 1694; that the election of members to these biennial Parliaments shall be distributed among the counties and boroughs

according to some rule of equality or proportion,...to render the House of Commons (as near as may be) an equal representative of the whole, and in order thereunto, that a present consideration be had to take off the elections of burgesses for poor, decayed, or inconsiderable towns, and to give some present addition to the number of Parliament members for great counties that have now less than their due proportion.

This is the principle of the redistribution of seats which was applied nearly two centuries later in the Reform Bill of 1832. (3) Other novel provisions anticipate the Cabinet system of the next century in so far as relates to the range of its powers. These establish a Council of State, with power over foreign negotiations and a general superintendence over the disposal of the militia. Unlike the old Privy Council, the members of which were only the King's servants, appointed, consulted, and dismissed at his pleasure, the Council of State was to be named in the first instance in the Constitution itself, and its members were "to continue in that power...for the certain term not exceeding seven years". The idea of a Council of State with definite functions was probably derived from the Committee of Both Kingdoms,[1] and it reappears in the later constitutions of the time. (4) The ecclesiastical settlement of the *Heads of the Proposals* anticipates the Toleration Act of 1689. The restoration of Episcopacy was not prevented, but all coercive power was to be taken away from the bishops; all Acts "enjoining the use of the Book of Common Prayer and imposing any penalties for neglect thereof" were to be repealed; and the taking of the Covenant was not to be enforced. Thus the sects were protected from persecution—either by bishops on the one hand, or presbyteries on the other; and in this way practical toleration was to be fully secured. If the King should accept these terms, his adherents were to be far more leniently dealt with than in any preceding treaty. Not more than five were to be left to the justice of Parliament; the composition payable by the rest was to be reduced; and Royalists were only to be excluded from office and Parliament for five years.

Although Cromwell and its author Ireton succeeded in carrying this scheme in the Council of the Army, it was violently opposed there by the extremer democrats to whom the name of Levellers was now beginning to be given. In *The Case of the Army truly stated*, a manifesto presented to Fairfax on October 18 on behalf of Lilburne and his followers, manhood suffrage was advocated; and both by implication in the document and express statement in debate, its authors threw over both the monarchy and the House of Lords. The result was to bring out the danger of an organisation like the Council

[1] Gardiner, *Civil War*, iii. 161.

of the Army where men were divided upon fundamental questions, and the generals decided to bring its activities to an end. On November 8, 1647, the Agitators were sent back to their regiments, and a mutiny which broke out on November 15 was easily put down. From this time forward the control and expression of army opinion fell once more into the hands of the Council of Officers, and the Grand Council of the Army became extinct.[1] The *Heads of the Proposals*, although still a scheme for a constitution, had already ceased to be a basis for negotiations with the King. Charles expected to gain everything by the dissensions of his enemies, and on November 11 he put an end to the possibility of negotiations being reopened by his flight from Hampton Court to Carisbrooke, where he hoped to put himself once more into touch with the Presbyterians and the Scots. In 1644 the Scots had crossed the border to fight for Presbyterianism against Episcopacy, and they were now ready to cross the border again to fight for Presbyterianism against the sects. They opened negotiations with the King at Carisbrooke, and on December 26 the *Engagement* was signed,[2] by which Charles undertook to establish Presbyterianism in England for three years, and to take "an effectual course" for "suppressing the opinions and practices" of the sects. On their part, the Scots agreed that no one should suffer in his person or estate for not submitting to the Presbyterian discipline, provided that he did not belong to any of the obnoxious sects. By the *Engagement* the King broke the last link that bound him to the army, and staked everything upon the success of the Scots in the field.

The alienation of the Scots was a serious danger for Independency and the army. They could put down riots in London and deal easily enough with disorderly civilians; but Scotland disposed of an army, and when troops met troops the result might be very different. Moreover, it was not with Scotland only that the army would have to deal, for clouds were gathering on every side. In the beginning of 1648 there was a stir among the Royalist

---

[1] Firth, *Army*, p. 362.
[2] Printed in Gardiner, *Documents*, pp. 347-352.

refugees on the Continent, and a rumour came from the Hague that it would be "no wonder to see ten thousand merry souls then lying there, and cursing the Parliament in every cup they drank, venturing over to make one cast more for the King". In February a rising took place in Pembrokeshire which spread through the rest of South Wales; and on April 3 the Parliamentarian Lord Inchiquin went over to the Royalists in Ireland. On April 21 the young Duke of York escaped from London; and a week later Sir Marmaduke Langdale seized Berwick for the King, thus opening the road for an advance from Scotland. On May 1 the other border-fortress, Carlisle, was taken by Sir Philip Musgrave; and soon after, the Eastern Counties—the stronghold of the earlier Puritan resistance —sent a petition to Parliament praying for the King's restoration "to the splendour of his ancestors". There was a formidable Presbyterian riot in London; a revolt in Kent and Essex; and a part of the fleet, stationed off the Kentish coast, declared for the King. On July 8 the Scottish army, 10,000 strong, crossed the Border, declaring that they had come to put down "that impious toleration, settled by the two Houses contrary to the Covenant".

But armed Independency was strong enough to defy all its enemies. The rising in Kent was put down by Fairfax, and Cromwell subdued Wales, and then, marching north with only 8600 men, fell on the whole Scottish army, now reinforced and said to number 21,000,[1] at Preston on August 17, and won the third great victory of his career. Marston Moor and Naseby had been victories of Presbyterianism over Episcopacy. Preston is a greater and still more glorious victory—of armed Independency over Presbyterianism. From this time forward the army is supreme.

[1] Gardiner, *Civil War*, iii. 437.

The Rule of the Purged Parliament

ABOUT a fortnight before the battle of Preston was fought, the two Houses had decided to reopen negotiations with the King. These began at Newport in the Isle of Wight on September 18, 1648, notwithstanding the fact that a petition, signed by 40,000 persons living in or near London protesting against a settlement which would retain the monarchy and the House of Lords, had been presented to the House of Commons on September 11. The petitioners claimed that the House of Commons "as chosen by and representing the people" was "the supreme authority of England". "It is impossible for us to believe", they said, "that it can consist with the safety or freedom of the nation to be governed by two or three supremes".[1] The victorious army also was equally hostile to the proposed settlement, and the sinister demand began to be made for justice upon the "chief delinquent".

As early as the autumn of 1647 the Levellers had added to their declarations in favour of constitutional reform the suggestion that punishment should be executed upon Charles as the cause of the shedding of blood; but at that time their argument had made little impression. It was otherwise after the web of intrigue which he had spun from Carisbrooke had plunged the nation into another civil war. The responsibility for the first war had been laid upon the King's evil counsellors; the responsibility for the second was laid upon the King himself.[2] In a great prayer-meeting at Windsor, held at the end of April, 1648, not long before the troops separated for the Welsh campaign, the officers, as one of them afterwards wrote,[3]

came to a very clear and joint resolution...that it was our duty, if ever the Lord brought us back again in peace, to call Charles Stuart, that man of blood, to an account for that blood he had shed and mischief he had done to his utmost against the Lord's cause and people in these poor nations.

[1] Firth, *Lords*, p. 202.   [2] Firth, *Cromwell*, p. 209.
[3] Adjutant-General Allen: Cromwell's *Letters and Speeches*, i. 310.

When the army returned again victorious, this vindictive feeling broke out afresh, and petitions began to come in to Fairfax from the regiments praying that impartial justice might be done "upon all criminal persons".[1] On November 18 the Council of Officers adopted *The Remonstrance of the Army*, which included the demand "that the capital and grand author of our troubles...may be speedily brought to justice for the treason, blood, and mischief he is...guilty of", and this was presented to Parliament on November 20.[2] The Presbyterian majority ignored it, and pursued their negotiation with the King. The result was the application of force upon both parties to the negotiation—upon the King and upon Parliament itself. Just as in 1647 Charles had been carried off by troops from Holmby House to Newmarket to enable the army to negotiate with him, so now he was removed from Carisbrooke to Hurst Castle on December 1 to prevent his negotiating with the Parliament. And on December 6 Colonel Pride went down with soldiers to the doors of the House of Commons, and on that day and the next arrested forty-five members, and prevented ninety-six more from entering the House. Only seventy-eight members were left in the House, and as about twenty of these refused to sit until the imprisoned members were released, the "Rump" Parliament consisted of less than sixty members, forty being required for a quorum.[3] Later on, old members were readmitted and new ones elected, but for the first six months of 1649 the largest attendance at a division was only seventy-seven, and even as late as 1652 the numbers did not rise above 125. As a rule, fifty was considered a good House.[4]

"Pride's Purge" had transferred all power to what had hitherto been the Independent minority in Parliament,

---

[1] Gardiner, *Civil War*, iii. 487.

[2] *Ib.* iii. 508. *Cf.* Cromwell's letter to Fairfax of November 20: "I find a very great sense in the officers of the regiments of the sufferings and the ruin of this poor kingdom, and in them all a very great zeal to have impartial justice done upon offenders; and I must confess, I do in all, from my heart, concur with them; and I verily think and am persuaded they are things which God puts into our hearts" (*Letters and Speeches*, i. 390).

[3] Firth, *Lords*, p. 205.   [4] *Ib.* p. 218.

and they were at the orders of the Council of Officers, so the way was now clear for the trial and execution of the King. At the eleventh hour, however, an effort was made to save him. Some of the officers doubted the wisdom of killing Charles I to make Charles II king—"to exchange a king in their power for a king out of their power, potent in foreign alliances and strong in the affections of the people".[1] A last overture was accordingly made to Charles on the basis of his surrendering the right to veto bills passed by Parliament, giving up the lands of the Church, and "abjuring" the Scots. But this, as someone said, would be to make him "no more...than a Duke of Venice".[2] Charles preferred to lose his life rather than part with his regal power, and he refused to see the messenger. On January 2, 1649,[3] the Commons sent up to the Lords an Ordinance creating a special court to try the King, accompanied by a resolution that "by the fundamental laws of this kingdom it is treason in the King of England for the time being to levy war against the Parliament and kingdom of England". The Ordinance appointed three judges to try the King, together with 150 commissioners in place of a jury, of whom twenty were to form a quorum. The House of Lords unanimously rejected both the Ordinance and the resolution, and the three judges declined to serve. But the army was not to be stopped by obstacles which it regarded as only technical; and on January 6 the House of Commons threw over both the King and the House of Lords in three democratic resolutions which proceeded strangely from the purged remnant of a Parliament which had long ceased to be representative:

That the People are, under God, the original of all just power; that the Commons of England in Parliament assembled, being chosen by and representing the People, have the supreme power in this nation; that whatsoever is enacted or declared for law by the Commons in Parliament assembled, hath the force of law, and all the people of this nation are concluded thereby, although the consent and concurrence of King or House of Peers be not had thereunto.[4]

---

[1] Gardiner, *Civil War*, iii. 553.   [2] *Ib.* iii. 554.
[3] *Commons' Journals*, vi. 107, 108.   [4] *Ib.* vi. 111

Two days later, by order[1] of the Lower House alone, a new High Court of Justice was instituted, consisting of some 150 commissioners who were to act both as judge and jury. Even the republican Algernon Sidney criticised the court. He told his colleagues that there were two reasons why he could not take part in their proceedings: first, the King could not be tried by that court; secondly, no man could be tried by that court. To which Cromwell replied, with characteristic impatience of forms when his mind was once made up, "I tell you, we will cut off his head with the crown upon it".[2] On January 30, 1649, the King of England was brought to the scaffold outside his own palace of Whitehall. In his last speech he said, "God's judgments are just. An unjust sentence that I suffered to take effect is now punished by an unjust sentence upon me"; and in all probability "the bright execution axe" under which he fell was the axe which had beheaded Strafford.[3] By this deed militarism, in the moment of its triumph, began to prepare the way for the Restoration. We may say of Charles I, as Heath[4] did of Lord Capel, "with Samson, he may be said to have done these Philistines more harm at his death than in all his life".

The men who had executed the King had no use for the House of Lords. As early as 1646 Lilburne had claimed that the "Commons of England" were "the original and fountain of power",[5] and Overton had said,[6] "I acknowledge none other to be the Supreme Court of Judicature of this land but the House of Commons, the knights and burgesses assembled in Parliament by the voluntary choice and free election of the people thereof". In 1648 the *Remonstrance of the Army* had demanded that "the supreme power and trust" should be in representative assemblies, "without further appeal to any created standing power".[7] From this it was but a short step to the resolution carried

---

[1] Printed in Gardiner, *Documents*, p. 357. The name of Ordinance, which had been used of legislation in which both Houses concurred, was now dropped (Gardiner, *Civil War*, iii. 561).
[2] Firth, *Cromwell*, p. 218.   [3] *Ib.* pp. 227, 228.
[4] James Heath, *A Chronicle of the late Intestine War*, p. 229.
[5] Firth, *Lords*, p. 157.   [6] *Ib.* p. 160.   [7] *Ib.* p. 204.

in the Purged Parliament without a division on February 6, 1649, "That the House of Peers in Parliament is useless and dangerous, and ought to be abolished".[1] At the time when this was passed, the attendance of peers at this dangerous House had dwindled to about six. On the following day another resolution declared

that it hath been found by experience...that the office of a King in this nation, and to have the power thereof in any single person, is unnecessary, burdensome, and dangerous to the liberty, safety, and public interest of the people of this nation, and therefore ought to be abolished.[2]

Thus the monarchy and the House of Lords perished together, and "in their death they were not divided".

On February 14, 1649, the Purged Parliament elected its first Council of State. Its forty-one members included Bradshaw the regicide, as well as Fairfax, Cromwell, and Skippon. Of those originally nominated, only Ireton and Harrison were rejected by Parliament.[3] On May 19 England was declared to be "a Commonwealth and Free State". A new Great Seal was designed, with a map of England and Ireland and the arms of the two countries on one side, and on the other a representation of the House of Commons, with the inscription, "In the first year of freedom by God's blessing restored". The statue of Charles I was thrown down, and on the pedestal the words were engraved, *Exit Tyrannus, Regum ultimus*.[4]

In spite of all its democratic professions, the "Commonwealth and Free State" was merely the rule of the Purged Parliament under another name. All the authority formerly exercised by the Crown in Parliament was now transferred to the remnant of the Lower House, which also appropriated to itself both executive and judicial functions, interfering by means of committees even with the courts of law.[5] It was this which led Cromwell to describe it long

---

[1] *Commons' Journals*, vi. 132.

[2] *Ib.* vi. 133. Acts in accordance with these resolutions, one abolishing the office of King and the other the House of Lords, were passed on March 17 and March 19 respectively (see Gardiner, *Documents*, pp. 384 and 387).

[3] Gardiner, *History of the Commonwealth and Protectorate*, i. 6.

[4] Goldwin Smith, i. 572.   [5] Firth, *Lords*, p. 241.

afterwards as "the horridest arbitrariness that ever was exercised in the world".[1] The only new institution that was created was the Council of State, and this was nothing more than a committee of the Rump, appointed for a year at a time, and liable to constant interference from the parent body, which was in continual session. Only in one way was the Council constitutionally strong against the Assembly which had called it into being. Of its forty-one members, no less than thirty-one were also members of Parliament, and as the average attendance in Parliament was not more than fifty-six, the Council could in theory command a majority upon questions on which it was unanimous. But as the average attendance in Council was not more than fifteen, and the members were rarely unanimous, "the Council had no such masterful weight in Parliament as has been sometimes ascribed to it".[2]

The system thus established was not at all in accordance with the ideas of the army. These are to be found in a document entitled *The Agreement of the People*,[3] presented to the Purged Parliament on behalf of the army on January 20, 1649. This is based on the earlier *Agreement of the People* which had been presented by the Levellers to the Council of the Army on October 28, 1647,[4] and this derived in turn from *The Case of the Army truly stated*. As the result of long discussion in the Council of Officers, the later *Agreement* differs from the earlier on important points, and it was put forward, not as a complete and immediate solution of the constitutional problems awaiting settlement, but as a rough sketch for a written constitution,

[1] April 21, 1657: *Letters and Speeches*, iii. 99.
[2] Gardiner, *Protectorate*, i. 9.
[3] Printed in Gardiner, *Documents*, pp. 359–71. This contemplated the establishment of Triennial Parliaments; a Council of State (to which a position of commanding importance was unintentionally given); and an established Church with freedom of worship to the sects whom it did not include. But its most interesting feature is the idea of reserving certain points as fundamental, which Parliament could not alter or repeal. Unlike the American Constitution, however, which was hereafter to adopt the principle of a " law paramount", the *Agreement of the People* provides no machinery by which the reserved parts of the constitution could be revised.
[4] Printed in *ib.* pp. 333–5.

to be discussed and amended by the wisdom of Parliament, and tendered to the nation whenever a convenient time should arrive.[1] The convenient time did not arrive, although on September 27, 1650, Parliament made a belated attempt to carry out the religious ideas of the framers of the *Agreement* by passing an Act to repeal all penalties for not going to church.[2] The Act, however, required instead,

to the end that no profane or licentious persons may take occasion by the repealing of the said laws (intended only for relief of pious and peaceably-minded people from the rigour of them) to neglect the performance of religious duties,

that

all and every person and persons within this Commonwealth and the territories thereof shall (having no reasonable excuse for their absence) upon every Lord's Day, days of public thanksgiving and humiliation, diligently resort to some public place where the service and worship of God is exercised, or shall be present at some other place in the practice of some religious duty, either of prayer, preaching, reading or expounding the Scriptures, or conferring upon the same.

The Government of the Commonwealth was exposed to attack from three sides at once.

The Presbyterians were now entirely hostile, some of their divines preaching against the regicides and praying for Charles II. The strength of the party lay in London, Lancashire, and the large towns, but it included the middle classes everywhere. Since the ejection of the Episcopalian clergy, the livings had been filled for the most part by ministers chosen by the parishes and confirmed by ecclesiastical synods after the Presbyterian order; thus, broadly speaking, the beneficed clergy were Presbyterians. The protection of the Commonwealth against attack from this side lay in the fact that they were not yet ready to co-operate cordially with the Royalists. In the first place, the two parties desired different things. The Presbyterians still wished for a Presbyterian Church settlement and the restoration of the monarchy on the lines of the later negotiations with the King, while the Royalists desired

---

[1] Firth, *Army*, p. 363.
[2] Printed in Gardiner, *Documents*, pp. 391–4.

the restoration of Episcopacy and the re-establishment of the monarchy as it was before the war began. In the second place, each party distrusted the other, and the Royalists could not yet forgive the Presbyterians for their share in the Great Rebellion. As one of them said, "The Independents cut off the King's head, but it was the Presbyterians who brought him to the block".[1] Thus attacks on the Government from the Presbyterian side were never pressed home; they contented themselves with vague talk and passive resistance.

The Royalists, although beaten in the field, were still formidable by means of the press. Ten days after the King's execution *Eikon Basilike* appeared in print. It was really written by Dr Gauden, afterwards Bishop of Exeter, but everybody believed that it contained a record of the King's thoughts and feelings set down by his own hand.[2] Dr Watson, preaching before Charles II at the Hague, said, "Our Royal Martyr hath not only the crown and trophy of a title, but the everlasting, stupendous monument of a book—raised higher than the Pyramids of Egypt in the strength of language, and well-proportioned, spiring expression".[3] *Eikon Basilike* was not quite all this, but it was admirably adapted for creating and maintaining the pious legend of the martyr-King, who in the hour of supreme trial prayed for the forgiveness of his persecutors. The book caused a remarkable revival of Royalist sentiment, and drew from Milton his *Eikonoklastes*, in which he denounced "the inconstant, irrational, and image-doting rabble",[4] who "with a besotted and degenerate baseness of spirit" are "ready to fall flat and give adoration to the image and memory of this man, who hath offered at more cunning fetches to undermine our liberties and put tyranny into an art than any British king before him".[5] *Eikon Basilike* itself was followed by a swarm of vigorous pamphlets containing violent attacks upon the regicides. For instance, the pedigree of Cromwell is drawn out thus:

Cain was the first gentleman of his family; Judas was the second

---

[1] Quoted in Firth, *Cromwell*, pp. 243–4.
[2] *Ib.* p. 240.   [3] Quoted in Masson, iv. 131.
[4] *Prose Works*, i. 496.   [5] *Ib.* i. 313.

that bore arms (three elder-trees and a halter); Korah, Dathan, and
Abiram his uncles by the mother's side; Achan his godfather;
Absalom his schoolmaster; Machiavel his counsellor; Faux and
Fairfaux his companions in evil.

The pamphlet ends with a mock will, beginning thus:

In the name of Pluto, Amen; I, Noll Cromwell, alias the Town
Bull of Ely, Lord Chief Governor of Ireland, Grand Plotter and
Contriver of all Mischiefs in England, Lord of Misrule, Knight of
the Order of Regicides, Thieftenant-General of the Rebels at
Westminster, Duke of Devilishness, Ensign of Evil, Scoutmaster-
General to his Infernal Majesty, being wickedly disposed of mind,
of abhorred memory, do make this my last Will and Testament in
manner and form following.[1]

No less violent than the Royalists were the extreme
Levellers and the fanatics of army democracy. "Men's
minds had so far drifted from the anchorage of use and
wont", says Gardiner,[2] "that to some of them every
counsel of perfection seemed capable of immediate realisation". "The execution of the King and the transition
from monarchy to a republic", says another writer,[3]
"could not take place without general disturbance. The
fountains of the political deep were broken up" and "there
ensued a carnival of wild sects and chimaeras". Thus there
appeared within the party of the Levellers, and covered
by the same term, groups of socialistic republicans, who
sought to abolish private property and buying and selling,
and to make all things common. On another wing were
to be found the Fifth Monarchy men—the religious
fanatics—who presented a petition to the Council of
Officers in February, 1649, asking that the Church should
be the sole depository of civil authority, and that the
government of the country should be handed over at once
to a general assembly elected by the congregations, in
order that the reign of Christ and his saints upon earth
might at once begin.[4] But far more dangerous than these

---

[1] *A New Bull-Baiting* (August 7, 1649), quoted in Masson, iv. 57 *n.*
[2] *Protectorate*, i. 32.   [3] Goldwin Smith, i. 575.
[4] "According to the wild system of the universal chronology then in
vogue, the past History of the World on this side of the Flood had consisted
of four great successive Empires or Monarchies—the Assyrian, which
ended B.C. 531; the Persian, which ended B.C. 331; the Macedonian, or

were the political or democratic Levellers, of whom John
Lilburne was the leader and mouthpiece. The seventeenth
century had produced two leading political ideas, which
were quite inconsistent with each other but which were
both influential upon the minds of men: the idea "that
good and religious men had a right to rule the evil and
irreligious, and that the nation ought to be governed
according to the wishes of its representatives in Parliament".[1] The demands of the Fifth Monarchy men were
founded upon the former idea, and it was upon this that
the Commonwealth was ultimately based, for its Parliament
was not representative and it depended for support upon
the officers of the army. The demands of the political
Levellers, on the other hand, were based upon the second
of these ideas, and thus there was a fundamental antagonism
between them and the Government of the Commonwealth.
This was expressed in Lilburne's famous pamphlet,
England's New Chains Discovered, presented to Parliament
on February 26, 1649. Lilburne attacked the Council of
State as a body which intervened to prevent direct government by the elected representatives of the people, and
demanded that it should be superseded by "committees
of short continuance, frequently and exactly accountable
for the discharge of their trusts"; and he asked that
Parliament should remain in permanent session in order
to keep these committees in check. Further, the Levellers'
suspicion of the influence of the higher military officers,
as something which interfered with true representative
government almost as much as did the Council of State,
was expressed in a demand that Parliament should put
in practice once more the principle of the Self-denying
Ordinance, and consider how dangerous it was "for one
and the same persons to be continued long in the highest
commands of a military power".[2] What made Lilburne's

Greek Empire of Alexander, which was made to stretch to B.C. 44; and
the Roman, which had begun B.C. 44 with the accession of Augustus Caesar,
and which had included, though people might not see how, all that had
happened on the earth since then. But this last Monarchy was tottering,
and a Fifth Universal Monarchy was at hand" (Masson, v. 16).

  [1] Gardiner, *Protectorate*, i. 32.
  [2] See *ib*. i. 34–5.

pamphlet the more dangerous was, that the views which it expressed found a ready response among the private soldiers.

The movement of the Levellers was associated with a design to reappoint the Agitators and to revive the disused Council of the Army, in order that the soldiers might have an equal voice with the officers in determining the army's political action. Its promoters did not hesitate to incite the soldiers to mutiny, and they concentrated upon Cromwell in particular a furious attack. They called him a tyrant, an apostate, and a hypocrite. "You shall scarce speak to Cromwell about anything", said one of the pamphlets, "but he will lay his hand on his breast, elevate his eyes, and call God to record. He will weep, howl, and repent, even while he doth smite you under the fifth rib".[1] The Government of the Commonwealth could not afford to allow such attacks to go unpunished, and in March Lilburne and three others were brought before the Council of State. "You have no other way to deal with these men", said Cromwell, "but to break them, or they will break you".[2] Lilburne and his friends were sent to the Tower, but their proceedings led, in May, 1649, to a political mutiny in the army, which was put down with a strong hand by Cromwell. His pursuit of the mutineers led him to Royalist Oxford, and the University, now purged and Puritan, seized the opportunity to confer upon the great revolutionary soldier, with a fine incongruity, the honorary degree of Doctor of Civil Law.

The attacks of the Royalists on the one side and of the Levellers on the other constituted a real danger for the newly-founded Commonwealth. The Government had no command of literary ability, and when Milton refused to answer Lilburne, it was obliged to adopt measures which savoured a good deal more of an ancient despotism than of a new republic. (1) On July 17, 1649, an Act "declaring what offences shall be adjudged treason"[3] made a wide departure from the older conception of treason as mainly consisting of an overt act proving the traitorous imagination

---

[1] Firth, *Cromwell*, p. 248.   [2] *Ib.* p. 249.
[3] Printed in Gardiner, *Documents*, pp. 388–91.

of compassing the King's death or levying war against the King, and recast the law to meet the new circumstances of the case. It was now declared to be treason "if any person shall maliciously or advisedly publish, by writing, printing, or openly declaring", that the Government of the Commonwealth is

tyrannical, usurped, or unlawful; or that the Commons in Parliament assembled are not the supreme authority of this nation; or shall plot, contrive, or endeavour to stir up or raise force against the present Government or for the subversion or alteration of the same, and shall declare the same by any open deed.

An entirely new treason was also created to meet the case of a person "not being an officer, soldier, or member of the army" who should attempt "to stir up any mutiny in the said army". (2) To such legislation no objection need be taken, but the next act of the "Free State" was to gag the press. In September, 1649, an Act was passed forbidding the publication of any "book or pamphlet, treatise, sheet or sheets of news" without a licence, and imposing a penalty for spreading abroad scandalous or libellous books—not only on the author, printer, and seller, but also on the purchaser if he did not inform within twenty-four hours.[1] (3) On January 2, 1650, all men over the age of eighteen were required to take an engagement to be "true and faithful to the Commonwealth of England as it is now established, without a King and House of Lords",[2] and the Act directed that the courts of law should refuse justice to all "men" who had failed to do so.[3] (4) Finally, in March, 1650, a temporary High Court of Justice was established, to try without a jury all cases of treason to the Commonwealth and stirring up mutiny in the army. Of the sixty-four members of this new Star Chamber, at first not more than three were lawyers, but six judges were added soon after.[4]

In addition to the difficulties which threatened the Commonwealth from within, it had to deal also with external danger. In 1649 and 1650 Cromwell was busy reconquering

---

[1] Gardiner, *Protectorate*, i. 193.   [2] Gardiner, *Documents*, p. 391.
[3] Gardiner, *Protectorate*, i. 215.   [4] *Ib.* i. 277.

Ireland, where he pursued a policy which resembled in many ways that of Strafford fifteen years before. In 1650 and 1651 the resistance of the Scots was finally crushed at the decisive battles of Dunbar and Worcester. In 1652 and 1653 Blake conducted a successful naval war against the Dutch.

The Government of the Commonwealth was in some respects a good and efficient Government. The Council of State "consisted of country gentlemen of military or political experience, with a few lawyers, a few merchants, besides three or four professional soldiers", and "it contained a number of able men".[1] Thus the tone of the Council was set by the civilian of capacity and knowledge of affairs. The system of governing by committees of Parliament tapped new sources of administrative ability which the monarchy, with its tendency to appoint great personages to the offices of State, had failed to reach. Financially, also, the Commonwealth was far better off than the monarchy had ever been, for it was not only able to apply irresistible military force to the raising of taxes, but it was also rich in confiscations and Royalist compositions. In this latter respect it was living upon its capital, but it was not until later on that the disastrous consequences of this financial method began to be felt. The army was strong enough for all the purposes for which it was required. The men were well and regularly paid; pressing was no longer required to fill the ranks; and for both officers and men the army had become a regular professional career.[2] But foreign complications prevented the Government from attempting much in the way of positive reforms, and for several reasons it continued to decline steadily in public esteem. There was a general complaint of nepotism—that the members of the Purged Parliament used their power in the interests of their own families, and promoted their sons and nephews in the public service. In certain cases there was even a suspicion of corruption, especially in connexion with the Royalist compositions. It was said that delinquents could obtain a lighter assessment by bribing the assessment committee. In an entry relating

---

[1] Firth, *Cromwell*, p. 245.   [2] *Ib.* p. 247.

to November, 1652, Whitelocke[1] describes a conversation with Cromwell in which the latter referred to the "pride and ambition and self-seeking" of the members, "engrossing all places of honour and profit to themselves and their friends"; to their "design to perpetuate themselves and to continue the power in their own hands"; and to "their meddling in private matters between party and party". All this was leading up to a state of things that was becoming intolerable. The army began to have what Cromwell called "a strange distaste against them", and thus it had come about that "the nation loathed their sitting".[2]

What made the rule of the Rump appear more intolerable than it would otherwise have done was the fact that there was no prospect of its ever coming to an end, for it was the heir of the Long Parliament, and was therefore protected by the Act of 1641 against being adjourned, prorogued, or dissolved without its own consent. Yet no one could pretend that it was representative. The House of Commons of the Long Parliament consisted of 490 members; the Parliament of the Commonwealth never contained more than 125. The whole of Wales had only three members, London one, and some counties none at all, either as counties or through represented boroughs within their limits.[3] Yet this body, interested in various ways in retaining its power and with its ideas about itself limited and controlled by the ancient parliamentary tradition, claimed to be a sovereign assembly with an indefeasible right to rule. The army, on the other hand, had all along regarded the continuance of the Purged Parliament as a temporary expedient only, and as soon as it was free to turn its attention to politics once more, it began to agitate, first for reforms and then for the dissolution of Parliament. On August 2, 1652, the officers of the army presented a petition to Parliament enumerating a number of reforms which they wished to have carried into effect, and when Parliament did as little as possible, the movement for intervention grew. The debates of the

---

[1] *Memorials* (edition of 1853), iii. 470.
[2] Morley, *Cromwell*, p. 326.   [3] Firth, *Cromwell*, p. 235.

Council of Officers grew more frequent and their prayer-meetings longer and longer—the signs of a gathering storm. A news-letter of January, 1653, remarked significantly, "The officers have been seeking God two days; the grandees fear a design in hand".[1]

On January 13, 1653, the Council of Officers and the Council of State arrived at an understanding that a new Parliament should be elected;[2] but there was a practical difficulty to be faced. A freely-elected Parliament would almost certainly overthrow the Commonwealth and restore Charles II; so Cromwell and the officers advised that securities should be taken. The security which pleased the venal members of the Rump was that they themselves should retain their seats without any fresh election, and that they should be a committee with power to reject any new member whom they thought it desirable to exclude. There is also some reason for thinking that they even intended to make this system of "recruiting" apply to each successive Parliament, so that there would never be a General Election any more.[3] This was too much for Cromwell and the officers, who were determined at all costs to stop the "Perpetuation Bill" as someone called it.[4] On April 19 Cromwell had been assured by one of the leading members that nothing would be done in a hurry; on the morning of the 20th he was told that Parliament was busy passing the Bill.

It was Cromwell's view that the army, in whose hands the ultimate authority lay, was in a manner responsible for the misdeeds of the civil power.

"So", he says, "finding the people dissatisfied in every corner of the nation, and all men laying at our doors the non-performance of these things which had been promised and were of duty to be performed, truly we did then think ourselves concerned if we would (as becomes honest men) keep up the reputation of honest men in the world".[5]

The precise form which the intervention of the army would

[1] Firth, *Army*, p. 366.   [2] Gardiner, *Protectorate*, ii. 177.
[3] *Ib*. ii. 199, 200 *n*.
[4] See the "Declaration by the Lord General and the Council" of April 22, 1653, printed in Gardiner, *Documents*, pp. 400–4.
[5] *Letters and Speeches*, ii. 279.

be likely to take had been indicated long before[1] by
Cromwell himself. Ludlow tells us how an occasion arose
when the Long Parliament "were highly displeased with
the carriage of the army,...some menacing expressions
falling from some of them", whereupon "Lieutenant-
General Cromwell took the occasion to whisper me in the
ear, saying: 'These men will never leave till the army pull
them out by the ears'".[2] The soldiers had a short way
of dealing with assemblies, and when the Lord General
went down to the House he was accompanied by a file of
musketeers. It was not without reluctance that Cromwell
had come to the decision to expel the Parliament by military
force. It was an act, he said, "the consideration of the
issue whereof made his hair to stand on end".[3] But when
the decisive moment came, he shewed no hesitation. "The
spirit was so upon him that he was overruled by it; and
he consulted not with flesh and blood at all, seeing the
Parliament designing to spin an everlasting thread."[4]
Thus fell all that was left of the Long Parliament, after
an existence of nearly thirteen years. On the following
day it was found that someone had written on the door of
the Parliament House: "This house to let—unfurnished".[5]

With the failure of the brief and unsuccessful attempt
to establish an English Commonwealth upon a parliamentary basis, military force shewed itself, naked and
unashamed, as the sole source of power, the only basis of
government. Civil institutions had collapsed in ruin, and
the Lord General of the army was the only authority in
the kingdom that still remained. The final protest of the
civil power as it succumbed to military violence was not
without dignity.

"Sir", said Bradshaw to Cromwell when he came to dissolve the
Council of State, "we have heard what you did at the House
in the morning, and before many hours all England will hear it;
but, Sir, you are mistaken to think that the Parliament is dissolved;
for no power under Heaven can dissolve them but themselves:
therefore take you notice of that".[6]

[1] Gardiner assigns it to August, 1647 (*Civil War*, iii. 183).
[2] *Memoirs*, i. 147.   [3] Firth, *Cromwell*, p. 318.
[4] Quoted in Ranke, iii. 83 *n*.   [5] Gardiner, *Protectorate*, ii. 212.
[6] *Ib* ii. 211.

Bradshaw was at any rate right in this—that although the soldiers might destroy a Parliament they could not destroy that ideal of constitutional government of which Parliament was the expression. It is strange that the rest of Cromwell's life was to be spent in "a vain attempt to clothe" military force "in constitutional forms"[1]—only to find that the task was impossible. Cromwell was mortal: the ideal of constitutional government was immortal. It survived both him and his successor, and was able to find a fresh incarnation in another Long Parliament—the Long Parliament of the Restoration.

[1] Firth, *Cromwell*, p. 325.

The Parliament of Saints; the First Parliament of the Protectorate

ALTHOUGH the army had ended by force the rule of the Purged Parliament, it had no desire to appropriate political power for itself. To deal with the daily business of government a Council of State was appointed on April 29, 1653, consisting of thirteen persons, of whom nine were officers;[1] but the army was anxious to rebuild the civil institutions which it had destroyed. Cromwell said of himself that he sought "to divest the sword of the power and authority in the civil administration";[2] and with this end in view he embarked on the remarkable experiment known as the "Barebones Parliament".

This curious Parliament was a compromise between two different views. On the one side was Harrison the fanatic, who is described by Roger Williams as "a very gallant, most deserving, heavenly man, but most high-flown for the kingdom of the saints, and the Fifth Monarchy now risen, and their sun never to set again, etc."[3] He and those who followed him were in favour of entrusting power to a large Council of seventy selected members after the number of the Jewish Sanhedrin, hoping that in this way government would approximate more closely to the Divine pattern set up for imitation in the Word of God. Lambert, on the other hand, desired a small council supported by an assembly, and declared for a written constitution and a reversion to the principles of the *Agreement of the People*.[4] Cromwell followed Lambert in desiring a Parliament rather than a Council of Seventy, but he adopted Harrison's idea of the way in which it should be chosen. Falling back on one of the standing ideas of Army Independency, that the nation ought to be ruled by godly men, he decided to

[1] Masson, iv. 498.
[2] Speech of July 4, 1653 (*Letters and Speeches*, ii. 289).
[3] Quoted in Masson, iv. 549.
[4] Gardiner, *Protectorate*, ii. 220 and *n*. Cf. Firth, *Cromwell*, pp. 328–9.

summon a Parliament of Saints. But if such a Parliament was to be called, it was out of the question for it to be chosen by election, since no elective machinery could be devised which would not in practice return a considerable proportion of sinners. It was therefore decided to ask the Independent congregations of each county to suggest names, and out of these the Council of Officers made choice of 140 persons "fearing God and of approved fidelity and honesty". These were then called together by a direct summons issued in the name of Oliver Cromwell as Captain-General of the army "with the advice of my Council of Officers".[1] Since the 140 persons chosen included five representatives for Scotland and six for Ireland, the scheme established a novel principle. "For the first time in history a body was to meet in the name of the three peoples."[2]

This Assembly of Nominees gives us a curious insight into the political philosophy of Cromwell and his supporters in the army. The doctrine of the divine right of the godly to govern is here superimposed in a remarkable way upon the doctrine of direct popular representation. Cromwell himself placed the interests of the godly first, but he was never entirely satisfied with godliness as a basis for government.

"Of the two greatest concernments that God hath in the world", he said later on,[3] "the one is that of religion and of the just preservation of the professors of it: to give them all due and just liberty, and to assert the truth of God.... The other thing cared for is the civil liberty and interest of the nation. Which though it is, and indeed I think ought to be, subordinate to a more peculiar interest of God, yet it is the next best God hath given men in this world; and if well cared for, it is better than any rock to fence men in their own interests. Then, if anyone whatsoever think the interest of Christians and the interest of the nation inconsistent or two different things, I wish my soul may never enter into their secrets".

With the intellectual confusion which appears so often in

---

[1] The text of the summons, dated June 6, 1653, is printed in Gardiner, *Documents*, p. 405.

[2] Gardiner, *Protectorate*, ii. 232.

[3] To the Second Protectorate Parliament on April 3, 1657 (*Letters and Speeches*, iii. 30).

his speeches, Cromwell failed to grasp the fundamental
inconsistency between these two principles, and while
asserting the one he was always hoping to establish the
other also. The desire to establish the Government upon
a regular constitutional basis explains a great part of his
political action; and he welcomed the Parliament of Saints
as a step in that direction.

"Why should we be afraid to say or think", he said,[1] "that this may
be the door to usher in the things that God hath promised; which
have been prophesied of; which He has set the hearts of his people
to wait for and expect?...Indeed, I do think somewhat is at the
door: we are at the threshold....You are at the edge of the promises
and prophecies".

But in comparing the status of the Barebones Parliament
with the historic Parliaments which had preceded it, he
was careful to explain what it was that it lacked. "If it were
a time to compare your standing", he said,[2] "with those
that have been called by the suffrages of the people—
which who can tell how soon God may fit the people for
such a thing, and none can desire it more than I!"

Although Cromwell's mind was thus divided between
two inconsistent principles—the rule of the godly and the
sovereignty of the people—his practical common-sense
always told him how far towards the realisation of his
desires it would be safe for him to go. It was to be desired
that government should express the will of the people;
but the people must not be royalist, and they must accept
the principle of toleration, and they must choose and
establish the rule of godly men. If out of native perversity
they failed to do these things, it was the duty of the army
to control their political appetites for their own good.

It was with high expectations that the Parliament of
Saints began its sittings. Its members declared that "they
looked for the long-expected birth of freedom and happiness".

"All the world over amongst the people of God", they said, there
was "a more than usual expectation of some great and strange

---

[1] In his speech to the Barebones Parliament, July 4, 1653 (*Letters and
Speeches*, ii. 298).
[2] *Ib.* ii. 297.

changes coming upon the world, which we can hardly believe to be
parallelled with any times but those a while before the birth of our
Lord and Saviour Jesus Christ".[1]

Their first step was to declare themselves a true Parliament,
with all the powers and privileges of earlier Parliaments.
They next proceeded to elect a Council of State, adding
eighteen of their own body to the existing Council of
thirteen.[2] They then appointed twelve great committees
for the redress of every kind of grievance, and turned
eagerly to the work of reform.[3]

The majority of the saints were men of worth, substance,
and standing,[4] but they could not be made to endure the
irksome duty of constant attendance at the House.[5] The
fanatics, on the other hand, were numerically strong and
attended the debates regularly; so when it came to
legislation, they could often command a majority. Nevertheless, some useful work was done, and many of the
reforms which the Parliament projected and passed into
law are singularly modern in character. Among these
were: an Act establishing civil marriage and providing
for the registration of births, marriages, and deaths;[6] and
Acts for the relief of prisoners for debt, and for the better
custody of idiots and lunatics.[7] A committee was also
appointed to consider the simplification of the "tortuous,
ungodly jungle" of English law, in order, as a divine
announced from the pulpit, that "law should stream down
like a river freely, as for twenty shillings what formerly
cost twenty pounds, impartially as the saints please, and
it should run as rivers do, close to the doors".[8] Here the
reformers were unduly sanguine. They hoped that by their
means the laws might be made "easy, plain, and short",[9]
but it was soon discovered that this was not a business for
amateurs, and yet, as no lawyer sat in the Parliament of
Saints, there was no professional help available, even if it
had been efficacious in securing the end desired. Thus

[1] Firth, *Cromwell*, p. 331.
[2] Gardiner, *Protectorate*, ii. 239.   [3] Firth, *Cromwell*, p. 332.
[4] Morley, *Cromwell*, p. 345.   [5] Gardiner, *Protectorate*, ii. 258.
[6] *Ib*. ii. 242.   [7] *Ib*. ii. 261.   [8] *Ib*. ii. 216.
[9] *Ib*. ii. 253 *n*.: *cf.* Cromwell's speech to the First Parliament of the
Protectorate, September 4, 1654 (*Letters and Speeches*, ii. 353).

the project of reducing "the great volumes of the law" into "the bigness of a pocket-book" came to be recognised as "a thing of so great worth and benefit as England is not yet worthy of, nor likely in a short time to be so blessed as to enjoy".[1]

At two points, however, the saints touched problems that were difficult and contentious, and here they shewed that godly men are not always men of affairs.[2] (1) On August 5 they voted the abolition of the Court of Chancery after a single day's debate, and referred it to the Committee of Law to prepare a Bill to carry out this resolution and to consider how the equitable jurisdiction of the Chancery was to be exercised in the future.[3] The abuses of the Court were notorious. It was said that 23,000 causes of from five to thirty years' standing were lying there still undecided;[4] and the costliness of the procedure was as much a scandal in the seventeenth century as it was when Dickens wrote *Bleak House* in order to denounce it. The case for reform was unanswerable, but sudden abolition would have created chaos in a whole department of legal business. Thus, although attempts were made to provide a substitute, they failed to pass the House,[5] and the problem was ultimately left over to the Parliament of the Protectorate. From another point of view also the measure was impolitic, because it alienated from a Government by no means strong, one of the most influential vested interests in the country. "How did good people rejoice", says a writer of the time, "when they heard of that vote,... and how sad and sorrowful were the lawyers and clerks". "'Tis very fit", says another, "the extorting examiners and griping six clerks should suffer; for I think it was chiefly the excessiveness of their fees and the abuse of spinning out copies to so immoderate a length that

---

[1] Gardiner, *Protectorate*, ii. 253 *n*.

[2] When one of the godly members of the Purged Parliament moved that all profane and unsanctified persons be expelled the House, Henry Marten is said to have moved as an amendment, "that all the fools might be put out likewise, and then there would be but a thin House" (Traill, iv. 314).

[3] Gardiner, *Protectorate*, ii. 241.

[4] Firth, *Cromwell*, p. 332.

[5] Gardiner, *Protectorate*, ii. 262.

rendered the Court so burdensome".[1] All this was perfectly true, for the rapacity of the officials of the Court
was beyond question, but it is only sometimes and in some
circumstances that political courage is also political wisdom. (2) Parliament also attempted to deal with patronage
to livings and the payment of tithe, and it was over this
that the saints eventually came to grief. When the
Royalist and Anglican clergy were ejected for refusing to
take the Covenant, and were replaced by Presbyterians,
the Independents stood aloof, for they were not included
in the regular ecclesiastical organisation of the country.
The autonomous congregations of sects had been formed
outside the parochial system, and had claimed no share in
the disposal of livings or in the maintenance afforded by
tithe. But although the Independents did not desire tithe
for themselves, they did not view with any favour the
enjoyment of tithe by their ecclesiastical enemies the
Presbyterians, and thus one of the first proposals made to
the Barebones Parliament after it met was to the effect that
after three months no minister should receive his maintenance from tithe;[2] this was defeated by sixty-eight to
forty-three. Later on, however, the House resolved by
fifty-eight to forty-one to abolish patronage,[3] and soon
afterwards a carefully thought-out scheme for reforming
the old system of church patronage and making provision
for the ejection of incompetent clergy, was thrown out by
a majority of two[4] partly because it expressly retained
property in tithe and used it for the maintenance of the
clergy as heretofore.

While these things were going on in Parliament, the
extremists out of Parliament were attacking Cromwell.
The Fifth Monarchy men began to identify him with the
"Old Dragon" and the "Man of Sin", and one of them,
after expressing a wish that his words might be recorded
in heaven, proceeded to accuse him of "tampering with
the King" and "assuming exorbitant power". Cromwell's
reply was very much to the point. "I did not expect", he
said,[5] "when I heard you begin with a record in heaven,

[1] Gardiner, *Protectorate*, ii. 241 *n*.   [2] *Ib*. ii. 240.
[3] *Ib*. ii. 273.   [4] *Ib*. ii. 277.   [5] *Ib*. ii. 273.

that you would have told such a lie upon earth". It was somewhere about this time that he said in confidence to a friend: "I am more troubled now with the fool than with the knave".[1] The Levellers also began to hold up their heads again, and the indomitable Lilburne returned from banishment in defiance of an Act of the Purged Parliament which condemned him to death if he returned. The Council of State ordered his trial, but he conceived the happy idea of denying his own identity, and a sympathetic jury acquitted him amidst the plaudits of the populace.

The ecclesiastical policy of Parliament was opposed to Cromwell's sense of common honesty as well as to his idea of what was politic, and four years later he confessed that this constitutional experiment had been a failure. It was, he said to the Second Parliament of the Protectorate on April 21, 1657,

a story of my own weakness and folly. And yet it was done in my simplicity.... It was thought that men of our own judgment, who had fought in the wars, and were all of a piece upon that account, ...why surely these men will hit it, and these men will do it to the purpose, whatsoever can be desired.... And such a company of men were chosen and did proceed into action. And truly this was the naked truth, that the issue was not answerable to the simplicity and honesty of the design.[2]

Whether the Lord General would of his own accord have taken steps to end the Assembly which he had called into being is doubtful; but if he had done so he would have had the hearty support of the army, whose pay had been threatened by attacks on the monthly assessments, and its military honour touched by the readiness of the saints, in the notorious case of Sir John Stawell, to violate terms of surrender granted to the Royalist commanders.[3] But Cromwell was saved the trouble of another expulsion by the suicide of the Assembly. On Monday, December 12, 1653, the moderate party, having laid their plans, rose early and came down in good time to the House to move a resolution, "that the sitting of this Parliament any longer, as now constituted, will not be for the good of the Commonwealth,

[1] Gardiner, *Protectorate*, ii. 254. [2] *Letters and Speeches*, iii. 98.
[3] Firth, *Cromwell*, p. 336; Gardiner, *Protectorate*, ii. 257.

and that therefore it is requisite to deliver up unto the Lord General Cromwell the powers they have received from him".[1] As the House grew fuller, and more of the extremists were brought up, it seemed doubtful whether the motion would after all be carried. At this crisis the Speaker, who was himself one of the conspirators, suddenly rose from the chair, and without stopping to put the resolution to the vote, marched off to Whitehall, preceded by the mace and accompanied by fifty or sixty members, to sign a deed of abdication which had been already prepared. A minority of about twenty-seven stayed behind, but as they were not a quorum they could not continue the debate. They began to draw up a protest against the proceedings, but a couple of colonels with a force of musketeers turned them out. Meanwhile signatures were coming in to the deed of abdication, and in the end it was signed by eighty members—a clear majority of the whole House.[2]

Thus the failure of the great experiment stood confessed, and Cromwell found himself once more in possession of absolute power. "My own power again by this resignation", he says,[3] "was become as boundless and unlimited as before, all things being subjected to arbitrariness, and myself. . .a person having power over the three nations without bound or limit set".[4]

Once during the reign of the Purged Parliament Cromwell had a conversation with Whitelocke in which he had attacked the "exorbitances" of that body, and had urged that "some course must be thought of to curb and restrain them, or we shall be ruined by them". Whitelocke in reply had made the obvious constitutional objection that the officers themselves held their commissions from Parliament, and how could they curb and restrain it? To this Cromwell, with characteristic impatience of constitutional objections, made the memorable answer: "What if a man should take upon him to be King?"[5]

---

[1] Gardiner, *Protectorate*, ii. 279.
[2] Firth, *Cromwell*, p. 339; Gardiner, *Protectorate*, ii. 278–81.
[3] *Letters and Speeches*, ii. 373.
[4] See note on "Oliver Cromwell", Appendix, p. 282 below.
[5] Gardiner, *Protectorate*, ii. 174. The whole conversation is in Whitelocke, *Memorials*, iii. 468–74.

The establishment of the First Protectorate under the *Instrument of Government*[1] is, in a sense, a reversion to this idea. The standing difficulty of the army was the greed, inexperience, or folly of the assemblies which it called into being. It was therefore natural that in their new experiment the theorists of the army should appeal from the instability of a parliamentary system to the rigidity of a written constitution. "It was high time", they said, "that some power should pass a decree upon the wavering humours of the people, and say to this nation, as the Almighty Himself said once to the unruly sea: 'Here shall be thy bounds; hitherto shalt thou come and no farther'".[2] Nor is it surprising that in order to set up a standing check upon assemblies, they should re-establish under the name of "Protector" a restricted and limited King. In the *Instrument of Government*, as Gardiner remarked,[3] the absolute supremacy of Parliament is abandoned "in order to recur to the practice of the Elizabethan monarchy amended in accordance with the needs of the time".

Perhaps the most remarkable feature of the new Constitution is to be found in the character of the Triennial Parliaments provided for. The union of England, Scotland, and Ireland, and the redistribution of seats according to population, anticipate legislation, some of which came half a century later, some a century and a half, and some a generation later still. Now, as at the Reform Bill of 1832, the rising towns of Durham, Manchester, Leeds, and Halifax were enfranchised, and a host of unimportant places—including Old Sarum—lost their members. But while they thus displayed singular audacity of imagination in anticipating the future, the framers of the new Constitution did not lose sight of their own interests in the present. In so far as they were supported by public opinion at all, it was by the public opinion of the middle class, and so, as in 1832, it was to the middle class that the preponderant parliamentary weight was given. This meant getting rid of the small boroughs, which were for the most part under the influence of the neighbouring gentry. Whereas

---

[1] December 16, 1653: printed in Gardiner, *Documents*, pp. 405–17.
[2] Firth, *Cromwell*, p. 341.   [3] Gardiner, *Protectorate*, ii. 285.

in the Long Parliament there were 398 borough members, in Cromwell's First Triennial there were only 133; but on the other hand the representation of the counties rose from ninety to 265. This also explains why the forty-shilling free-holders disappeared, and were replaced in the counties by the owners of real or personal estate of the value of £200, while in the boroughs the narrow local customs which had formerly determined the franchise were allowed to revive.[1] The Government was still further strengthened in Parliament by a provision which left the distribution of the thirty-six seats each for Scotland and Ireland to the Protector in Council. In Ireland, where Roman Catholics and rebels were disqualified and only the English and Scottish settlers voted, the members elected were for the most part officers of the army; and in Scotland, by a judicious distribution it was not difficult to secure the election of Government nominees. Thus the Scottish and Irish representation played the same part under the Protectorate as ministerial pocket boroughs were to do hereafter in the political system of the eighteenth century.[2]

Another outstanding feature of the *Instrument* is the extensiveness of the powers which it confers on the executive, and especially on the Council of State. The Council was intended to serve as an efficient constitutional check upon the Protector. As its members held office for life, they were practically independent of him, and yet all his important political acts required their assent. The evidence available goes to shew that the control over him thus established by the Constitution was daily exercised in the actual business of government. In dealing with his Council, the Lord Protector, unlike Elizabeth or Charles I, was compelled to rely upon influence rather than authority. "We know enough to convince us", says Gardiner,[3] "that the ordinary belief that Oliver was an autocrat and his councillors mere puppets, is a very incorrect view of the situation". But having thus established an effective control over the Protector, the constitution-makers of 1653 did

---

[1] *Ib*. iii. 6–7. [2] *Ib*. iii. 8.
[3] *Cromwell*, p. 86.

not hesitate to confer upon the Protector-in-Council the most extensive powers. A provision of the *Instrument* authorised him "to make laws and ordinances for the peace and welfare of these nations where it shall be necessary, which shall be binding and in force until order shall be taken in Parliament concerning the same". The Constitution was adopted on December 16, 1653, and the date fixed by it for the meeting of the first Triennial Parliament was September 3, 1654, and thus for nearly nine months Cromwell and his Council had a free hand. The result was a period of reforming activity almost unique in English history. Between December, 1653, and September, 1654, no fewer than eighty-two Ordinances were passed, most of which were afterwards approved by Parliament; and although a great many of these were only administrative, some of them rise to the higher levels of statesmanship. It is in this period that we find the answer to Hallam's depreciation of Cromwell in comparison with Napoleon.[1] It is certainly untrue to say that Cromwell "never shewed any signs of a legislative mind, or any desire to fix his renown on that noblest basis, the ameliora-tion of social institutions".[2]

The more important of Cromwell's Ordinances[3] fall into three groups, and, taken together, they furnish the key to his whole domestic policy in so far as it was a policy of social reform. He aimed (1) at the reform of the law; (2) at the reformation of manners; and (3) at the re-organisation of religion.

(1) An Ordinance of January 19, 1654, annulled the engagement to be faithful to the Commonwealth, as a burden and snare to tender consciences;[4] and another of the same date remodelled the law of treason to meet the case of government being lodged in the hands of a Single Person.[5] An Ordinance of February 28[6] revived and continued the special jurisdictions and privileges of the

---

[1] Firth, *Cromwell*, p. 346.   [2] Hallam, *Constitutional History*, ii. 264.
[3] An abstract of Cromwell's Ordinances is given in Masson, iv. 558–65.
[4] *Acts and Ordinances of the Interregnum*, ed. C. H. Firth and R. S. Rait, ii. 830.
[5] *Ib.* ii. 831.   [6] *Ib.* ii. 844.

County Palatine of Lancaster; and another of June 9 provided that assizes should be held at Durham by the judges of the Northern Circuit.[1] On June 13[2] the Protector equipped himself with a High Court of Justice to try cases of treason arising under the Ordinance of January 19, consisting of thirty-two commissioners, three of them being judges; the court had power to inflict the death penalty by appointing offenders to be "beheaded or hanged only". Finally, a long and complicated Ordinance of August 21[3] solved one of the problems which had baffled the Parliament of Saints, by regulating and limiting the jurisdiction of the Court of Chancery and establishing ī fixed scale of reduced fees.

(2) For the reformation of manners, an Ordinance of March 31, 1654[4], suppressed cock-fighting, since it had been found by experience "to tend many times to the disturbance of the public peace" and to be "commonly accompanied with gaming, drinking, swearing, quarrelling, and other dissolute practices". Another Ordinance, of June 29[5], was directed against "challenges, duels, and all provocations thereunto", described as "a growing evil in this nation", "displeasing to God, unbecoming Christians, and contrary to all good order and government". Legislation of June 30[6] provided for "the better suppressing of drunkenness and profane cursing and swearing" among "carmen, porters, watermen, and others" employed upon the River of Thames, who "are very ordinarily drunk and do... blaspheme". An Ordinance of July 4[7] prohibited horse-racing for six months, in view of "divers mischievous plots and designs" pursued by enemies of the public peace, who were accustomed "to take advantage of public meetings and concourse of people at horse-races" for "instilling such their purposes into the minds of others who are peaceably affected".

(3) The reorganisation of the Church by Ordinance was a more complicated business. The Parliament of Saints had sought to abolish tithe; but Cromwell's point of view

[1] *Ib.* ii. 907. [2] *Ib.* ii. 917. [3] *Ib.* ii. 949.
[4] *Ib.* ii. 861. [5] *Ib.* ii. 937. [6] *Ib.* ii. 940.
[7] *Ib.* ii. 941.

was entirely different. "For my part", he said afterwards,[1] "I should think I were very treacherous if I should take away tithes till I see the legislative power to settle maintenance" to ministers "another way". The Protector's plan was not to abolish tithe but to restrict the enjoyment of it to fit persons. Thus an Ordinance of March 20, 1654,[2] in view of the fact that to fill vacant livings "many weak, scandalous, popish, and ill-affected persons" had "intruded themselves, or been brought in, to the great grief and trouble of the good people of this nation", set up a Commission of "Triers", by whom all persons to be hereafter appointed to benefices by private patrons should be first approved as of "holy and unblameable conversation" before they could receive any income derived from endowments. "After provision for the appointment of the fit", the Protector proceeded to "the elimination of the unfit",[3] and by another Ordinance, of August 28, 1654,[4] local commissions of "Ejectors" were appointed in every county to remove clergy and schoolmasters who were "scandalous, ignorant, and insufficient". In defining what "shall be deemed and accounted scandalous", the Ordinance placed the use of the Book of Common Prayer side by side with "blasphemous and atheistical opinions", "profane cursing or swearing", "common haunting of taverns and ale-houses", "frequent playing at cards or dice", and other more serious offences. In connexion with education, it should also be noticed that by an Ordinance of September 2, 1654,[5] Cromwell appointed commissioners to visit the University of Oxford and a similar Board for Cambridge; and the same commissioners were empowered to visit the great schools—the Cambridge commissioners visiting Eton, and the Oxford commissioners Winchester and Merchant Taylors, while the visitation of Westminster was assigned to the visitors of both Universities.

Cromwell set much store by the comprehensiveness of his ecclesiastical arrangements. "Here are three sorts of

---

[1] In his speech of September 17, 1656 (*Letters and Speeches*, ii. 538).
[2] *Acts and Ordinances*, ii. 855.
[3] Firth, *Cromwell*, p. 358.   [4] *Ib.* ii. 968.
[5] *Ib.* ii. 1026.

godly men that you are to take care for", he said to his
Second Parliament,[1] referring to Presbyterians, Baptists,
and Independents; "if a man be of any of these three
judgments, if he have the root of the matter in him he
may be admitted". The Triers were drawn impartially
from all three, and outside the circle of beneficed clergy
who consumed tithe, there were innumerable free congregations scattered over the country, either supporting
a minister of their own or worshipping without any
authorised minister at all.[2] The establishment of religious
liberty as the sects understood it was dearer to the hearts
of Cromwell and his advisers than any other single
political object, and it might almost be said that the main
purpose of the *Instrument of Government* was to make this
unassailable for ever. But religious liberty as the sects
understood it "was not extended to Popery or Prelacy",
and the use of the Prayer Book was still unlawful.

Other legislation of this prolific nine months included
"the better amending and keeping in repair the common
highways within the nation";[3] the "preservation of the
works of the Great Level of the Fens";[4] the relief of poor
debtors;[5] "the regulation of hackney-coachmen in London
and the places adjacent";[6] the reorganisation of the Post
Office;[7] and the maintenance of the Poor Knights of
Windsor.[8]

The First Parliament of the Protectorate, called in
accordance with the *Instrument of Government*, met on
September 3, 1654, and its first act was to question the
right of private persons to draw up a Constitution and
impose it upon the whole nation. It refused to recognise
the binding force of the *Instrument*, and claimed that
government should be settled in Parliament alone. In this
the Parliamentarians received the support of the London
clergy, and we are told that on the Sunday after the meeting
of the assembly "the parsons generally prayed for the
Parliament...but not much concerning the Single Per-

---

[1] On April 21, 1657 (*Letters and Speeches*, iii. 120).
[2] Trevelyan, *Stuarts*, p. 311.
[3] *Acts and Ordinances*, ii. 861. [4] *Ib*. ii. 899. [5] *Ib*. ii. 911.
[6] *Ib*. ii. 922. [7] *Ib*. ii. 1007. [8] *Ib*. ii. 1019.

son".[1] In reply to this attack upon the Constitution under which they were acting, the Protector and his Council declared their willingness to accept an amended Constitution from the House, provided that certain points could be guaranteed. In a speech to the members, the Protector distinguished between "circumstantials", which he was ready to allow the House to alter, and "fundamentals", upon which he intended to stand firm.[2] The "fundamentals" were four in number: (1) government by a Single Person and a Parliament; (2) that Parliaments should not make themselves perpetual; (3) that there should be liberty of conscience; and (4) that neither the Protector nor Parliament should have exclusive control over the power of the sword. Having thus defined his position, the Protector required the members of the House to sign an undertaking "to be true and faithful to the Lord Protector and the Commonwealth" and not to "alter the government as it is settled in a Single Person and a Parliament".[3] For refusing this "Recognition", as it was called, ninety of the extremer Republicans were excluded from the House. The remainder of the members then proceeded to discuss the Constitution, clause by clause, with a view to amending it in such a way as to make it more parliamentary without coming to an open breach with the Protector and those who acted with him. They speedily accepted the first two fundamentals by approving government by a Single Person and a Parliament and adopting the principle of triennial elections; but an important modification of the *Instrument* was carried which would profoundly affect the character of the executive. It was proposed to make the Council of State dependent upon Parliament by substituting for indirect election and tenure for life, nomination by the Protector with the approval of Parliament and tenure only until forty days after the meeting of a new Parliament unless the Councillors received "a new approbation" of Parliament[4]. Over the

---

[1] Gardiner, *Protectorate*, iii. 22.   [2] *Letters and Speeches*, ii. 381–5.
[3] Gardiner, *Protectorate*, iii. 32.
[4] See the Bill of November 11, 1654, for a Parliamentary Constitution printed in Gardiner, *Documents*, pp. 427–47.

other two fundamentals the House came into direct collision with the Protector, for (1) it sought to limit the toleration which the *Instrument* had guaranteed, by excepting such "damnable heresies" as should be afterwards enumerated[1] —a term which was likely to cover many of the sects which Cromwell was desiring to tolerate; and (2) it decided to restrict the Protector's control of the army to Cromwell's lifetime. An attempt was also made by a financial committee to reduce the army from the 57,000 at which it now stood to the 30,000 named in the *Instrument*, and to cut down the soldiers' pay. For the reduction of the army there were very strong reasons, as the national expenditure was more than four times what it had been under Charles I, and with the army at 57,000 men there was a deficit of nearly half a million on the year's working.[2] Nevertheless, these were precisely the measures which Cromwell and his officers could never sanction. The prospect of the disbanding of nearly half the army brought officers and men alike into line against the Parliament, for arms had now become their profession in life and thus there was a great vested interest against reduction. But there was also a more unselfish reason. The army was the sole guarantee of toleration, and it was feared that if the control of it fell to the Parliament, this would mean, sooner or later, the persecution of the sects. None knew better than the army leaders how slight was the hold of the principle of toleration upon the country at large, and how easy it would be for Parliament to overthrow it. "Indeed, that hath been one of the vanities of our contests", said Cromwell,[3] "every sect saith, 'O, give me liberty', but give him it, and to his power he will not yield it to anybody else".

It is scarcely surprising to find the Protector taking the earliest opportunity which the Constitution gave him to get rid of his first Parliament. "It looks", he said,[4] "as if a laying grounds for a quarrel had rather been designed than to give the people settlement". He therefore dissolved the

---

[1] See Gardiner, *Documents*, p. 443.
[2] Gardiner, *Cromwell*, p. 97.
[3] September 12, 1654: *Letters and Speeches*, ii. 383.
[4] January 22, 1655: *ib.* ii. 419.

7

Assembly on January 22, 1655, after it had sat for the five months prescribed by the *Instrument*, but only for five *lunar* months. The House had discussed and amended the *Instrument of Government*, and had quarrelled with the Protector over its provisions, but it had never approved it, and thus the ultimate foundation of the Government was still military. The assent of the representatives of the nation had not been obtained, and the new Constitution, although it had been working for more than a year, still derived its sanction from the Council of Officers which had drafted it. The Swedish Chancellor Oxenstiern, in conversation with Whitelocke, had counselled the Protector to "get him a back and breast of steel", and when pressed for an explanation he said: "I mean the confirmation of his being Protector to be made by your Parliament, which will be his best and greatest strength".[1] It was precisely this that Cromwell could not do.

[1] Bulstrode Whitelocke, *A Journal of the Swedish Embassy* (ed. H. Reeve, 1855), i. 328.

The Second Parliament of the Protectorate

THE Constitution of the Protectorate was exposed to attack from two sides. The *Instrument of Government* failed to satisfy the extremer Republicans; for the creation of a permanent executive authority, to a great extent independent of Parliament and wielding very large constitutional powers, was the death-blow to their favourite scheme—of government by the direct action of a representative assembly. To men who were disposed to press to its most literal applications the doctrine that all power is from the People, it was intolerable that the assembly of the People's representatives should be relegated to the third place in the Constitution, in favour of a permanent Protector and an irremovable Council of State. If this was the view of the political fanatics, the religious fanatics also were on the same side. The Fifth Monarchy men, who daily expected the millennium, were not prepared to see the Kingdom of Christ usurped by Cromwell. One preacher denounced him as "the dissemblingest perjured villain in the world".[1] Another prayed in public, "Lord, thou hast suffered us to cut off the head which reigned over us, and thou hast suffered the tail to set itself up and rule over us in the head's place".[2] "O, thou black Whitehall", said another,[3] "fah! fah! it stinks of the brimstone of Sodom and the smoke of the bottomless pit. The flying roll of God's curses shall overtake the family of that great thief there". Others identified the Protector with the little horn spoken of by Daniel the prophet[4], "which waxed exceeding great, toward the south, and toward the east, and toward the glorious land", and cast down the host of Heaven, "and it cast down Truth to the ground, and it did its pleasure, and prospered".[5]

On the other hand, it was all in favour of the *Instrument*

---

[1] Quoted in Masson, iv. 547.   [2] Gooch, p. 264.
[3] John Rogers: see Gardiner, *Protectorate*, iii. 114.
[4] E. Jenks, *The Constitutional Experiments of the Commonwealth*, p. 79.
[5] Daniel, viii. 9–12.

that it faithfully reflected the ideas of the army as they had been set forth four years earlier in the *Agreement of the People*. The dangers of the time called for a stronger and more permanent executive than the *Agreement* had contemplated, but its essential features were all there—Parliaments at fixed intervals sitting for a stated time, election on a basis of population, a Council of State governing in the intervals of Parliament, and the maintenance of a "preaching ministry" with full security for toleration. The continuance of the army itself was also secured.

"From the publication of the *Instrument of Government*", says a modern writer,[1] "I think we may date the satisfaction of the bulk of the army with the settlement, and consequently the beginning of Cromwell's settled power. Its chief provisions remained intact during Oliver's lifetime, and except for the question about the Crown, he had no serious difficulty with the army".

Another merit of the *Instrument of Government* is that it marks an advance towards reasonable constitutional principles. Hitherto the history of Puritanism on its political side had been the growth of one of the two conflicting principles which influenced the political thought of the revolutionary period at the expense of the other—the growth of the principle of the government of the godly at the expense of the principle of the sovereignty of the people. One Parliament after another had been purged and expelled to vindicate the right of the godly to govern, and in the Assembly of Nominees, where an election was not even pretended, the claims of political Puritanism had reached their highest point. What makes the Protectorate so important a landmark is, that it registers the turn of the tide. It is true that the system established by it was not in its inception elective at all, for the Protector and the large majority of the Council of State were named in the *Instrument* itself, and although the executive was immensely powerful, Parliament could only influence the composition of it by degrees, as vacancies arose, and then only indirectly. But in spite of all safeguards and reservations, the *Instrument* did establish a Parliamentary system which admitted

[1] Jenks, p. 78.

sinners as well as saints, and it even contemplated the return of the Royalists to politics after a sufficient lapse of time.

By the dissolution of his First Triennial, Cromwell was left in 1655 in very much the same position as that in which Charles I had found himself in 1629 when he quarrelled with his Third Parliament before it had granted him supplies. For the King it had meant ruin, but the Protector was entirely at his ease. His ordinary revenue fixed by the *Instrument* was beyond the control of Parliament, and he also continued to act upon the Customs Ordinance of December 29, 1653, quoting the clause in the *Instrument* which left the settling of ways and means to the Protector in Council. Some of the lawyers objected that the Ordinance had no binding force, but the Protector had a legal case, and he attached little weight to criticisms that were merely technical. "The people...", he said to his First Parliament in the speech announcing the dissolution, "will prefer their safety to their passions, and their real security to forms, when necessity calls for supplies".[1] If this argument failed to convince, he fell back on force. "'Tis against the will of the nation", one man is represented as saying to him. "Very well", he replied, "but what if I should disarm the nine, and put a sword in the tenth man's hands? Would not that do the business?"[2] Although he preferred to work under constitutional forms if possible, Cromwell was quite ready to fall back upon the principles on which beneficent despotisms are founded, and to follow the example of Strafford.

In a more literal sense also, the Protector was prepared to "put a sword in the tenth man's hand". The dissolution of Parliament in January, 1655, had been followed by a series of insurrectionary movements and assassination plots, and of these the Royalist rising in the West, known as Penruddock's Insurrection, in March, 1655, met with a momentary success. Government was at that time enormously strong against attacks of this kind, but the Protector took steps to make it stronger. "We did find

---

[1] *Letters and Speeches,* ii. 425.
[2] J. H. Jesse, *Memoirs of the Court of England,* iii. 67.

out a little, poor invention."[1] He embodied in June a new
local militia of some 6000 horse, consisting of volunteers
from among the known supporters of the Government,
and placed them under the command of eleven "Major-
Generals",[2] each controlling a district of from two to seven
counties and disposing of about 500 men. The scheme was
an application to the whole kingdom of Desborough's
appointment as "Major-General of the West" which the
Protector had made on an emergency for the particular
purpose of putting down Penruddock's Insurrection.[3]
The Major-Generals were not, at this stage, intended to
supersede the local magistrates, but rather to stimulate
them to a more active discharge of their duties and to
place an efficient police force at their disposal;[4] but they
received a very wide commission, and their zeal for the
reformation of public and private morals led to an irritating
interference with personal freedom.

During the summer and autumn of 1655 the Protector
tried, by reducing the numbers and pay of the army[5] and
by effecting economies in other directions, to bring his
expenditure within the limits of his income; but at the end
of the year he had to face a deficit of about £230,000.[6]
Under the terms of the *Instrument of Government* this
deficit was clearly the business of Parliament, for it had
been caused partly by the maintenance of a larger army
than the 30,000 which the Constitution provided, and
partly by war expenditure occasioned by the conflict with
Spain. But the Protector proposed to meet it by throwing
over the *Instrument* altogether, and enlarging the area of
taxation by executive authority. He had already imposed
on the Royalists a "Decimation tax" of ten per cent. to
meet military expenditure, and he proposed to extend the
tax to all persons whose income or property was sufficient
to bring them into the wealthier class of taxpayers.[7] The
course which he recommended was both illegal and un-
constitutional, but the difficulties of the Protector's position

---

[1] *Letters and Speeches*, ii. 530.
[2] See Gardiner, *Protectorate*, iii. 172, 196.
[3] *Ib.* iii. 138.   [4] *Ib.* iii. 174.   [5] *Ib.* iii. 170, 171.
[6] *Ib.* iii. Supplementary chapter, p. 4.   [7] *Ib.* p. 7.

had long since forced upon him "the habit of playing fast
and loose with the *Instrument* whenever he considered that
a necessity had arisen",[1] and his Straffordian conception
of government enabled him to justify himself in his own
eyes. Now, however, he found himself confronted by the
united opposition of soldiers, civilians, and lawyers alike,
and in the end he was obliged to give way. The Second
Triennial was summoned for September, 1656, to deal
with the financial situation and to vote supplies for the war
with Spain.

The cry at the elections was, "No courtiers nor swords-
men",[2] and a large number of Cromwell's opponents were
returned. But the resources of the Government were not
exhausted, for experience had shewn that Parliaments
could be purged. A clause of the *Instrument* had provided
that members of Parliament "shall be such (and no other
than such) as are persons of known integrity, fearing God
and of good conversation, and being of the age of twenty-
one years"; and another clause had empowered the Council
of State "to peruse the...returns, and examine whether
the persons so elected and returned be such as is agreeable
to the qualifications, and not disabled to be elected". By
a strained interpretation of these clauses—regarding, in
particular, "known integrity" as meaning, not integrity
of character but integrity "to the Government"—the
Council converted a moral into a political test, and excluded
most of Cromwell's opponents. Out of 460 members
about a hundred were thus excluded, and fifty or sixty
more abstained from taking their seats.[3] Sir Charles
Firth's analysis of the constituencies from which they
came[4] shews how feeling in the electorate had changed.
The counties had been the strongest supporters of the
Parliament in the Civil War, but now no less than seventy
of the hundred excluded members represented counties.
Out of the fifty-seven members elected by the counties
included in the old Eastern Association which had furnished Cromwell's Ironsides, twenty-nine were now to be

[1] *Ib.* p. 8.   [2] Firth, *Cromwell*, p. 420.
[3] C. H. Firth, *The Last Years of the Protectorate*, i. 16.
[4] *Ib.* i. 17.

reckoned among his enemies. On the other hand, the boroughs provided him with steady support. Out of the twenty-five members representing Eastern Association boroughs, only four were against him; and of forty-four members for the twenty-two larger boroughs, only seven were in opposition. This suggests that the middle classes, and the traders and manufacturers generally, supported the Protectorate. Nevertheless, the exclusion of so many members caused deep discontent. One writer asked whether to exclude one hundred was not "a crime twenty-fold beyond that of the late King's in going about to seclude the five members".[1] The French Ambassador said that the people were more angry at this exclusion than at any other attack upon their liberties.[2]

The members of the Second Triennial who survived the exclusion were for the most part supporters of the Protector and his policy, and from these there proceeded a further constitutional experiment.

Regarded as a permanent settlement of the nation, the *Instrument of Government* was not altogether satisfactory. There was no means either of amending it or of interpreting it, for the idea of a Supreme Court by which the framers of the American Constitution solved the problem did not occur to the seventeenth century. The need for an interpreting authority was brought home to the Protector by the case of James Nayler, the mad visionary of Bristol, who claimed to be Christ. The Second Triennial, refusing to be limited by the terms of the *Instrument* and claiming to possess the judicial powers which had belonged to former Parliaments, voted without a division that he was "guilty of horrid blasphemy, a grand impostor, and a great seducer of the people",[3] and inflicted upon him a sentence of unexampled savagery. This was to throw over the *Instrument* altogether, and it was a claim which the Protector, as trustee of the Constitution, could not possibly allow. It appeared to him to be of vital importance that some authority should be set up to interpret the *Instrument* and to arbitrate between him and his Parliament, and this

---

[1] Firth, *Protectorate*, i. 21 *n.*   [2] *Ib.* i. 23.
[3] *Ib.* i. 88.

was what turned his thoughts to the creation of a Second Chamber. It was one of the most cherished convictions of the army that it was necessary in the interests of liberty to limit the power of Parliament, and later on Cromwell, addressing the officers on the need for a Second Chamber, pressed the point home.

"By the proceedings of this Parliament", he said,[1] "you see they stand in need of a check or balancing power,...for the case of James Nayler might happen to be your own case. By their judicial power they fall upon life and member, and doth the Instrument in being enable me to control it?"

Meanwhile, other considerations were pointing to the necessity of amending the Constitution in a different direction. In January, 1657, Sindercombe's plot to assassinate the Protector was discovered; this, if it had succeeded, would have spelt ruin. "I believe", said one of the members, "none of us that sit here had been safe, if this design had prospered".[2] If Cromwell should die, who would succeed him? Would not his death be the signal for a period of inglorious intrigue, followed by an outbreak of anarchy? Might not the army itself split asunder under rival generals, and the country be once more involved in a disastrous civil war? Thus to a case for the revival of a Second Chamber was added a case for the revival of hereditary monarchy.

The latter idea was not quite new, for in the early days of the Second Triennial, on October 28, 1656, an Irish member had proposed in the House that the *Instrument* should be amended so as to make the office of Protector hereditary instead of elective,[3] and since then the question of the succession had been several times discussed. It was suggested that the danger of anarchy might be avoided if the Protector were given power to nominate his successor, and this met with some support, even in the army, which was on the whole opposed to change. The new conditions, however, led to a more audacious suggestion—that the Protector should be offered the title of King.

[1] February 27, 1657; *Letters and Speeches*, iii. 488.
[2] Firth, *Protectorate*, i. 119.   [3] *Ib.* i. 64.

At the end of January or the beginning of February, 1657, soon after the discovery of Sindercombe's plot, some of Cromwell's supporters drew up in private meetings a new Constitution to replace the *Instrument*, an essential feature of which was that, in order to checkmate the assassins, the Protector should be invited to assume "the name, style, title, and dignity of King".[1] On February 23 this paper made its first appearance in the House on the initiative of Sir Christopher Packe, a tenacious and boring member, who during a debate at the Committee of Trade had made thirty speeches and "was very angry he could not be heard *ad infinitum*", so that "the committee was forced at last to come to a compact with him, that he should speak no more after that time".[2] Packe was, however, supported by some influential members of the Council of State, and it was decided by 144 votes to fifty-four that the paper should be read.[3] In the discussion which followed, the lawyers and country gentlemen were in favour of the kingship, and most of the officers who had seats in the House were against it; but its supporters commanded a majority. On February 27 a hundred officers, including the Major-Generals, waited upon the Protector and prayed him to refuse the title of King; but at this stage they did not receive, nor could they expect, a definite answer. On March 2 the House decided to postpone the question of the kingship until the rest of the document should have been considered; but in the end the civilians triumphed over the soldiers, and on March 25 it was carried by 123 votes to sixty-two that the Protector should be asked to be King.[4]

Among moderate men the government of Cromwell was beginning to be accepted as a permanent settlement of the kingdom. Cromwell himself was a man of sense and sober judgment, and his rule was a guarantee against the excesses of the Levellers and extremer Republicans. His foreign policy appeared effective and patriotic, and it had made a great impression upon observers at home and abroad. His championship of the Vaudois, the war with

---

[1] Firth, *Protectorate*, i. 128, 129 *n.*, 131.   [2] *Ib.* i. 130.
[3] *Ib.* i. 131.   [4] *Ib.* i. 135, 139, 148.

Spain, the acquisitions in the New World, and the efficient protection given to English trade by sea, had gratified at once the religious feeling, the acquisitiveness, and the national pride of Englishmen. They could now feel that the hostile monarchies of Europe, although their dynastic sympathies were with Charles II, respected and feared what has been called the "pariah state". Moreover, like other men who have achieved greatness, Cromwell had risen to his responsibilities, and his bearing as head of the State did no discredit to the country over which he ruled. As early as 1654 the French Ambassador had recorded his impressions: "Towards the foreign ambassadors", he wrote, "the Protector deports himself as a king, for the power of kings is not greater than his"; and a little later he added, "Some say he will assume the title and prerogatives of a Roman Emperor".[1]

But it was not to Cromwell's virtues only that we trace the disappearance among moderate men of their natural hesitation to raise him to a higher office than that of Protector. Their strongest motive was the desire to return from a military to a constitutional government. As a contemporary observer remarked,[2] "They are so highly incensed against the arbitrary actings of the Major-General, that they are greedy of any powers that will be ruled and limited by law". The title of King was the only title which carried with it the traditional constitutional limitations to the power of Government; and it was the only title which implied a settlement that was really permanent, for all others could be regarded as only temporary, leaving it open to Charles II to claim to be King *de jure*.

"It is a change of name only", they said, "and you are desired to take it by the agreement of the representatives of three nations in Parliament. It is the ancient way by which good kings were ever made. All Israel gathered themselves together at Hebron to make David king".

To the Protector the changes in the Constitution which

---

[1] Jesse, iii. 62–3.
[2] Probably John Rushworth: see *Clarke Papers*, iii. 91–2.

were now proposed were acceptable in the main, although he had criticisms to make upon points of detail. "I am hugely taken with the word *settlement*", he said, "with the thing and with the notion of it. And indeed I think he is not worthy to live in England that is not".[1] He had expressed the view much earlier[2] that "a settlement of somewhat with monarchical power in it would be very effectual"; and if his feet could be set once more upon the ancient and well-beaten track of the Constitution, many of his difficulties would solve themselves. It was generally believed that, in spite of the opposition of a large part of the army, Cromwell would accept the Crown, but after three days consideration he declined it, and as the House had decided that the new scheme must be accepted or rejected as a whole, this meant that it fell to the ground. Although they were discouraged and disheartened by this refusal, the moderate majority in Parliament persevered in their plan. On April 7 they addressed the Protector again, asking him to accept the draft Constitution which had now come to be called *The Humble Petition and Advice*,[3] only to hear from him "a speech so dark, that none knows whether he will accept it or not".[4] On April 9 the House appointed a large committee of nearly a hundred members to try to remove the Protector's doubts and scruples, and a series of conferences with him took place.[5] At one of these a new argument made its appearance which carried great weight with the members—that Henry VII's Act of Treason protected those who adhered to a king *de facto*, and would therefore protect Cromwell's supporters if he were made King. This Act was afterwards pleaded in Sir Harry Vane's case at the Restoration, and was disallowed by the judges precisely on that ground—that the usurper was not a king. So strong was the feeling in Parliament in favour of the kingship, that Thurloe told Henry Cromwell that nothing else would satisfy them.[6]

[1] *Letters and Speeches*, iii. 87.
[2] In 1651: Whitelocke, *Memorials*, iii. 374.
[3] Printed, with the "Additional Petition" of June 26, 1657, in Gardiner, *Documents*, pp. 447–64.
[4] Firth, *Protectorate*, i. 169.   [5] *Ib.* i. 170.   [6] *Ib.* i. 176.

"The title is not the question", he said, "but it's the office, which is known to the laws and this people. They know their duty to a king and his to them. Whatever else there is will be wholly new, and be nothing else but a probationer, and upon the next occasion will be changed again. Besides, they say the name Protector came in by the sword out of Parliament, and will never be the ground of any settlement; nor will there be a free Parliament so long as that continues; and as it savours of the sword now, so it will at last bring all things to be military. These and other considerations make men who are for settlement steady in their resolutions as to this government now in hand; not that they lust after a king, or are peevish upon any account of opposition, but they would lay foundations of liberty and freedom, which they judge this the next way to".[1]

For these reasons the moderate party continued earnestly to press the Protector to give way. He sought to gain time by suggesting amendments to the other parts of the *Humble Petition and Advice*, but Parliament promptly accepted all his proposals, and pressed him again for a positive answer; and on May 8 the answer came. It was generally expected that under this pressure from his supporters Cromwell would accept the Crown, and he told several of the members privately that he intended to do so.[2] But on May 6 he made the discovery that not only his brother-in-law Desborough, but also Fleetwood and Lambert—the three great officers on whom he specially relied—were determined to withdraw from all public employment if their General should become King. A petition promoted by Colonel Pride was signed by the majority of the field-officers of the army then in London, asking Parliament not to press the Protector to any further answer touching the *Petition and Advice*. These clear indications were enough for Cromwell, and in the long-expected answer to Parliament, while approving the proposed Constitution, he said definitely, "I cannot undertake this government with that title of King".[3] This answer was reluctantly accepted, and after long debates, on May 25 the *Humble Petition and Advice* was once more offered to Cromwell, but now without the title of King. This time he consented to it without hesitation.[4]

---

[1] Thurloe, *State Papers*, vi. 219: quoted in Firth, i. 176–7.
[2] Firth, *Protectorate*, i. 190.　　　[3] *Letters and Speeches*, iii. 129.
[4] Firth, *Protectorate*, i. 198.

Although Cromwell had refused the Crown, the *Humble Petition and Advice* amended the Constitution in such a way as to restore something not altogether unlike the old kingship.

(1) The Protector was empowered to nominate his successor, and thus to establish a form of monarchy which would be certain in time to become hereditary.

(2) The Parliamentary Constitution set up by the *Instrument of Government* was amended so as to establish a Second Chamber, and the Protector was empowered to nominate not less than forty nor more than seventy life-peers to make up this "Other House", subject in each case to the approval of the elected House. It should be observed that Cromwell chose the Lords of his Second Chamber with the greatest care, selecting them from among the influential members of the party which supported the Protectorate. They included a number of high officials —judges and members of the Council; seventeen military officers of high rank; and about a dozen country gentlemen of family and property.[1] Seven members of the old peerage were also summoned, but only two consented to sit,[2] and this deprived the Other House of a good deal of influence and reputation.

(3) Instead of a revenue of uncertain amount to be raised from such sources as the Council of State should determine, there was to be a fixed revenue of a million for the army and navy and £300,000 "for the support of the Government", and this was not to be altered, nor was any fresh taxation to be laid upon the people, "without common consent by Act of Parliament".

(4) The Council of State, which had been all powerful under the *Instrument of Government*, was relegated by the *Humble Petition and Advice* to the subordinate position of a Privy Council. Its members were no longer to be appointed for life by a complicated system of nomination, but they were to be chosen by the Protector, with the consent of his Council and of Parliament, and might be removed by him with the consent of Parliament; while in the intervals of Parliament the Protector-in-Council might

---

[1] Firth, *Protectorate*, ii. 12.   [2] *Ib.*

suspend any councillor "for just cause". The number of the Council was limited to twenty-one persons, and these "such as are of known piety and undoubted affection to the rights of these nations, and a just Christian liberty in matters of religion".

(5) The religious settlement of the *Petition* is not materially different from that of the *Instrument*, for about this the most influential men of the Protectorate had all along been agreed. It contemplates a comprehensive Church endowed and established, with toleration for the various sects remaining outside it, but this toleration was rather less wide than that of the *Instrument*, for it did not include Unitarians, while blasphemy and profaneness were added to the licentiousness hitherto held to be a disqualification for liberty of worship. Another novelty was that, like Henry VIII, Cromwell, in consultation with his Parliament, was to put forth a Confession of Faith. This was not to be a final test of orthodoxy, but was to be "recommended to the people of these nations", and no one was to be permitted to "revile or reproach" it. This last clause was directed against the Quakers, whose practice of interrupting the service in churches in order to say to the officiating minister, "Come down, thou deceiver, thou hireling", and to call him a "dead dog", was rather disconcerting.

(6) It should be observed also that the Protector surrenders in the *Petition and Advice* the power which he had claimed under the *Instrument* of excluding by executive authority members of Parliament who were hostile to his Government on the ground that they were not properly qualified. He guarantees "the ancient and undoubted liberties and privileges of Parliament", and promises in particular "that those persons who are legally chosen by a free election of the people to serve in Parliament" shall not "be excluded from sitting in Parliament to do their duties but by judgment and consent of that House whereof they are members".

The *Humble Petition and Advice* was afterwards criticised by Vane, who stated the objections taken to it by the Republican party. He argued that it would only revive monarchy and lead straight to a Stuart restoration. "Shall we be under-builders to supreme Stuart?" he said. "If you be minded to resort to the old government, you are not many steps from the old family."[1] It was precisely because it was a reversion to the old government that the *Petition* was acceptable to so many, and as long as Cromwell lived, there could be no question of a return to the old family. The reversion to the old order affected Cromwell's external state, for at his installation on June 26, 1657, instead of the plain black velvet which he had hitherto affected, he was robed in purple and ermine, and to the civil sword which had served as the symbol of his authority was added a golden sceptre.[2] The critics of the man and his system were not, however, silenced. Cromwell had accepted the *Petition and Advice* on May 25, and *Killing no Murder* appeared within a week after, although it had been written when it was supposed that he was about to accept the Crown. It appealed to the soldiers "to pull down this Dagon".

His bed, his table is not secure, and he stands in need of other guards to defend him against his own. Death and destruction pursue him wherever he goes; they follow him everywhere like his fellow-travellers, and at last they will come upon him like armed men.[3]

On January 20, 1658, the Second Parliament of the Protectorate reassembled for its second session. The hundred members who had been excluded now took their seats in accordance with the terms of the *Petition*, while about thirty of Cromwell's ablest supporters were removed to the Other House.[4] This meant that both the leadership and the majority passed to the Republicans, and they at

---

[1] *D.N.B.* viii. 124.

[2] The robe of purple velvet, the sword, the sceptre, and a richly-gilt Bible were gifts to the Protector from his Parliament. "What a comely and glorious sight it is", said the Speaker, "to behold a Lord Protector in a purple robe, with a sceptre in his hand, a sword of justice girt about him, and his eyes fixed upon the Bible! Long may you prosperously enjoy them all, to your own comfort and the comfort of the people of these three nations!" (Masson, v. 148.)

[3] Firth, *Protectorate*, i. 228.

[4] *Ib.* ii. 19. The writ summoning Richard Cromwell to the Other House is printed in Gardiner, *Documents*, p. 464.

once launched an attack upon the Other House. The Lower House had claimed for itself all the traditional rights of the House of Commons; what would happen to the liberties of England if the Upper House should claim the rights of the House of Lords? "The Commons of England", said Haslerig,[1] "will quake to hear that they are returning to Egypt". The Other House was too full of soldiers, who had power to check and control the representatives of the people; and it did not contain enough representatives of landed property. "They are not a balance, as the old Lords were, as to matter of estate."[2] Nor did the Republican leaders confine their opposition to vague talk. They opened communications with the opponents of Cromwell, both in the army and in the City of London, and, anticipating the Chartists, they prepared a monster petition, directed to the House of Commons under the title of "the Parliament of the Commonwealth of England", as if the Other House were no part of Parliament, praying for the restoration of a single chamber with uncontrolled authority. The petition also took up the grievances of the soldiers, and it was rumoured that Fairfax would head the deputation which was to present it to the Lower House.[3] Where the army was concerned, Cromwell was a man of swift decision and prompt action. The petition was to have been presented on February 4, but he determined to forestall it by a dissolution. Between 10 and 11 in the morning he came down to Westminster and summoned the Commons to meet him in the House of Lords. His son-in-law Fleetwood tried to dissuade him from any extreme step, but he replied, "You are a milksop: as the Lord liveth I will dissolve the House".[4] In an angry speech he reviewed their shortcomings, pointing out that the establishment of a Second Chamber was one of the conditions upon which he had accepted the *Humble Petition and Advice*. "I would not undertake it", he said, "without there might be some other body that might interpose between you and me on the behalf of the Commonwealth, to prevent a tumultuary and popular

---

[1] Quoted in Firth, *Cromwell*, p. 430.
[2] Firth, *Protectorate*, ii. 23.   [3] *Ib.* ii. 30–4.   [4] *Ib.* ii. 37.

spirit".[1] He then accused the Republicans of endeavouring to pervert the army, and concluded his speech with a sentence that has become famous: "And if this be the end of your sitting and this be your carriage, I think it high time that an end be put to your sitting. And I do dissolve this Parliament. And let God be Judge between you and me".[2]

The principal difficulty created by the Protector's quarrel with his Parliament was financial. At the time of the dissolution the pay of the soldiers was many months in arrear,[3] and in the summer of 1658 there was a debt of at least a million and a half; but the position was by no means hopeless, and another Parliament was in contemplation from which he expected to obtain better financial support. But on September 3, 1658, the anniversary of his victory at Dunbar and of the "crowning mercy" of Worcester, the great Protector died. "Let us all not be careful", he had written just ten years before,[4] "what use men will make of these actings. They shall, will they, nill they, fulfil the good pleasure of God, and so shall serve our generations. Our rest we expect elsewhere; that will be durable".

[1] *Letters and Speeches,* iii. 505.
[2] *Ib.* iii. 192: *cf.* also the version given in iii. 508.
[3] Firth, *Protectorate,* ii. 257, 266.
[4] On September 1, 1648: *Letters and Speeches,* i. 350.

"FOR some weeks", as has been well said, "Oliver ruled England from his urn".[1] The accession of Richard Cromwell, whom his father on his death-bed had nominated as his successor, was well received, and he was to all appearance secure upon the throne. The acute observer Thurloe, writing to Henry Cromwell immediately after the proclamation of the new régime,[2] said: "It hath pleased God hitherto to give his Highness your brother a very easy and peaceable entrance upon his government. There is not a dog that wags his tongue, so great a calm are we in". But a note of warning had been struck already. "The machine is strong", wrote a contemporary, "but I do not deem it durable, for it is violent". Even during his father's lifetime, Henry Cromwell himself had asked a pertinent question: "Does not your peace depend upon his Highness's life, and upon his peculiar skill and faculty and personal interest in the army as now modelled and commanded?"[3] And Thurloe, in the letter to Henry Cromwell quoted above, goes on to lay his finger upon the essential weakness of Richard Cromwell's position. "But I must needs acquaint your Excellency that there are some secret murmurings in the army, *as if his Highness were not general of the army, as his father was.*" Here we have the fundamental difference between Oliver Cromwell and his son. Oliver Cromwell had been a military man of great reputation, who as commander-in-chief of the army possessed its complete confidence and unquestioning obedience. Richard Cromwell was only a civilian, and a particularly unmilitary civilian—a florid, inoffensive country gentleman, who, we are told, was "bred in the country, and led a life that delighted much in hunting, and other rural sports". In a word, Oliver was Protector because he had been Lord General; Richard was only Lord General because he was

---

[1] Gooch, p. 283.
[2] September 7, 1658 (Thurloe, vii, 374).
[3] Henry Cromwell to Thurloe, June 30, 1658 (Thurloe, vii. 218).

Protector. But this claim of a civilian to hold the highest military office failed to satisfy the army, and it was not long before this dissatisfaction took shape in a military agitation.

The new Protector had been proclaimed at the beginning of September, 1658. Towards the end of October the officers began to hold weekly meetings at St James's, and "a very eminent spirit of prayer appeared" among them. For a time they kept off politics and contented themselves with expounding the Scriptures, but at last they "began to break out, and to hint at some alterations made in the army, as if good men were put out and worse put in"— in other words, they claimed a veto upon the Protector's choice of officers.[1] It was also decided to petition for the appointment of a commander-in-chief who should be a soldier and have the appointment of inferior officers, and that for the future no officer should be dismissed but by the sentence of a court-martial.[2] Such security of tenure, which would prevent the modelling and purging of the army on political grounds, would be a popular demand in an army that had come to be regarded as a profession for life.

The Protector was conciliatory, and succeeded in allaying the agitation for a time, but it was impossible for him to entertain the idea of granting these demands. To make Fleetwood or Lambert Lord General would be to surrender the power of the sword; and Richard Cromwell, in obedience to the same instinct which had guided Charles I, refused to make his officers thus greater than himself. He declared that he himself was Lord General, as his father had been before him, and that Fleetwood was only Lieutenant-General under his orders.

Although the army was thus disaffected, the lawyers and statesmen rallied round the new Protector, and by their advice he summoned a new Parliament. In summoning this assembly the terms of the *Humble Petition and Advice* were not strictly adhered to. On the one hand, the "Other House" was called together in accordance with the *Petition*, but on the other, the revised scheme of con-

---

[1] Firth, *Army*, pp. 376–7.   [2] Thurloe, vii, 434, 436.

stituencies for the representative House was thrown over altogether, and the Government reverted to the system of the days before the Civil War.[1] The old boroughs were revived, and with them the preponderance of the borough over the county representation. The union with Scotland and Ireland was, however, retained, and they were duly represented by sixty members, nearly all Government officials. The exclusion of the Royalists was naturally still maintained.

This curious Parliament, blended of new and old, so far from giving the Protector the support which he needed against the army, was destined to throw everything into confusion. Although the presence of the sixty Scottish and Irish members gave the Government an assured majority upon all important questions, the Republicans were still remarkably strong, and it was their policy to oppose the Protector in every possible way. They were in favour of the abolition of the "Other House", a strict definition of the Protector's functions, and direct government by the elected representatives of the people; and in order to gain these ends they practised what is now known as "obstruction", but was then entitled to a more poetic description. "All that could be done", says Ludlow, "was only to lengthen out their debates, and to hang on the wheels of the chariot, that they might not be able to drive so furiously."[2]

These quarrels between parties in Parliament gave the army leaders their opportunity. They pressed upon the Protector the encouragement afforded by the dissensions in Parliament to Royalist plotters; their own special grievance of want of pay; and in particular they revived their original demand that the military office of Lord General should be separated from the civil office of Lord Protector, and should be given to Fleetwood, the Protector's brother-in-law. The line taken by the Parliament on this important question, called into existence

---

[1] The fourth clause of the *Petition* had reserved the number and distribution of the members for further consideration by Parliament; but under this no action had been taken. See Masson, v. 429.

[2] *Memoirs*, ii. 55.

again in an aggravated form the old controversy between the civil and the military power. To the Parliament it appeared an intolerable thing that a military force, paid by Parliament and in theory subordinate to the civil power, should make demands and issue decrees as though it were a separate estate of the realm. Accordingly, on April 18, 1659, the representations of the officers were met by two drastic votes. The first prohibited any council or meeting of the officers of the army while Parliament was sitting "without the direction, leave, and authority of his Highness the Lord Protector and both Houses of Parliament". The other, due to the fact that London was full of disorderly bodies of troops which threatened the liberty of Parliament, required every officer to pledge himself in writing never to interrupt the deliberations of the Houses. "It would fare ill with Parliament", the members said, "if it could no longer order them to return to their posts". But it soon became evident that the army would not obey the Assembly, but would repudiate the control of the civil power. The officers met in spite of the prohibition; fresh regiments were summoned to London in defiance of the orders of the Government; and even the Protector's own guard deserted him. A deputation of officers called upon him to dissolve Parliament, and waited outside his door until the order for a dissolution was handed over to them; while members who tried to resume their sittings were turned away from the Parliament House by the troops. If he had cared to appeal to force, the Protector might have summoned to his aid the Scottish army of occupation under Monk and the Irish army under his brother Henry Cromwell; but this would have involved another civil war. The remark attributed to him at this time is not without dignity: "I will not have a drop of blood spilt for the preservation of my greatness, which is a burden to me".[1] But, failing such an appeal to force, nothing was open to him but a surrender to the army, and even a surrender did not save him. Fleetwood and Desborough had at first intended to work through the Protectorate, and to maintain Richard Cromwell "a duke

[1] *D.N.B.* xiii. 189.

of Venice for his father's sake who raised them",[1] but the inferior officers and the Republican party in the City of London were too strong for them. The army declared for a pure republic, without government by a Single Person; the Protector soon after abdicated: and the "Year of Anarchy" began.

Parliament was dissolved on April 22, 1659, and within a fortnight the army leaders were compelled by pressure from the Republicans, supported by the inferior officers of the army, to recall the Purged Parliament—the only case of a government in England which had been republican in form. On May 7 forty-two of the old members took their seats, and their number was afterwards increased to nearly ninety.[2] This had the effect of sweeping away all the constitutional checks of the Protectorate, for there was now no Protector, no written Constitution, no Second Chamber, no real representation of the constituencies, and no limitation of the arbitrary power of the single House. It was impossible that in the long run the army could be satisfied with such an arrangement, and within a week they demanded the establishment of an assembly that should be representative of the people, with the addition of "a select Senate coordinate in power". Of this last, one of the pamphleteers observed that it was "as like the Other House as an ape is like a monkey".[3] A barren discussion of constitutional problems followed, ended by an open breach between Parliament and the army; and on October 13 Lambert and the troops stationed in London expelled the Purged Parliament again, although Monk and the regiments in Scotland supported the Parliament. Thus the army itself was divided, but for the time being power rested with that part of it which was on the spot. The officers established a military Committee of Safety, which appointed an advisory body "to prepare such a form of government as may best suit and comport with a free state and commonwealth, without a single person kingship or House of Peers".[4] So far as the nature of their proposals is known, they would have included a written Constitution,

---

[1] *Ib.*
[2] Firth, *Lords*, p. 260.
[3] *Ib.* p. 261
[4] *Ib.* p. 265.

two elected Houses, and the appointment of twenty-one "Conservators of Liberty" to interpret the Constitution and see that it was faithfully observed.[1] But before the new scheme could be approved, another revolution took place. The opposition to military rule was so general, that on December 26, 1659, the officers were obliged to recall to Westminster the members of the Purged Parliament and to reconstitute the earlier situation.

So far, the history of the period of transition between the death of Oliver Cromwell and the restoration of King Charles II has exhibited in a striking manner the power of the army. Cromwell had become great by means of it, and after his death it still existed, ready to make someone else great. One Assembly after another attacks it, and goes down at once before it, at a mere touch of the armed hand. It appears almost as if the army could go on making constitutions and overthrowing them to the end of time, for public opinion, although not without influence, was in the last resort powerless against military force. This, however, was only true as long as the army was of one mind. The situation was entirely changed by a third intervention from Scotland.

General George Monk had been ruling Scotland since 1654 with conspicuous success. He had under his command a disciplined army of 10,000 men entirely devoted to himself—a result partly due to his personal popularity among the soldiers, but still more to the fact that he was a master of the Cromwellian art of "purging". As Sir John Bramston put it in his *Autobiography*,[2] Monk had established his ascendency "by garbling his army".

As long as Richard Cromwell was in power, Monk's respect for his father kept him loyal. He is represented as saying, "Richard Cromwell forsook himself, else I had never failed my promise to his father or regard to his memory".[3] But the Royalists had already perceived in Monk the instrument best fitted to effect the King's restoration. "He commandeth...a better army than that in England is", wrote Colepeper,[4] "and in the King's

[1] Firth, *Lords*, p. 266   [2] Camden Society (1845), p. 113.
[3] *D.N.B.* xxxviii. 152.   [4] *Ib.* xxxviii. 153.

quarrel can bring with him the strength of Scotland". It is with the appearance of Monk, therefore, that the Restoration really begins. Hitherto the civil power had been helpless before the army. This second Cromwell declared for the civil power, and placed an army at its disposal; and there was little doubt what the civil power would do as soon as it was freed from military domination.

On October 17, 1659, Monk received the news of the expulsion of the Purged Parliament. The same night he made arrangements for the occupation of Berwick, and announced his intention of intervening in English politics "to assert the liberty and authority of Parliament". "I am engaged, in conscience and honour", he had said earlier, "to see my country freed from that intolerable slavery of a sword government, and I know England cannot, nay, will not endure it".[1] Whether at this stage he had already determined to restore the King is doubtful, but events moved fast. The Committee of Safety in London sent Lambert against him, and it was during Lambert's absence that the Purged Parliament was again restored. On January 2, 1660, Monk crossed the Tweed at the head of 5000 foot and 2000 horse. As early as November, 1659, he had been in negotiations with Fairfax—the one Parliamentary general left of high character and entirely unstained reputation—and on January 1 Fairfax and his friends had occupied York in arms. This was an accession of vital importance, for his influence was still strong among the soldiers he had once commanded, and this may very well have been one of the causes of the disintegration of Lambert's army. He found that he could not rely on his troops, and his force retired before Monk's advance, slowly breaking up on the way. Monk was now able to clear the road either by disbanding Lambert's regiments or by purging them and adding them to his own. A military riot in London itself enabled him to suggest that some of Fleetwood's men should be displaced to make room for his own; and on February 3, 1660, he entered the capital in force.

[1] Firth, *Army*, p. 384.

It was not difficult to deal with the Parliament, for the members owed everything to Monk, and in the circumstances it was impossible to resist him. Thus, in alliance with the Presbyterian City of London, he demanded and obtained the restoration of the members of Parliament who had been excluded by "Pride's Purge". But these had been Presbyterians, and under the pressure of the Protectorate the Presbyterians had become Royalists, for they were ready to make any sacrifice in order to emancipate the country from the domination of the soldiers. Before they took their seats, Monk obtained from them a pledge that they would dissolve the present Parliament within a month; call a new Parliament for April 20; appoint a new Council of State; and settle the government of the army. Faithful to their promises to the man who had restored them to their seats, the Presbyterians, now once more in a majority in Parliament, gave Monk all that he desired. They appointed him general-in-chief of all the land-forces of the three kingdoms and joint commander of the navy; they filled the new Council of State with his friends; and they dissolved themselves on March 16, first taking the significant step of annulling the engagement to be faithful to the Commonwealth hitherto required of all persons in office.

Meanwhile Monk was dealing in his own effective way with the really serious danger of a military revolt. He removed Fleetwood's troops from London, quartered the regiments in small sections, and replaced the inflexible republicans among the officers by men whom he could trust. So complete were his measures that when Lambert escaped from the Tower and gave the signal for a rising, he was only joined by a small force, and so was speedily recaptured.

As could easily have been foreseen, the first free Parliament was a Royalist Parliament. The writs professed to exclude those who had served under Charles I, but such was the state of public feeling that nobody took any notice of the prohibition. On April 25 the two Houses met again after the old order, the Peers once more returning to Westminster. On May 1 they took into consideration the

Declaration from Breda,[1] which promised: (1) an amnesty for all persons not specially excepted by Parliament; (2) liberty of conscience for all whose views do not disturb the peace of the realm; (3) the settlement in Parliament of all claims to landed property; and (4) the payment of arrears to the army. On this a vote was carried that "according to the ancient and fundamental laws of this kingdom, the government is and ought to be by King, Lords, and Commons". On May 10 we find the Commons busy voting furniture and upholstery to the King, with "a rich coach also, the inside crimson velvet, richly laced and fringed"; with "liveries for two coachmen and two postillions suitable".[2] On May 25 the King landed at Dover, where he was welcomed by Monk, whom he kissed and called "Father"; by the Mayor of the town, who presented him with "a very rich Bible", which he said he "loved above all things in the world"; and by a great concourse of people. On May 29 he entered London,

"With a triumph of above 20,000 horse and foot, brandishing their swords and shouting with inexpressible joy; the ways strewed with flowers, the bells ringing, the streets hung with tapestry, fountains running with wine. . . . I stood in the Strand and beheld it", continues Evelyn,[3] "and blessed God. And all this was done without one drop of blood shed, and by that very army which rebelled against him; but it was the Lord's doing, for such a restoration was never mentioned in any history, ancient or modern, since the return of the Jews from the Babylonish Captivity; nor so joyful a day and so bright ever seen in this nation, this happening when to expect or to effect it was past all human policy".

"Were you here", wrote another Londoner to a friend in Paris, "you would say, good God! do the same people inhabit England that were in it ten or twenty years ago? Believe me, I know not whether I am in England or no, or whether I dream".[4]

Generally speaking, it is true to say that the revolutionary Government which had been established by military power could only be overthrown by the same means. Oliver Cromwell at the head of an army had founded the Protectorate; and now George Monk, also at

[1] Printed in Gardiner, *Documents*, p. 465.
[2] *Parliamentary History*, iv. 41.
[3] *Diary* for May 29, 1660.   [4] Quoted in Gooch, p. 321.

the head of an army, had accomplished the Restoration.
But there were contributory causes to Monk's success.
(1) In the history of the Restoration, as in that of the fall
of the monarchy, finance plays an important part. In the
first instance the revolutionary Government had commanded abundant supplies, for it could apply irresistible
force to the raising of taxes, and, unlike the monarchy,
it was hampered by no constitutional restrictions. Even
under the Long Parliament, the householders of Colchester,
when they were slow in paying the monthly assessment,
had been "quickened" by having troops quartered in their
houses; and soon after the first Civil War the Puritan
county of Essex had sent a petition to Parliament praying
that the country might not be "eaten up, enslaved, and
destroyed" by the army raised for its defence.[1] In 1654
a merchant named Cony, on whom the mantle of John
Hampden appeared to have fallen, refused to pay a
custom on imported silk levied under Cromwell's Customs
Ordinance, on the ground that he could not be taxed save
in Parliament. The Protector dealt with him much as
Charles I might have done during the eleven years of
arbitrary government. He was summoned before a Committee of the Council and fined £500, and was then
committed to prison for refusing to pay the fine. The case
ultimately came into the law-courts, and when Cony's
three counsel argued that the Ordinance under which he
was charged was invalid, the Council at once committed
all three of them to prison until they should retract their
argument. In the end Cony paid and the lawyers retracted,
for it was ill contending with a government based upon
military force. In addition to the income provided by
taxation, the Governments of the Interregnum had control
of a vast capital, raised from Royalist compositions and
the sale of the confiscated estates of the Crown and the
Church. But long before the Restoration, these resources
were getting used up. "We are so out at the heels here",
wrote Thurloe in April, 1658,[2] "that I know not what
we shall do for money"; and in July he refers to "our

---

[1] Gardiner, *Civil War*, iii. 34.
[2] Thurloe to Henry Cromwell, April 20, 1658 (Thurloe, vii. 84).

great necessities which much increase every day".[1] The result was that the pay of the troops fell more and more into arrear, and there was a growing dissatisfaction with a government which failed to meet its obligations. Nothing in the Declaration from Breda was more efficacious in promoting the Restoration than the promise to pay the arrears of the army, and this promise was faithfully kept.[2]

(2) Monk's task of removing republican officers was made easier because the officers themselves, by their attitude upon the question of arrears, had to a considerable extent forfeited the confidence of their men. One of the devices forced upon the Government by their inability to make both ends meet, was the payment of the troops by promises instead of cash. They revived the practice, which had originated in 1647, of issuing to them debentures secured upon "the public faith". Like the seamen's tickets of Pepys's time, this paper currency became very much depreciated, and some of the officers, in haste to enrich themselves, bought up the debentures of their own soldiers at low prices. This intrusion of speculative usury into the relations between officers and men caused deep dissatisfaction among the soldiers, and deprived the officers of that influence over them which in the earlier days of army history had enabled the Council of Officers to speak in the name of the whole army.[3]

(3) Public opinion made itself felt, even in the ranks of a professional army; and the popular odium in which they found themselves took all the heart out of Fleetwood's and Lambert's men.

"The soldiers here", wrote a Londoner in December, 1659, "are so vilified, scorned, and hissed, that they are ashamed to march; and many officers when they go into the City dare not even wear their swords for fear of affronts; and thus God hath blasted them, and they are become vile in the eyes of the people".[4]

Thus, although the force at Lambert's disposal was larger on paper than the army of Monk, when the critical moment came it suffered a kind of disintegration. "The

---

[1] The same to the same, July 20, 1658 (*ib.* vii. 282).
[2] Firth, *Army*, pp. 207–8.
[3] See *ib.* pp. 202–7.　　　　　　　　　　[4] *Ib.* p. 384.

current", said Cowley,[1] "was so irresistible, that the strongest strove against it in vain, and the weakest could sail with it to success". Yet after all, if Monk had played his cards less skilfully, the Restoration could hardly have been accomplished without a civil war of the sanguinary kind which Cromwell had once predicted.[2] We owe it to Monk that the transition from a military despotism to a free Parliament was accomplished by means of a peaceful revolution.

At one time it was the fashion to regard the period of the Interregnum as abortive, and it is true that its experiments in constitution-making were for the most part dismal failures; but at any rate it did not leave things as they were before. (1) We owe it to the statesmen of the Great Rebellion that absolute monarchy failed to establish itself in England. (2) We owe it to the military energy and genius of Cromwell that the three kingdoms of England, Scotland, and Ireland came together as one State, instead of three hostile governments, one controlled by Independency, the second by Presbyterianism, and the third by Rome. (3) The period of the Rebellion thrust upon Parliament, from the necessities of the case, a great part of the business of governing, and thus the Commons for the first time learned the art of government. Parliament absorbed one department of public business after another, and controlled them by means of committees. Under the Tudors, Parliament had no business with the army, or with the navy, or with religion, or with trade; under the Commonwealth it had special committees for all these things. Thus for the old tradition of the functions of Parliament which warned it off three-fourths of the province of government as a jealously guarded mystery of State, was substituted the more modern tradition which justified and encouraged parliamentary interference in every department. This new tradition, although born in the revolutionary

[1] Quoted in Firth, *Cromwell*, p. 448.

[2] "If God did not hinder, all would but make up a confusion. We shall find there will be more than one Cain in England, if God did not restrain, and we should have another more bloody Civil War than ever we had in England" (*Letters and Speeches*, iii. 174).

period, survived the Restoration, and in this way the gulf between the Council Government of the Tudors and the Parliamentary Government of the Georges was bridged by the experience of the seventeenth century.[1] (4) The revolutionary period exhibited an extraordinary fertility in political ideas. In the politics of the nineteenth and twentieth centuries there is scarcely a speculation which the seventeenth century has not already anticipated. In February, 1652, Winstanley the "Digger" dedicated to Cromwell a pamphlet advocating the establishment of a collectivist society in which all worked for the good of all under the superintendence of overseers elected by the community.[2] Other pamphlets of the period demand the disestablishment of the Church; a single-chamber republic; equal electoral districts; the abolition of rotten boroughs; women's suffrage; the ballot; freedom of trade; freedom of the press; schemes of local government; the reform of the law; and the establishment of a national bank. "It is hardly necessary to insist", says Professor Jenks,[3] "upon the immense importance of such a crop of ideas, regarded as an element in constitutional history".

The general enthusiasm with which Charles II was welcomed back from exile, was a natural and spontaneous expression of the national joy at being relieved from the intolerable pressure of military government. Dryden, who had just been celebrating the greatness of Cromwell with "Heroic Stanzas, consecrated to the glorious Memory of his most Serene and Renowned Highness Oliver, late Lord Protector of this Commonwealth, etc., written after the celebration of his Funeral", now hastened to the foot of the throne with "*Astraea Redux*, A Poem on the Happy Restoration and Return of his Sacred Majesty, Charles II", in which he took occasion to make disparaging references to the Protectorate. Fuller[4] notes that the King's birth on May 29, 1630, "was accompanied with two notable

---

[1] See Jenks, pp. 2–5. [2] See Gardiner, *Protectorate*, ii. 5.
[3] *Constitutional Experiments*, p. 5.
[4] *Worthies*, ii. 416. Hamon L'Estrange also refers to the child's baptism: "June the 27 he was in most refulgent pomp carried to the Sacred Font" (*The Reign of King Charles* [edition of 1656], p. 112).

accidents in the heavens. The star Venus was visible all day long.....And two days after, there was an eclipse of the sun..."; and he then proceeds to quote Hamon L'Estrange's loyal interpretation:

To behold this babe Heaven itself seemed to open one eye more than ordinary. Such asterisks and celestial signatures affixt to times so remarkable as this usually are ominous, prophetically hinting and pointing out somewhat future of eminent contingency.

Cambridge condemned "the violence and treason of those vehement men who maliciously endeavoured to divert the stream of succession from its ancient bed"; and Oxford, with a still more fervent repudiation of the Great Rebellion, declared that the University "would never depart from those religious principles by which it was bound to obey the King without any reserve or limitation whatever". All this enthusiasm did not, however, alter the fact that in several important particulars the Restoration of 1660 was not a complete restoration.

(1) It was natural that the doctrine of Divine Right should reappear, because it was the form in which the seventeenth century stated the paramount duty of obedience to the law. But although Divine Right reappears, the doctrine of "absolute power" which had been grafted on to it does not. Its place as an influential political super-stition is now taken by "non-resistance", and this, as Gneist acutely remarks,[1] is "the Royalist theory *on the defensive*".

(2) The Restoration did not restore the criminal juris-diction of the Privy Council. The duty of general super-vision over the process of law which the Council had formerly exercised fell partly to the Court of King's Bench; but in many cases the only way of remedying the injustices of the ordinary law was by means of private bill legislation. Nor did the Restoration restore the Star Chamber or the High Commission Court. Thus for all purposes of conflict with the legislature, the executive was greatly weakened.

(3) The Restoration did not restore the power which Charles I had claimed of levying taxes without consent of

[1] ii. 281.

Parliament. From this time forward, no attempts were made to take advantage of legal technicalities in order to raise impositions, benevolences, or forced loans. When he was in exceptional need of money, the King now proceeded in quite a different way. The department of foreign affairs, which the Crown still controlled, was made financially productive. Charles II raised funds by selling himself to France.

(4) Nor did the Restoration restore the practice of attempting exceptional legislation by the agency of the Council. All legislation is henceforth grounded upon clear majorities in legally elected Parliaments. The method of Charles II is rather to influence Parliament itself; although both he and his successor made what use they could of the last relics of authority over legislation left to them—the dispensing and suspending powers.

In these various ways the Restoration failed to restore the monarchy to the position which it had occupied before the Civil War; and this is why Gardiner speaks of it[1] as "a restoration of Parliament, even more than a restoration of the King".

The Restoration settlement was mainly the work of the Long Parliament of the Restoration, better known as the "Pension" Parliament; but certain preliminary questions were dealt with by the Convention Parliament by which the King had been recalled. How far were Cromwell's Acts to bind the restored monarchy? Were the Cavaliers to be rewarded for their loyalty by the spoils of the sects? Were the present holders of land to retain possession, or were they to surrender them to those who had held them before the war? Were the regicides to be punished? and if so, how many? Of these the most pressing question was that of a general amnesty, which had been promised in the Declaration from Breda, subject to such exceptions as Parliament might make. The Convention Parliament excepted the regicides only, of whom twenty-six were still living; and an attempt of the Pension Parliament to introduce thirteen more exceptions was resisted by the King and his advisers, to their lasting credit. The regicides were

[1] *Student's History of England*, p. 580.

all executed at Charing Cross, with their faces towards the Banqueting House at Whitehall from the window of which the King they had condemned had stepped out upon the scaffold. They all died bravely; Pepys saw Colonel Harrison's execution, and wrote in his *Diary*[1] that he looked "as cheerful as any man could do in that condition".

The Convention Parliament considered the question of the settlement of lands, but upon this an agreement was never reached. A Bill was introduced to give indemnity to all who purchased land during the Interregnum; but in the end it was decided to restore the alienated Crown and Church lands by statute, but to leave individuals to the ordinary process of law. This restored their lands to Royalists who had been dispossessed by force, but gave no redress to the far larger class of those who had sold their lands in order to pay the compositions and the decimation tax. This was why the Act of Oblivion and Indemnity came to be called an Act of indemnity for the King's enemies and of oblivion for his friends.[2] The Cromwellian officers were dispossessed who had invested in Church or Crown lands the money they had acquired by buying up the debentures of their men; and thus a new kind of landed proprietor which the period of revolution was creating in England disappeared. In Ireland, on the other hand, the confiscations made by the revolutionary governments were maintained, and there the Cromwellian officer established on the land came to exercise an important influence upon the later development of the country.[3]

[1] For October 13, 1660.
[2] Burnet, *History of his Own Time* (edition of 1724), i. 165. "The average Cavalier declared, with Roger L'Estrange, that these measures 'made the enemies to the Constitution masters, in effect, of the booty of three nations'" (Feiling, p. 101).
[3] Firth, *Army*, p. 208.

The Pension Parliament

THE Pension Parliament sat for eighteen years, from 1661 to 1679. In two respects only its composition differed from that of the Parliaments before the Civil War. (1) Since in 1625 the peers had established the principle that every peer was to be summoned to Parliament by refusing to sit without the Earl of Bristol,[1] from whom a summons had been withheld by the Crown, the increase in the peerage which had been going on since the beginning of the century was reflected in the numbers of the House of Lords. These, including the bishops, now stood at 168.[2] (2) On the other hand, the increase in the numbers of the House of Commons came finally to an end. In 1674 the City and County of Durham were incorporated into the representative system of the country; but when in 1681 Charles II attempted to revive his father's prerogative of creating boroughs, and enfranchised by royal charter the town of Newark, the attitude of the House of Commons was so hostile that no second attempt was made. As the principle had been already established under James I that boroughs once enfranchised were entitled thereafter to receive writs, the numbers of the Lower House remained fixed at 513 until the Act of Union with Scotland in 1707.[3]

Although the composition of Parliament was thus but little altered, its power and position had completely changed, for the Great Rebellion had profoundly affected the English political imagination. The prerogative of the King had never rested upon armed force, but "on custom and respect for law, and to some extent on...an acceptance of the existing order of things as a part of the scheme of nature".[4] The power of kings had been a mysterious uncertainty, for when in English history a king had been

---

[1] See L. O. Pike, *Constitutional History of the House of Lords*, p. 238.
[2] Gneist, ii. 290 *n.*
[3] Porritt, *The Unreformed House of Commons*, i. 392.
[4] Anson, vol. ii. pt. i. p. 31.

deposed, it had always been by another king, whose claim
to the throne might conceivably be held in Heaven to be
a better claim. The one great exception was the successful
revolt of the United Provinces against Spain; and the
significance of this had been missed in England, partly
because it was a foreign instance, and partly because the
King was a Catholic, and the subjects who successfully
revolted against him were Protestants who were aiming
first of all at religious freedom. But now the Civil War
had proved that a king could be beaten in the field, like
any other general, by superior numbers and more efficient
organisation, and that he could even be brought to the
scaffold like any other man. The deep impression which
this had made is recorded in the Service for King Charles
the Martyr, which used to be said in churches on January
30 every year. This contains a Collect which points the
moral of the Great Rebellion thus:

Almighty and Everlasting God, whose righteousness is like the
strong mountains and Thy judgments like the great deep; and who
by that barbarous murder (as on this day) committed upon the sacred
person of Thine Anointed, *hast taught us that neither the greatest
of Kings nor the best of men are more secure from violence than from
natural death*....

This knowledge of the King's weakness perhaps accounts
for the latitude which was allowed to the restored monarchy.
Parliament now knew that in the last resort the King could
be kept within the law unless he had an armed force
behind him, and the King knew that without an armed
force he could not in the long run resist the will of Parliament, for he did not wish to "go on his travels again".
Thus the ultimate sovereignty had passed from the Crown
to Parliament. "The Civil War had reversed the relation
between Whitehall and Westminster; the members now
feared nothing from Court, but courtiers feared much from
Parliament."[1] This was recognised by the French Ambassador when he told Louis XIV that the members of
Parliament "are not only allowed to speak their mind
freely, but also to do a number of surprising, extraordinary
things; and even to call the highest people to the Bar".[2]

[1] Trevelyan, *Stuarts*, p. 375.   [2] *Ib.* p. 340.

The Pension Parliament also differs from its predecessors in that it was affected by the decay of high religious feeling which is characteristic of the Restoration period. In this we see "an overflowing vitality" which

followed the melting of the frosts of Puritanism—the external coating of ceremony and refinement, the essential core of animalism, rough, irrepressible relaxation, and abounding license; the polite world behaving like a troop of vicious children in its impatience of seriousness and its contentment with anything at all in the shape of amusement; the Court turning gladly from the task of politics to the business of dissipation, and the Royal circle from a discussion of the small-pox to a game of blindman's buff or hunt the slipper.[1]

It would be too much to say that religion had already ceased to be the centre of interest; that change was to be deferred until the eighteenth century. The sober Puritans of the Rebellion were sober Puritans still, although now they lay under a cloud, and the open profligacy of the Court, although it made profligacy the fashion, did not affect to any considerable extent the habits of the great unfashionable mass of the people. The general tone of thought was still religious.

"The Stuart Government", says Seeley,[2] "was judged by a public strongly influenced by Puritanic ideas, and almost as much disposed to condemn it for the Plague and the Fire, as marks of Divine anger, as for the defenceless condition of the Thames".

But the fact remains that there is a much lower tone about the politics of the Restoration period than had prevailed in the days of Hampden and Pym. The country gentry had been impoverished by the Civil War; their family life had been broken up; and their needy heirs had suffered a kind of degeneration, either in exile abroad or in poverty at home.[3] Corruption in politics in all probability began with the Purged Parliament of the Commonwealth, but in

[1] The author very much regrets that he has no note of the source of this picturesque passage. It was taken from a review published a good many years ago in one of the literary journals.

[2] ii. 154.

[3] Trevelyan, *Stuarts*, p. 350. It was pointed out at the time that there were few Royalist captains fit to command at sea, and in the counties there were "few of the old stock of people left who had formerly managed business, and few of the new who knew which way to go about it" (Feiling, p. 107).

the Pension Parliament of the Restoration there was a still more abundant supply of material ready prepared for the influences of corruption to work upon, and among the conditions which favoured corruption must certainly be reckoned the tone of the time.

Another consideration which affected the position of the Pension Parliament was the growing power of public opinion, which was now beginning to be organised outside Parliament. The Restoration period is the period of the coffee-houses, and these, as Macaulay reminds us,[1] might have been "not improperly called a most important political institution". "Sir, for news or town discourse", says a letter-writer of 1673,[2] "I must not pretend to know much, being I visit not taverns nor coffee-houses, nor do I converse much with any persons that do"; but this negative statement at any rate recognises where it was that all the news came from. So much was the political influence of the coffee-houses felt by the Government, that in 1675 they were all suddenly closed by proclamation; but the measure met with such general resistance that they were speedily reopened, although under some restrictions. We realise the extent to which they discharged some of the functions of the modern newspaper, when we find Shaftesbury in a speech on the Dutch War using the words, "The coffee-houses were not to be blamed for their last apprehensions".[3] The period of the Restoration is also the period of political clubs. In 1675 the Green Ribbon Club was founded as the head-quarters of the country party organisation, and this was the first English club to acquire a local habitation. It had rooms at the King's Head Tavern at the end of Chancery Lane, opposite the Inner Temple; and here elections were organised, petitions set on foot, political literature handed round, and motions drafted for Parliament.[4] These methods were, however, directed to the organisation of opinion in London alone.

[1] i. 179.
[2] James Hicks to Sir Joseph Williamson, July 21, 1673 (*Williamson's Letters*, Camden Society, 1874, i. 112).
[3] Speech of February 5, 1673, printed in Christie, *Life of Shaftesbury*, ii. Appendix, pp. lxiii–v.
[4] Trevelyan, *Stuarts*, p. 393.

The gossip of the coffee-houses only reached the country in the form of weekly news-letters, and these were subject to the press regulations. On the other hand, the Government of the Restoration, as would naturally be the case, was far more sensitive to public opinion than governments had been before the Civil War.

The first business of the Pension Parliament was to confirm the Acts of the Convention Parliament, and to make its own contribution to the Restoration settlement.

The settlement on its financial side[1] was mainly the work of the Convention Parliament. A committee appointed to examine the records of Charles I's reign reported that between 1637 and 1641 the royal revenue had been about £900,000 a year, of which at least £200,000 had been raised in ways not warranted by law. On the other hand, the expenditure had, on the average, amounted to about £200,000 more than the receipts. They therefore advised that the ordinary revenue of Charles II should be fixed at £1,200,000 a year. Towards this the Crown lands contributed £100,000, and the customs, now consolidated and simplified and charged at reduced rates, about £400,000. The policy of the "Great Contract" was now carried through, and the King accepted £100,000 a year in place of the feudal dues. It was scarcely possible for him to do anything else, for the Court of Wards which collected them had ceased to sit in 1645, and the Commonwealth had converted all military tenures into common socage, and had abolished purveyance and pre-emption. As land had been bought and sold since as if free of these burdens, Parliament had no alternative but to confirm their abolition by an Act. In order to raise the £100,000 a year required to compensate the King, Parliament adopted the expedient copied from the Dutch by Pym in 1643, and levied an excise upon inland trade. The list of excises had originally begun with drinks brewed in the country, and had been gradually extended by the Governments of the Interregnum until it came to include a large number of the articles of inland trade. At the Restoration these were reduced to drinks again—chiefly beer and cider, but including also

[1] See S. A. Dowell, *History of Taxation* (1884), ii. 17 ff.

the new fashionable drinks, tea, coffee, chocolate, and sherbet. The removal of tobacco from the excise list (although it still paid custom) caused an increase in the practice of smoking, and this was further stimulated by the Plague, when Pepys[1] and others chewed tobacco as a disinfectant. Smoking had been discouraged by the Puritans, but even at the great Protector's funeral, which Evelyn[2] calls "the joyfullest funeral I ever saw", the soldiers were observed taking tobacco in the streets. As the yield from Crown lands, customs, and excise failed to make up the £1,200,000 required, the Pension Parliament in 1662 imposed a new tax called "hearth-money", which was in effect a tax upon houses. This was extraordinarily unpopular—partly because it was borrowed from France; partly because it reached a class of persons who were untouched by other direct taxation; partly because it was farmed out, and was exacted by the farmers to the uttermost farthing; and still more because the visits of the "chimney-men" were regarded as an intrusion upon domestic privacy.[3]

These sources supplied the ordinary revenue of the Crown. As benevolences and forced loans had now disappeared, the King's extraordinary revenue was derived entirely from Parliamentary grants. The old subsidy was levied for the last time in 1663, and its place was thereafter taken by the "monthly assessment", now borrowed from the Commonwealth and incorporated into the permanent financial system of the country. The special value of this method of taxation lay, first, in the frequency with which it brought money into the Exchequer, and, secondly, in the way of escape which it provided from the vicious

[1] *Diary*, June 7, 1665.
[2] *Diary* for October 22, 1658.
[3] This appears in the curious epitaph of Rebecca Rogers of Folkestone, who died August 22, 1668 (Dowell, iii. 190):

> "A house she hath; it's made of such good fashion,
> The tenant ne'er shall pay for reparation;
> Nor will her landlord ever raise her rent,
> Or turn her out of doors for non-payment;
> From chimney-money too this cell is free—
> To such a house who would not tenant be!"

traditions of the subsidy. The method of assessment for subsidy had been extraordinarily loose; all kinds of allowances had been made to taxpayers for which there was no statutory authority—especially for large families, and for what was vaguely described as "expenses of position"; men who ought to have been on the subsidy books escaped altogether; and there was never any fresh assessment, as each subsidy was levied upon the basis of the last. Under the new system it was possible to assess taxpayers at what they were really worth; to sweep away all the allowances; and to reassess from time to time, as wealth increased, diminished, or changed hands. This change of system also resulted in the abolition of the separate taxation of the clergy. Under the Commonwealth the clergy had been taxed as laity, and when the assessment replaced the subsidy, it was found convenient to continue taxing them as laity instead of applying to Convocation for separate clerical grants. A constitutional consequence of this was that from this time forward the parochial clergy were permitted to vote for members of Parliament.

The important feature of the Restoration settlement on its military side is the revival by statute in 1662[1] of the militia organisation of the counties under the lords-lieutenant, which had fallen into decay under the Commonwealth because it was eclipsed by the great professional army. As Gneist points out,[2] it now appears as "a counter organisation to the republican army and as an armed force of the wealthy classes". It is true that the lords-lieutenant were once more nominated by the Crown, but in actual practice the choice of the Crown was limited to the magnates of the shire. The lords-lieutenant themselves appointed the officers, and this had the effect of restricting these posts to the landed gentry; while to the ranks only well-to-do farmers and citizens were admitted. The expenses of the force were to be defrayed by an annual rate which was not to exceed a quarter of the monthly assessment. Following the earlier Militia Act of 1661,[3] the preamble

---

[1] 14 Car. II, c. 3.   [2] ii. 278 n.
[3] 13 Car. II, c. 6. Extracts are printed in C. Grant Robertson, *Select Statutes, Cases, and Documents*, 1660–1832, pp. 28–30.

of the Act of 1662 declared in the most solemn manner that the

"sole supreme power, government, command, and disposition of the militia... is, and by the laws of England ever was, the undoubted right of his Majesty and his royal predecessors, kings and queens of England", and that "both or either of the Houses of Parliament cannot nor ought to pretend to the same";

but this declaration failed to recognise that in reality the power of the sword had passed to the magnates of the shire. This was their guarantee against military government and arbitrary power; and it was this force which drove out James II and accomplished the Revolution of 1688.

It goes without saying that this military settlement failed to satisfy the King. It has been pointed out that nothing more conclusively proves the political ability of Charles II than the way in which he borrows and adapts to his own purposes the ideas of the Cromwellian period; and one of these ideas was that government could be founded upon the support of a standing army. His policy, and that of his successor, was therefore to intrigue for an armed force of his own. On the evening of Sunday, January 6, 1661, a number of Fifth Monarchy men under Venner a cooper, issued from their conventicle in Coleman Street, where they had been inflaming each other with discourses on the Apocalypse, and attempted to inaugurate the millennium by knocking the City guard on the head. They were easily dispersed by Monk with a troop of horse, but "Venner's Insurrection" gave the King, who was just then paying off the professional army, an excellent pretext for retaining a bodyguard of trustworthy troops. He kept two regiments, one of horse and one of foot, besides a third which was in garrison at Dunkirk; and these formed the nucleus of a new standing army. This soon grew under Charles II to 5000, and at the accession of James II it stood at 8700.

The legal position of the military force at the command of the younger Stuarts was, however, very precarious. There was nothing to prevent the King raising troops by contract or voluntary enlistment; but they had to be fed, and lodged, and paid, and kept under military discipline.

The Petition of Right made it illegal to quarter soldiers upon householders, or, unless they were on actual service in time of war, to control them by martial law; and the Crown had no money to spare for paying an army. At a later time the problem was solved by Parliament itself granting funds for a standing army and establishing discipline by means of a Mutiny Act; but the Parliaments of Charles II would do nothing of the kind, for the period of Cromwell had made as deep an impression upon the country gentry as it had done upon the King. Before the Civil War the popular objection to an army had been that it was oppressive to those who were required to serve in it, and this was what had led the Long Parliament to pass an Act to abolish impressment. But the experience of the Interregnum had changed all this. "Henceforth the objections to a standing army are not so much that it involves hardship to the men who compose it, as that it is an instrument of despotism. The soldier is no longer an injured citizen; he is a danger to the State."[1] Thus for more than a century after the death of Cromwell, the country gentry, always haunted by his spectre and fearing lest he should reincarnate himself in some other great general, were suspicious of a standing army. In 1674, and again in 1677, the House of Commons passed resolutions against it; at the Peace of Ryswick Parliament cut the army down in spite of the menacing European situation and the protests of William III; and as late as the time of the younger Pitt an excellent scheme for building barracks was rejected in the Commons, lest barrack life, by separating soldiers from civilians, should render them dangerous once more to civil liberty.[2]

On the ecclesiastical side, more than on any other, the settlement of Charles II's reign involved a complete restoration. In many churches worship after the old order was restored as soon as the King was proclaimed and before he landed in England. An entry in the register of a Durham parish for May 12, 1660—the day of the proclamation there—is typical: "on which day I, Stephen Hogg, began to use again the Book of Common Prayer".

[1] Anson, vol. ii. pt. ii. p. 171.   [2] Gardiner, *Cromwell*, p. 106.

But the reversion to the old order of worship did not of itself settle outstanding ecclesiastical questions. The Presbyterian party, which had contributed so much to the Restoration, had a claim upon Charles which could not be ignored, and there were alternative ways in which this claim might be met—either by including the Presbyterians within the Church or by allowing them freedom of worship outside it. The policy of comprehension was the policy of Clarendon, and at first this seemed likely to carry the day. Bishoprics were offered to several Presbyterian divines—among them, to Richard Baxter—and in October, 1660, Clarendon drafted for the King a Declaration on Ecclesiastical Affairs, offering to accept a revision of the Prayer Book, concessions in ritual, and the establishment of limited episcopacy on the lines of "Archbishop Ussher's Model" of 1641. This was really a kind of Presbyterianism, for it regarded the bishops only as the presidents of annual diocesan synods which were to settle by vote all questions arising within the diocese, and it contemplated also the establishment of monthly synods within each rural deanery.

If Clarendon alone had had the management of the negotiations, it is possible that they might have been successful, but the King's sympathies were with toleration rather than comprehension. The Romanising tendency of the younger Stuarts is a fundamental fact of the Restoration period. Charles II was not a religious person,[1] and the judgment of Dr James Welwood, written in 1700, is probably not very wide of the mark.

His religion was Deism, or rather, that which is called so; and if in his exile or at his death he went into that of Rome, the first was to be imputed to a complaisance for the company he was then obliged to keep, and the last to a lazy diffidence in all other religions,

---

[1] "A Collect was also drawn for the Parliament, in which a new epithet was added to the King's title that gave great offence and occasioned much indecent raillery: he was styled 'our most religious King'. It was not easy to give a proper sense to this and to make it go well down; since whatever the signification of religion might be in the Latin word, as importing the sacredness of the King's person, yet in the English language it bore a signification that was no way applicable to the King" (Burnet, i. 183).

upon a review of his past life and the near approach of an uncertain state.[1]

But he had learned from the period of Cromwell to appreciate the political strength of the sects in England, and he had conceived the design of so handling the idea of toleration as to secure religious freedom for the Roman Catholics under the pretext of conferring it on the sects. Thus he could only with difficulty be dissuaded from adding to Clarendon's draft Declaration a clause in favour of the repeal of the penal laws and the grant of toleration to Papists and sectaries alike. This policy wrecked the chances of limited episcopacy, for Anglicans and Presbyterians were both opposed to it, and when a Bill was introduced into the Convention Parliament to give effect to the King's Declaration, it was rejected by a small majority. The result of this was that the Church settlement was left over to be dealt with by the Pension Parliament; and when the new Parliament met on May 8, 1661, it took the question out of the hands of Clarendon and the King, and ignoring both comprehension and toleration, proceeded to legislate on lines of its own.

The "Clarendon Code", of which Clarendon was not the originator, consisted of four statutes.

(1) The Corporation Act of 1661[2] required all persons holding municipal office to renounce the Covenant—a test which excluded many of the Presbyterians; to take an oath of non-resistance—a test which excluded Republicans; and to take the Sacrament according to the rites of the Church of England—a test which excluded Roman Catholics, as well as some of the sects. Thus the general effect of the Act was to confine municipal office to Royalist Anglicans; and this was the more important because in many towns the corporations elected the members of Parliament.

(2) The Act of Uniformity of 1662[3] achieved five things. (a) It imposed upon the clergy a revised Book of Common Prayer which was substantially the Prayer Book

[1] Quoted in W. H. Hutton, *A History of the English Church*, 1625–1714, p. 180.
[2] 13 Car. II, st. ii. c. 1: printed in part in Grant Robertson, *Statutes*, pp. 34–7.
[3] 14 Car. II, c. 4: printed in *ib.* pp. 37–53.

of Elizabeth, but with certain valuable additions:[1] the Prayer for All Sorts and Conditions of Men, probably composed by Peter Gunning; the General Thanksgiving, by Bishop Reynolds; the Prayer for the High Court of Parliament, probably written by Laud in 1625; and the Prayers to be used at Sea, which indicate the new importance of the Navy. But the chief objections of the Puritans were entirely ignored, and Baxter and those who thought with him gave up all idea of allowing themselves to be comprehended in the restored Church. (*b*) The Act imposed upon the clergy a declaration of "unfeigned assent and consent to all and everything contained" in the Book of Common Prayer, and those who failed to make the declaration before the Feast of St Bartholomew (August 24), 1662, were to be deprived of their livings. (*c*) A decision of momentous importance for the Church of England was taken when a clause of the Act[2] imposed a penalty of £100 upon any person who administered the sacrament before he had been made a priest by episcopal ordination. Hitherto, although this had been usual it had not been regarded as absolutely essential, and from time to time foreigners ordained after the manner of the Continental Protestant Churches had been admitted to English benefices.[3] (*d*) The Act imposed upon all persons in Holy Orders and all teachers in schools and in the Universities a declaration against the Covenant, another denying the lawfulness of taking arms against the King, and a third of intention to "conform to the liturgy of the Church of England as it is now by law established". (*e*) Schoolmasters and tutors were to be licensed by the bishop of the diocese. The effect of the Act was that when the Feast of St Bartholomew came, more than 2000 clergy —about a fifth of the whole number—were deprived of their livings, and it is to this exodus of 1662 that the origin of modern Dissent is to be traced.

The Act of Uniformity may be defended as a measure of definition; the last two Acts of the Clarendon Code were merely measures of persecution.

[1] Gwatkin, pp. 352–3.   [2] § 14.
[3] Goldwin Smith, ii. 16

(3) The Conventicle Act of 1664[1] was intended to prevent the ejected clergy from preaching to unauthorised congregations of their own. It imposed penalties upon all persons over the age of sixteen who were present at a conventicle—this being defined as any meeting for religious worship at which five or more persons were present besides the household—and authorised the magistrates to "dissolve and dissipate, or prevent" such unlawful meetings.

(4) The Five Mile Act of 1665[2] forbade ejected clergy to come within five miles of any city, borough, or corporate town, or of any parish or place where they had preached in a conventicle or had had regular cure of souls. It also forbade persons not belonging to the Established Church to teach in any school, or to take "any boarders or tablers that are taught or instructed by him or herself". The Act had the effect of carrying the best Puritan teaching into remote parishes.[3] It has also been suggested that the strength of Nonconformity in modern Birmingham is due to the fact that the group of villages out of which the city grew were all more than five miles from any city, borough, or corporate town, and thus the Dissent of the Midlands tended to collect there.

Although Clarendon had abandoned the policy of comprehension, Charles II clung tenaciously to the policy of toleration, and during his reign he made three attempts to carry it out. (1) Immediately after the passing of the Act of Uniformity in May, 1662, he tried to suspend its operation for three months, but was frustrated by the united and determined opposition of the bishops and the constitutional lawyers. (2) In December, 1662, he issued

---

[1] 16 Car. II, c. 4. Grant Robertson (p. 70) prints the second and severer Conventicle Act of 1670.

[2] 17 Car. II, c. 2: printed, with some omissions, in Grant Robertson, pp. 67–70. It should be noticed that the limitation of five miles had appeared in earlier legislation. Elizabeth's Act against Popish Recusants (1593) had forbidden them to travel more than five miles from their usual places of abode (J. R. Tanner, *Tudor Documents*, p. 160); and one of Cromwell's proclamations (1658) had placed the same restriction upon the movements of Royalists (Firth, *Protectorate*, ii. 68).

[3] Gwatkin, p. 355.

his First Declaration of Indulgence, by which he undertook, if the concurrence of Parliament could be obtained,
to exercise on behalf of the Dissenters that dispensing
power which he held to be "inherent in the Crown"; and
steps were taken to procure an Act to confirm his claim to
dispense with laws enforcing religious conformity or
requiring oaths. But in February, 1663, the Commons
vigorously protested against any scheme for "establishing schism by a law",[1] and the King was unable to proceed. (3) Finally, in March, 1672, he issued his Second
Declaration of Indulgence[2] declaring the suspension
of "the execution of all and all manner of penal laws
in matters ecclesiastical against whatsoever sort of non-
conformists and recusants". Parliament was, however,
again too strong for him. In February, 1673, the House
of Commons passed a resolution, by 168 votes to 116, that
"penal statutes in matters ecclesiastical cannot be suspended but by Act of Parliament",[3] and it became evident
that there would be no supplies unless the King gave way.
On March 8 the Declaration was therefore recalled, after
it had been in force for just a year, and no other attempt
at toleration was made during the reign.

The complete failure of Charles II to carry his ecclesiastical policy against the opposition of Parliament,
illustrates the change in the position of Parliament which
had taken place since Tudor times. The Elizabethan
Church settlement had been mainly the work of the Queen
and Cecil, and when the Commons tried to criticise it, they
were warned off the province of the ecclesiastical supremacy.
The Church settlement of the Restoration was mainly the
work of Parliament. The King had other views, and he
did his best to carry them out; but he was beaten by the
resistance of Parliament at every point.

The Parliament which thus accomplished the Restoration settlement and restored the Church of England to
something more than her old position, at first contained a
great Royalist majority; although it has been shewn that
the minority was vastly stronger than has been commonly

---

[1] Hutton, p. 196.   [2] Printed in Grant Robertson, pp. 74–77.
[3] For these proceedings see *ib.* pp. 77–80.

supposed.[1] On the motion that the Solemn League and Covenant should be burned by the common hangman, the majority of 228 was opposed by a minority of 103; and the Conventicle Act was only carried by 145 to 109. It has also been shewn that the Pension Parliament was not so much out of touch with the constituencies as the fact that it sat for eighteen years might suggest. When it was first elected, the proportion of quite old men in it was unusually large, and this meant that many seats were vacated early, either by the death of the holders, or by sons in the Commons succeeding to peerages and being called to the Upper House. Moreover, many Royalists in the Commons were made peers as a reward for loyal service. The result was that when Danby came to power in 1674, 242 seats in the Commons had already changed hands, and there were more than 200 members sitting in the House who had not been there in 1661.[2] These frequent bye-elections affected the complexion of the House of Commons in two ways. (1) At first the tendency was for the followers of Clarendon to be replaced by new men, specially interested in trade and finance, who grouped themselves round Ashley, and looked to the King rather than to the Chancellor for their reward. We have here, although with many differences, something not altogether unlike the party of "King's friends" in Parliament which was to enable George III a century later to emancipate the Crown from the power of the Whigs. But (2) later on, the bye-elections worked the other way. The vacancies became most frequent during the time of the War, the Plague, and the Fire, and the new members faithfully reflected the growing hostility to the Court. The earlier loyalty was slowly giving way under the strain of bad finance, bad administration, and the flaunting profligacy of Whitehall. It was now that corruption became a necessity. The increased salaries attached to the principal public offices had made them well worth having, and the degeneration of tone in the politics of the time had led

---

[1] See Professor Wilbur C. Abbott's articles on "The Long Parliament of Charles II" in *E.H.R.* xxi. 21–56, 254–285.

[2] *E.H.R.* xxi. 261.

men to believe that wealth and place were the only things worth seeking. As a large part of the royal revenue was not under the control of Parliament, a secret service fund was possible, and there was a perpetual scramble going on for those grants from the Treasury which were not attached to any office and passed under the name of "pensions". The list of the recipients of these came to include some of the leading statesmen of the time, and no one seemed to have any shame about taking money from the Court. The members of the Pension Parliament were in their hearts almost as critical of Charles II as the members of the Long Parliament had been of his father; but he could threaten them with a dissolution, and under the system of influence, a dissolution meant the loss of the pensions which had given the Parliament its name.

The Policy of Exclusion

T HE new position of authority which Parliament now enjoyed, even in relation to the Crown, appears elsewhere than in the Restoration Church Settlement. The King had once said to the Earl of Essex that

he did not wish to be like a Grand Signior, with some mutes about him and bags of bowstrings to strangle men as he had a mind to it; but he did not think he was a king as long as a company of fellows were looking into all his actions, and examining his ministers as well as his accounts.[1]

Yet the Pension Parliament impeached two of his ministers, Clarendon and Danby, broke up the Cabal by the Test Act, and in the interests of financial reform took steps to look into his accounts.

Of these measures the last-named comes first in order of time. In 1665 Parliament established appropriation of supply, and in 1667 it set on foot the first Parliamentary Commission of Public Accounts. It was in 1667 also that Clarendon fell. As Seeley points out,[2] he had risen to a position of such eminence that it can only be compared to that of Mazarin. "He was father-in-law to the heir to the throne, father of the future Queen, grandfather of the royal children, and besides all this, leading Minister, restorer and nursing father to the Anglican Church, and Chancellor." Yet he was unable effectively to resist the attacks made on his administration by the new men who, under the leadership of Ashley, were forming themselves into an anti-Clarendonian party in Parliament.[3] He was attacked, somewhat as Buckingham had been attacked, first on account of the Portuguese marriage and the sale

---

[1] Burnet, i. 345.   [2] ii. 178.

[3] These new men returned to the Pension Parliament at bye-elections were more interested in trade than in religion, and were much more competent to criticise finance than their predecessors had been. The simple contrast between Anglican and Presbyterian which had prevailed when the Parliament was first elected was being replaced by new and quite different political divisions (see E.H.R. xxi. 44).

of Dunkirk, and afterwards for the inadequate naval preparations which allowed the Dutch to force the Medway. Charles I had dissolved Parliament in order to save Buckingham; Charles II refused to think of dissolving the Pension Parliament in order to save Clarendon. It is true that Charles II was not personally anxious to retain Clarendon, as Charles I had been to retain Buckingham; but there is also a change in the situation. It was now far more important than before that the King should be on good terms with Parliament; and the fall of Clarendon is the next step after the case of Buckingham towards vesting in the House of Commons the power of dismissing an unpopular minister. Buckingham was impeached in order to get rid of him, and the attempt failed. Clarendon was dismissed before his impeachment[1] because he was attacked in Parliament, and the King could not afford to retain his minister at the cost of a breach of the good understanding between the Crown and the House of Commons.

The fall of Clarendon was for the King a kind of emancipation, for he was now able to pursue a policy of his own, and this policy was tolerationist. He began by consulting Buckingham, the Zimri of Dryden,[2] who had a strong connexion among the Independents, and Arlington, whose sympathies were with the Roman Catholics. The next to be called into his counsels was Ashley, whose special sphere was trade, and who contributed to the toleration controversy an able paper in which he supported toleration to all except Fifth Monarchy men as a measure necessary in the interests of trade. Clifford, who came next, was a Roman Catholic. Lauderdale was the intimate personal friend of the King, but he busied himself almost entirely with the affairs of Scotland. The Government of

---

[1] The articles of impeachment are printed in Grant Robertson, pp. 565–6.

[2]
> "A man so various that he seemed to be
> Not one, but all mankind's epitome;
> Stiff in opinions, always in the wrong,
> Was everything by starts and nothing long;
> But in the course of one revolving moon
> Was chymist, fiddler, statesman, and buffoon."
> (*Absalom and Achitophel.*)

the Cabal was strong and capable. Its common basis of action was not only toleration, but devotion to foreign affairs, to trade and plantations, and especially to financial reform.[1] But its tone was low, and "henceforth ability rather than character takes the first place in political life".[2]

The Cabal, able as it was, had to encounter a strong opposition in Parliament, for in spite of the bye-elections and the measures of influence, the majority of the members still held tenaciously to the upholding of Anglicanism, the maintenance of the supremacy of Parliament, and hostility to France. As the King and his advisers were aiming at toleration, emancipation from the control of Parliament, and a secret alliance with France, a good deal of clever management would be required to hoodwink Parliament and prevent an open breach. This breach came over the very question of toleration which, more than any other, enabled the members of the Cabal to meet upon common ground. The fear of the fanatics which had led to the Clarendon Code was giving place to fear of Catholicism and arbitrary power;[3] and when the Pension Parliament met again in 1673 it was not content to compel the withdrawal of the Declaration of Indulgence issued in the previous year. By an alliance between moderate Churchmen and Dissenters—a kind of rehearsal of the similar alliance which was to accomplish the Revolution of 1688 —the Test Act[4] was passed, providing that all persons holding any office of trust should (1) publicly receive the Sacrament according to the rites of the Church of England; (2) take the oath of supremacy; and (3) subscribe a declaration against transubstantiation. The object of the Act was to make a clean sweep of all Roman Catholics holding office under the Crown, and this it successfully achieved. The Duke of York resigned the post of Lord High Admiral, and Clifford surrendered the Lord Treasurership. Ashley, now Earl of Shaftesbury, who had discovered that he had been duped over the secret clause

[1] *E.H.R.* xxi. 47.   [4] *Ib.* xxi. 46.
[3] *Ib.* xxi. 256.
[4] The more important provisions of the Act are printed in Grant Robertson, *Statutes*, pp. 81–4.

of the Treaty of Dover,[1] supported the Test Act and was dismissed by the King before the end of the year. Buckingham was also dismissed not long after, and followed Shaftesbury into opposition, and thus the Cabal was finally broken up.

When Clifford lost the Treasurership, it was given to Sir Thomas Osborne, soon afterwards made Earl of Danby, an Anglican of the Clarendon type, who hated France and Catholicism. The importance of this appointment from the point of view of the constitutional historian lies in the fact that Osborne was selected mainly because he was acceptable to the two Houses. It is a recognition on the King's part that toleration was unobtainable.[2]

In the period of Danby the corrupt influence of the Crown in Parliament during the seventeenth century reached its highest point. His party in Parliament was made partly by drawing together the remnants of the old Royalist churchmen who had followed Clarendon, but partly also by direct bribery and the free distribution of official favours, places, and pensions.[3] Along with this went a remarkable development of the arts of influencing constituencies, and the struggle over the power of determining elections was beginning which was to end with the writs of *quo warranto*.[4]

"In the purchase of votes", says Professor Wilbur C. Abbott,[5] "the wholesale bribery of constituencies, the pressure on corporations, the use of Court and ministerial influence, of government servants, even of soldiers, the corruption of election officers, the suborning of sheriffs, and various methods of family and financial pressure on electors, we observe a skill and resource generally

---

[1] Mr Feiling (p. 150) finds reason to believe that Shaftesbury had "veered over" before he made this discovery, "for earlier in the session he had been in touch with leading members of the Opposition and had shown clearly enough his sympathy with the Test".

[2] "Danby's administration has this permanent importance—that almost for the first time a minister who drew his entire resources from Parliament presented the King with a clear and coherent programme of action. His plans were threefold: to restore the Crown's independence by wholesale financial reform, to bring it into accord with national opinion on questions of foreign policy, and to achieve these objects through a Parliamentary majority built on the old foundation of Church and King" (Feiling, p. 154).

[3] *E.H.R.* xxi. 264.   [4] *Ib.* xxi. 54.   [5] *Ib.* xxi. 257.

ascribed only to a much later and more sophisticated age of political corruption".

The Cabal had gone far upon this road but Danby went farther, and the management of Parliament on the one hand and of the constituencies on the other, developed into a fine art.

It was in the administration of Danby that the Pension Parliament made its first successful encroachment upon the prerogative in the province of foreign affairs.[1] In 1677 the House of Commons presented an address to the King praying him to make such alliances as would secure the kingdom, quiet the people, and save the Spanish Netherlands, and it was intimated that as soon as the desired alliances had been entered into, plentiful supplies would be forthcoming. Thus the Commons penetrated into the King's own territory, and negotiated with him there like an independent and victorious power. A little later, the House became more definite, and demanded an alliance with the Dutch against France. Charles replied,

You have intrenched upon so undoubted a right of the Crown that I am confident it will appear in no age (when the sword was not drawn) that the prerogative of making peace and war hath been so dangerously invaded.[2]

Should he consent, no prince in Europe "would any longer believe that the sovereignty of England rests in the Crown". He ordered the adjournment of the two Houses, but when they met again, the European political situation had changed, and he was able of his own accord to announce an alliance with Holland and Spain against France. The King was not forced into a surrender, for it never came to a fight, but the episode serves as another illustration of the immensely strong position which the Parliaments of the Restoration period had come to occupy as against the Crown.

In the administration of Danby we find foreign influences at work in English politics, not, as heretofore, through indirect and subterranean channels, but by direct

[1] On this see *E.H.R.* xxi. 269–71.
[2] *Parliamentary History*, iv. 889.

impact upon the English Constitution itself. The warlike and anti-French influence in England was the Pension Parliament led by Danby, and it was worth the while of Louis XIV to spend a good deal of money in order to prevent the naval power of England being thrown on the side of the United Provinces in their conflict with France. His policy was therefore directed towards silencing the Pension Parliament, and to this end money could be profitably applied in two directions. (1) He could pay Charles II to keep Parliament prorogued. In 1676—in spite of Danby, who was too monarchical in his ideas to invade the King's own sphere of foreign policy—Charles bound himself by a secret treaty, which he copied and sealed with his own hands, to make no engagements with other powers without the consent of France, on condition that he received a pension of £100,000 a year. Again, in 1677 he accepted £1,600,000 for a timely prorogation, which saved Louis just at a moment when it was almost certain that his victories in the Spanish Netherlands would lead Parliament to demand war with France. (2) Louis XIV also found that he could spend money to advantage among the leaders of the Parliamentary opposition itself, and in 1678 he distributed large sums through the agency of the French Ambassador. The necessity for this arose in the first instance out of that marriage of incalculable importance which Danby had brought about in 1677 between the Duke of York's daughter Mary and William, Prince of Orange—a marriage to which the King yielded mainly because he hoped it would detach William from Shaftesbury and the Opposition, and smooth the difficulties which were beginning to shew themselves in the way of his brother's accession to the throne. But this marriage seemed dangerous to France, not only because it removed the last obstacle in the way of an Anglo-Dutch alliance but also because Charles, whose policy was always dynastic, could no longer be trusted not to turn against France. These fears appeared only too well founded when the Pension Parliament, now in close accord with the King, began in 1678 to make preparations for war. But Louis XIV was not at the end of his resources. He played with the utmost skill upon the fears of the Opposition about a standing army, and made use of these to neutralise their hostility to France. In the end they were persuaded to abandon their European policy, and to direct their efforts towards getting rid of the army of 30,000 men which they had voted the King the means to raise, lest he should use it to re-establish Catholicism by armed force. It was the striking success of the French King in the English Parliament which provoked Seeley's audacious remark that the leader of the Opposition in the last session of the Pension Parliament was Louis XIV himself.[1]

"There were two inchanting terms", says Bishop Parker, "which at the first pronunciation could, like Circe's intoxicating cups, change men into beasts, namely, *Popery* and *the French Interest*".[2] In 1678 these spells were both at work, and they produced the dangerous state of public feeling which preceded the Popish Plot. The way for the panic had been prepared by the Plague and the Fire, which had "unsettled men's reason...and charged the political air with thunder".[3] A plot to assassinate a Protestant king to make way for a Catholic heir did not appear impossible to the grandsons of the men who had seen the life of Elizabeth assailed by assassins in order that she might be succeeded by Mary Queen of Scots; and the idea of a general massacre did not seem absurd when men thought of St Bartholomew. We now know that the Popish Plot is to be classed "with the terrible illusions bred at Athens by the mutilation of the Hermae, and in New England by the alarm of witchcraft",[4] but in the circumstances of the time it is not altogether surprising that the concoctions of Oates and Dangerfield should have found credence. A resolution was carried in both Houses without a single dissentient on November 1, 1678,

that there hath been, and still is, a damnable and hellish Plot, contrived and carried on by the Popish recusants, for the assassinating and murdering the King, and for subverting the government, and rooting out and destroying the Protestant religion.[5]

[1] ii. 241.   [2] Samuel Parker, *History of his Own Time*, p. 379.
[3] Trevelyan, *Stuarts*, p. 361.   [4] Goldwin Smith, ii. 41.
[5] *Commons' Journals*, ix. 530; *Lords' Journals*, xiii. 333.

The militia were called out, cannon planted round White-hall, and guards were stationed in the vaults under the Parliament House where Guy Fawkes had stored his gunpowder more than seventy years before. A period of wild proscription set in for the Catholics, and in London especially fresh batches of innocent persons were con-demned daily on the evidence of the informers alone.

The most important result of the Plot, so far as Parlia-ment was concerned, was that out of it the Exclusion Bill was born. The protagonists in Parliament were Danby on the one side, and Shaftesbury, who was, with the exception of Pym, the ablest Parliamentary tactician of the century, on the other. Each intended to use the Plot for his own purposes, but the advantage lay with the more adroit intriguer. Shaftesbury can scarcely have believed in the Plot, but the temptation to use it in order to recover power for himself and to take revenge upon his enemies was irresistible. His plans first took shape in an attempt in the Pension Parliament to obtain the exclusion of the Duke of York from all share in the Government, and this developed in later Parliaments into a movement for his complete exclusion from the throne. In November, 1678, an address was moved in both Houses praying the King to remove the Duke from his person and counsels, and as a concession to Parliament Charles prevailed on his brother to cease attending the meetings of the Privy Council. This did not prevent a Bill[1] from passing both Houses before the end of the month "disabling Papists from sitting in either House of Parliament", an exception in favour of the Duke of York being only carried in the Commons by a majority of two, by means of a muster of all the placemen, "including", as someone put it, "the aged and infirm". This was practically a further extension of the policy of the Test Act.

Another result of the Plot was the impeachment of Danby and the dissolution of Parliament. So strong a supporter of the monarchy as Danby was scarcely prepared to denounce the King in public for receiving money in

[1] Printed in Grant Robertson, pp. 86–92, under the title "The Test Act No. 2".

secret from Louis XIV as the price of England's neutrality; and yet as the King's chief minister he could scarcely avoid the knowledge of what was going on. Thus he soon found himself in a position in which he was conniving at the dealings of Charles with France while maintaining his own anti-French policy publicly in Parliament. This was all right as long as nothing leaked out, but in an evil hour Danby quarrelled with Montagu, the English Ambassador in Paris, and Montagu betrayed him to Shaftesbury and the Opposition. In the state of the public temper created by the Plot, a statesman who had connived at secret negotiations with France could expect no mercy; and the fact that he had from the first discredited the fictions of Oates was now turned against him. He was described in the impeachment as "popishly affected", and it was stated that he had "traitorously concealed the late horrid Plot" after he had had notice of it.[1] To save his minister and to protect himself against the inconvenient disclosures which the trial of the impeachment would almost certainly involve, the King dissolved the Pension Parliament on January 24, 1679.

Although the Parliament of 1661 to 1679 is called "Royalist" and "Cavalier", it had carried almost every point against the King on which it cared to fight him. It had compelled him to give up toleration, to abandon his French policy, to curtail his extravagance, to reduce his army, and to surrender his opposition to Holland by sanctioning the marriage of William and Mary. In the growth of this immensely strong and successful Opposition in the Pension Parliament, the Revolution of 1688 may be seen casting its shadow before it. "In any case, the history of this Parliament greatly modifies the idea that the Revolution of 1688 was in any sense a conspiracy of great lords far in advance of their time and more or less independent of popular sentiment."[2]

During the Pension Parliament three cases of great constitutional importance affected the permanent relations between the Upper and the Lower House. In 1668

[1] *D.N.B.* xlii. 298.
[2] *E.H.R.* xxi. 285.

Skinner v. *The East India Company*[1] raised the question of the legality of the original civil jurisdiction of the House of Lords. In 1661, 1671, and 1678 resolutions were passed in the Commons which had the effect of placing beyond dispute the privileges of the Lower House with regard to money bills.[2] Finally, in 1675 the case of *Shirley* v. *Fagg* raised the question of the appellate jurisdiction of the Lords in proceedings in Equity.[3]

When he dissolved the Pension Parliament, Charles appears to have cherished the illusion that the principal source of the power of the Opposition was Shaftesbury's success in making up factions in London, and if he could get together a new Parliament from the country, he would find it comparatively untouched by the excitement which had carried away the members of the old Parliament, exposed as they were to the contagion of the capital. But he had underrated the extent to which the country was in touch with London. The Opposition was disorganised, but only for a moment, and the electioneering energy of Shaftesbury and the Green Ribbon Club soon remedied the confusion which the unexpectedness of the dissolution had caused. The contest, says Macaulay,

was fierce and obstinate beyond example. Unprecedented sums were expended. New tactics were employed. It was remarked by the pamphleteers of that time as something extraordinary that horses were hired at a great charge for the conveyance of electors. The practice of splitting freeholds for the purpose of multiplying votes dates from this memorable struggle.[4]

Its result was that, with the exception at the most of about thirty members, the Opposition gained every seat. The placemen and pensioners of eighteen years all disappeared, and the King found himself confronted by an overwhelming Protestant majority. The first consequence was that Danby resigned the office of Lord Treasurer as soon as Parlia-

---

[1] See Anson, i. 359–60 and Grant Robertson, *Statutes*, pp. 355–61.
[2] See Anson, i. 269 and Grant Robertson, pp. 572–3.
[3] See Grant Robertson, pp. 368–79.
[4] Macaulay, i. 116. On the methods adopted in the election of this and the later Exclusion Bill Parliaments, see an article by Mr E. Lipson in *E.H.R.* xxviii. 59–85.

ment met; and it was not long before he was again impeached.[1]

Charles tried to conciliate Parliament by adopting a scheme put forward by Sir William Temple[2] which involved the admission of members of the Opposition to the Privy Council; but he was determined not to surrender on the vital point of his brother's succession to the throne. It is a remarkable fact about the last six years of Charles II's reign that Danby had no successor. The King, shaking off his disinclination for business, became his own minister, brought all his great political ability to bear upon affairs, and fought the battle of the dynasty with a tenacity and skill which won him a complete victory and prolonged the tenure of the Stuart House until the Revolution of 1688.

Charles was under no illusions about the strength of the forces arrayed against him, and he began by proposing to the Opposition important concessions.[3] He offered to impose by Act of Parliament four limitations with regard to the succession. (1) All ecclesiastical benefices and promotions to be conferred without the control or interference of a Popish successor. (2) No Papist to sit in either House of Parliament; the Parliament sitting at the King's death to remain sitting for a certain time afterwards; if no Parliament was sitting, the last Parliament to reassemble without any fresh summons. (3) No Papist to hold any office or place of trust; and posts in the Privy Council, the

---

[1] No less than five constitutional questions were raised by Danby's impeachment: (1) the legal responsibility of ministers for all acts done by them, whether done in obedience to the command of the Crown or not; (2) the practice of "general impeachments"; (3) the legality of pleading a pardon in bar of an impeachment; (4) the right of bishops to vote in capital cases; (5) the effect of a dissolution of Parliament upon a pending impeachment. These questions are discussed in T. P. Taswell-Langmead, *English Constitutional History* (8th edition), pp. 635–9. The articles of impeachment are printed in Grant Robertson, pp. 566–9.

[2] See Professor E. R. Turner's article on "The Privy Council of 1679" in *E.H.R.* xxx. 251–70.

[3] This policy had been to a certain extent anticipated by Danby's abortive Bill, introduced in 1677 with the consent of James, Duke of York, providing that if any future sovereign refused to take the declaration against transubstantiation his Church patronage and the education of his children should pass to the bishops (Feiling, p. 166).

Chancery, and the Courts of Common Law only to be filled up with the consent of Parliament. (4) Lords-lieutenant of counties, their deputies, and the officers of the navy to be nominated by Parliament or by a Commission appointed by Parliament. This last is the old question of the power of the sword.

The offered concessions went far towards satisfying all reasonable demands; nevertheless, the agitation for an absolute exclusion grew daily, for the Commons could not bring themselves to believe that any restrictions would bind a Popish King.[1] An Exclusion Bill was therefore brought in,[2] but as soon as it had passed the second reading, Charles, to save his brother, prorogued Parliament on May 27, but not before it had placed to its credit the notable legislative achievement of the Habeas Corpus Act of 1679.[3]

This dissolution brought the King no relief, for the Protestant tide still flowed as strongly as ever in the counties, and the elections held in October, 1679, returned a new Parliament which was as hostile to the Court as its predecessor had been. As soon as its composition was known, the King prorogued it before it met, and it did not actually sit until October, 1680.

It was in this lull before the crisis of the storm that we come for the first time upon the party names of Whig and Tory. The influence of Shaftesbury had caused a number of petitions to be sent up from those boroughs in which the Opposition was supreme, praying the King to call the

---

[1] They said it was but "binding Samson with withes" (Feiling, p. 182).

[2] Altogether three Exclusion Bills were introduced into Parliament—in 1679, 1680, and 1681. The substance of the Bill of 1680 is printed in Grant Robertson, pp. 102–4.

[3] Printed in Grant Robertson, pp. 92–101. Burnet's curious story of the accident by which the Bill was carried in the House of Lords may very well be true. "Lord Grey and Lord Norris were named to be the tellers. Lord Norris, being a man subject to vapours, was not at all times attentive to what he was doing; so a very fat lord coming in, Lord Grey counted him for ten, as a jest at first; but, seeing Lord Norris had not observed it, he went on with this misreckoning of ten; so it was reported to the House, and declared that they who were for the Bill were the majority, though it indeed went on the other side; and by this means the Bill passed" (Burnet, i. 485).

prorogued Parliament together upon an early day. In reply to these, the loyal corporations sent up addresses expressing their abhorrence of such petitions as an interference with the royal prerogative of summoning, proroguing, and dissolving Parliament at will. "Petitioners" and "Abhorrers" were thereupon coined as the first party names of the period, but they were soon supplanted by more famous terms. "Whig" and "Tory" were in the first instance derisive nicknames applied to each party by its opponents.[1] "Tories" were the half-barbarous Irish who infested the more desolate parts of the country in plundering bands after the Irish Rebellion. "Whigs" were the lawless Covenanters who held out in the Lowlands of Scotland after the failure of the Insurrection of 1679. Those who supported Exclusion were called Whigs by their enemies to imply that they were little better than Covenanting rebels; and those who desired the succession of a Catholic heir were nicknamed Tories by way of suggesting that they were only a set of Popish thieves. A passage in Oliver Heywood's *Diaries*[2] shews these names coming into use.

I being at Wallinwells, October 24, 1681, they were discoursing about a new name lately come into fashion for Ranters, calling themselves by the name of Torys. Mistress H. of Chesterfield told me a gentleman was at their house and had a red ribband in his hat, she askt him what it meant, he said it signifyed that he was a Tory. What's that, said she, he answered, an Irish rebel—Oh, dreadful, that any in England dare espouse that interest. I hear further since that this is the distinction they make instead of Cavalier and Roundhead—now they are called Torys and Wiggs, the former wearing a red ribband, the other a violet; thus men begin to commence war. The former is an Irish title for outlawd persons, the

---

[1] As in the earlier case of "Cavalier" and "Roundhead". "Cavalier", a gentleman trained to arms, had acquired a sinister meaning, and the term was applied to Rupert's plundering troopers by their victims. "Roundhead" was a contemptuous expression for the close-cropped London apprentices who chiefly composed the mobs at Westminster who "bawled against the bishops". Hacket tells the story of a vicar in Hampshire who gratified the Royalist part of his congregation every Sunday by singing lustily in the *Te Deum*, "O Lord, in Thee have I trusted, Let me never be a Roundhead" (*Life of Archbishop Williams*, Pt ii. p. 207).

[2] ii. 285.

other a Scotch title for fanaticks or dissenters, and the Torys will hector down and abuse those they have named Wigs in London and elsewhere frequently.

It was in the Parliament of 1680 that Shaftesbury reached the summit of his power.[1] As the defender of the Protestant faith against the schemes of the Jesuits, he was the most popular man in England, and for a time it seemed as if he must carry everything before him. But on the question of a successor to Charles if James should be excluded, the exclusionists themselves were divided. Shaftesbury had cast in his lot with the Duke of Monmouth, and, as Dryden put it, played Achitophel to his Absalom; and he was strong enough in the Lower House to carry an Exclusion Bill which, instead of naming Mary of Orange, was intentionally worded so as to leave the succession open to Monmouth's claims.[2] The Bill was carried by the Commons to the Upper House, but there it was already a lost cause, for no one believed Monmouth to be legitimate, and the pious legend of the "black box", mysteriously spirited away from Whitehall by the emissaries of the Pope, containing the proofs of his mother's marriage to the King, convinced no one who was not already pledged to be of Shaftesbury's following. Halifax the Trimmer spoke against the Bill, carrying with him all those exclusionists who supported the succession of the House of Orange, and the Bill was rejected in the Lords by sixty-three to thirty.

Meanwhile, the tide of popular excitement was on the turn, and the King, who knew better than any of his subjects how to read the signs of the times, once more dissolved Parliament, and summoned a new one to meet at Oxford on March 21, 1681. The first business of this Parliament was the reintroduction of the Exclusion Bill, but the invention of Oates and Dangerfield was shewing signs of exhaustion. An attempt was made to keep up the panic of the Plot by means of the case of Fitzharris,[3] which led to a furious controversy between the two Houses; but

[1] See note on "The First Earl of Shaftesbury", Appendix, p. 286 below.
[2] Trevelyan, *Stuarts*, p. 412.
[3] See Grant Robertson, pp. 569–70.

one morning the King came down in a closed sedan chair to the Geometry School at Oxford where the Lords were sitting, followed by another closed chair containing the robes of state, and in a few minutes the Oxford Parliament had ceased to exist. We hear nothing more of Exclusion, nor does another Parliament meet during the reign. And without a Parliament the Whigs were inarticulate and powerless. "Henceforth", says Hallam, using a Miltonic comparison, "they lay like the fallen angels, prostrate upon the fiery lake".[1]

In this emergency, the relations of Charles with France stood him in good stead. The Whigs imagined that they had him in their power because they could refuse supplies until the Exclusion Bill was passed. But the exclusion of James, whether in favour of a King Monmouth, whose foreign policy would be determined by the anti-French prejudices of the Whig leaders, or in favour of Louis XIV's greater antagonist, William of Orange, was not at all in the interest of France. The French Ambassador was therefore authorised to promise Charles a sum of five million livres if he should fail to come to terms with his Parliament.

Even more important was the fact that the King now had the country behind him. In the earlier days of the Plot, the Whigs, if silenced by a dissolution, might have appealed to the Protestant feeling of England, and fallen back on desperate measures. Shaftesbury

had on his side the fundamental principle that a nation cannot safely be governed by a ruler whose ideas on the most important question of the day are directly opposed to those of his subjects; and he was right, as the result shewed, in holding that in the seventeenth century a Catholic king could not satisfactorily govern a Protestant people.[2]

As yet, however, this was only a sentiment based upon a speculation concerning the future; and what Charles II appealed to was the practical experience of the past. It was not to be expected that the heir to the throne, whose hereditary claim was beyond dispute, would tamely retire

[1] ii. 451.
[2] Gardiner, *Student's History*, p. 618.

and accept the principle of Exclusion. But if he should resist, a civil war was certain, and of civil war the country had had enough. While the panic of the Plot lasted, the evil of a Popish successor appeared greater than the evil of another civil war; but this was not in accordance with the natural proportions of things. The King appealed from England drunk to England sober, and at the time of the Oxford Parliament England was getting soberer day by day. It is the great merit of Charles II's statesmanship at this juncture, that he realised that time was on his side and that it was his business to delay Exclusion rather than to resist it.[1] Then, with the utmost discrimination, he seized the moment for a final dissolution when the temperature was going down and the patient was beginning to see things once more as they really were. Whatever might have been the case in 1679 or 1680, in 1681 Charles was sure that if the Whigs resorted to violence they would no longer meet with any support; but he was careful to leave nothing to chance, and it was of set purpose that the Parliament of 1681 was summoned to meet at Oxford. London was Shaftesbury's stronghold, and there the City mob might intervene on behalf of Exclusion, as it had intervened against Strafford fifty years before. Oxford, on the other hand, was the traditional centre of Royalist feeling, and moreover the King had taken the precaution of occupying it beforehand with his guards. In spite of all, however, at the close of the Oxford Parliament England was upon the edge of civil war. The Whig leaders rode into Oxford attended by armed servants, and after the dissolution Shaftesbury tried to keep Parliament together in spite of it—an act which would have been then, as it had been in the case of the Scottish Assembly before the Bishops' War, a tocsin of revolution. But here the King's foresight had placed them at a disadvantage. They were no longer in London, supported by enthusiastic mobs and backed by the City authorities who could bring the train-

---

[1] "As a sword is sooner broken upon a feather-bed than upon a table, so his pliantness broke the blow of a present mischief much better than a more immediate resistance would perhaps have done" (Halifax, *A Character of King Charles II*, pp. 55–6).

bands into play; but in a place where local feeling was all against them and the armed force was on the other side. At this crisis the King owed much to the King's guards. If we might venture to follow the example of Hallam in attempting a Miltonic parallel, we might say that it was useless for the Whigs to attempt violence when they found Oxford "with dreadful faces thronged, and fiery arms".

The Revolution of 1688

BISHOP BURNET speaks of the fall of James II as "one of the strangest catastrophes that is in any history. A great king, with strong armies and mighty fleets, a great treasure and powerful allies, fell all at once, and his whole strength, like a spider's web, was...irrecoverably broken at a touch".[1] The explanation is to be found in another kind of Popish Plot—the Stuart plot against Protestantism—which had been abandoned by Charles II as impracticable, but which his successor, the chief conspirator, now revived. This had the effect of reviving also the policy of Exclusion, now cast into a more dangerous form.

James II's scheme was not without a certain plausibility. The main support of the restored Stuart monarchy was the restored Church of England; but the Church was not likely to allow herself to be Romanised, and thus her existence was one of the obstacles in the way of the King's plans. On the other hand, the career of Shaftesbury had revealed the great political power still wielded by the sects; and it was the King's design to substitute for the old alliance between the Crown and the Church a new alliance between the Crown and the Dissenters, and with their aid, purchased by the bribe of toleration for themselves, to obtain the repeal of the penal laws against the Catholics, and possibly something more. Nor did he expect resistance, for "non-resistance" was one of the cardinal doctrines of the restored Church. The bitter experience of the Great Rebellion was likely to serve him here, and the memory of this was revived at the very beginning of his reign by Monmouth's Insurrection. "I die a Protestant of the Church of England", Monmouth said at his execution, whereupon the divines who stood by said, "My Lord, if you be of the Church of England, you must acknowledge the doctrine of non-resistance to be true".[2] And if the Church was driven by the new policy into abandoning the

---

[1] i. 617. [2] Sir John Bramston's *Autobiography*, p. 189.

principle she had so often preached, then would be the time to take a leaf out of Cromwell's book, and to bring the standing army into play. We can see, of course, what enormous miscalculations were involved in all this, but the policy of James was not altogether at random. He may have misread history, but he did not refuse to read it at all. The forces on which he reckoned were real forces, although he so preposterously miscalculated their strength. He was not a king without a policy, but one who was embarking on a policy which a wiser man than he had already discarded because he saw that it was impossible to carry it out. But even James did not at once plunge headlong to his ruin. His brother died on February 6, 1685, and the new King spent the rest of the year in attempting to obtain his ends by means that were entirely constitutional, and only unwise because they could not possibly be successful. He began by asking Parliament to repeal the Test Act.

On James's accession he was supported by all moderate men, and this support was converted into something like enthusiasm when the insurrections of Argyle and Monmouth were successfully put down. It is improbable that the Bloody Assize and the other severities which followed the battle of Sedgemoor should have really created the reaction against the Government which Burnet attributes to them, for the traditional horror of treason was still too strong and little sympathy was felt for the men who had thus brought back the hateful memories of the Great Rebellion. Moreover, Parliament itself was packed with Tories.

"Great tricks and practices were used", says Luttrell,[1] "to bring in men well affected to the King, and to keep out all those they call Whigs or Trimmers; at some places, as Bedford, etc., they chose at night, giving no notice of it; in other boroughs, as St Albans, they have new regulated the electors by new charters, in putting the election into a selected number when it was before by prescription in the inhabitants at large; in counties they adjourned the poll from one place to another to weary the freeholders, refusing also to take the votes of excommunicate persons and other dissenters; noblemen busying themselves with elections, getting the writs and precepts

[1] *Brief Relation*, i. 341.

into their hands and managing them as they pleased;[1] King commanding some to stand and forbidding others, polling many of his servants at Westminster to carry an election; foul returns made in many places; and where gentlemen stood that they called Whigs, they offered them all the tricks and affronts imaginable".

But although his Parliament was thus favourably disposed to him, James found that upon the repeal of the Test Act they were adamant. Halifax warned him beforehand that the attempt would fail and refused to support the proposal, with the result that in October he was dismissed from the Privy Council; and the attitude of Halifax was typical of English statesmen generally. On the second Sunday after his accession, when James went to the Roman mass, the Duke of Norfolk, who carried the sword of state before him, had stopped at the door. "My Lord", said the King, "your father would have gone farther", only to draw upon himself the crushing retort, "Your Majesty's father would not have gone so far".[2]

There was at this time much in the European situation to justify the fears of English statesmen. The struggle in England between Protestantism and the Government was only one aspect of the greater conflict which was raging upon the Continent. The day after the dismissal of Halifax, on October 21, the decree revoking the Edict of Nantes was registered by the Parliament of Paris. The Bloody Assize was contemporaneous with the Dragonnades, in which Louis XIV was using force to stamp out Calvinism in France; and at the very moment when "this short military mode of dealing with religious questions" was proving effective there, "a Catholic king in England was seen struggling to obtain possession of a standing army".[3] All this seemed an object-lesson in the designs of Catholic

---

[1] *Cf.* Sir John Bramston's account (*Autobiography*, p. 173) of his own candidature for the borough of Maldon in Essex. At first his opponent had it all his own way, as he "came once or twice to the town and largessed the freemen", and "he appearing, I foresaw a charge, which I was troubled at"; but soon after, the Duke of Albemarle, who was Bramston's patron, not only undertook to bear a proportion of the expense, but met some of the voters at an inn and explained to them how they were to vote. "His Grace caressed them, called for wine, and drank to them, and they resolved they would do so."

[2] Hutton, p. 218.   [3] Seeley, ii. 255.

kings. As long as a Catholic was on the throne, the Test Act was an obstacle in the way of his filling all offices in the State with men who would assist him in his designs against the religion and liberties of England; it was therefore never less likely that it would be repealed. And yet James had been unwise enough to discount in advance the possibility of its repeal. The insurrection of Monmouth had enabled him to increase his army more than threefold, and in spite of the Test Act he had given commissions in the newly-raised regiments to Roman Catholic officers. When Parliament refused to regularise their position by repealing the Act, he informed the Houses that he was determined not to part with his officers although they were disqualified by law. The Commons offered to pass a Bill indemnifying them from the penalties already incurred, but they pointed out "that those officers cannot by law be capable of their employments, and that the incapacities they bring upon themselves thereby can no ways be taken off but by an Act of Parliament".[1] The King replied by proroguing Parliament on November 19, 1685, and although it was not dissolved until July, 1687, it did not meet again.

The King's object was to Catholicise the Government, and from the time when he quarrelled with and prorogued his Parliament, his progress along this perilous road was rapid indeed. The Crown still retained a formidable constitutional weapon in its control of the judicial bench, and James was able to obtain in the courts of law a decision on which his Catholicising policy could be safely rested. In the collusive action of *Godden* v. *Hales*,[2] tried in the Court of King's Bench, he claimed to override the Test Act in virtue of his dispensing power, and the decision of the Court was given in favour of the Crown. This momentous decision broke down at a touch the barrier which Parliament had erected in the way of a Catholic army, a Catholic civil service, and a Catholic Council; and during the years 1686 and 1687 the dispensing power was applied in four

---

[1] *Commons' Journals*, ix. 758.
[2] See note on "Godden *v*. Hales, 1686", Appendix, p. 289 below; and Grant Robertson, pp. 384–8.

directions. (1) The Roman Catholic officers already appointed to the army received dispensations from the penalties of the Test Act, and new officers were freely introduced. The King also busied himself in purging and modelling his army after the manner of Cromwell and Monk, and frequent reviews were held at the camp on Hounslow Heath. (2) A committee of the Council was appointed "to inspect the commissions of the peace throughout all the counties", and in many cases Protestant magistrates were replaced by Papists.[1] Sir John Bramston in his *Autobiography* describes the process as it went on in his own county of Essex. He himself was deprived of the office of High Steward of the borough of Maldon, which he had held since the Restoration, and "with myself were about 30 gentlemen put out of the commission of the peace, few of the old justices left in commission".[2] These were replaced for the most part by Levellers and Commonwealth's men, "the King judging that out of hatred to the Church of England, and out of desire to have the penal laws abrogated, they will also promote the taking away the Test too".[3] The same policy was pursued in a higher judicial sphere, for when two new Barons of the Exchequer had to be appointed, we are told that one was a papist, the other "phanatick".[4] (3) The King Catholicised the Privy Council itself. After the dismissal of Halifax in 1685 a Catholic cabal had been established outside the Council for the management of Catholic affairs, and this had soon come to advise the King upon affairs at large. It consisted of Sunderland, who had come to the front as chief minister after the retirement of Halifax, Father Petre the King's confessor—the English counterpart of Père La Chaise—Henry Jermyn, and Richard Talbot, better known as the Earl of Tyrconnel. But the decision of June, 1686, opened the Privy Council itself to the King's Catholic counsellors, and on July 17 Lord Powis, Lord Arundel of Wardour, Lord Bellasis, and Lord Dover were sworn in. Of these Bramston[5] notes that the three first were three of the five Popish lords impeached for the Plot. On October 17

---

[1] Bramston, p 251.　　[2] *Ib.* p. 304.　　[3] *Ib.*
[4] *Ib.* p. 311.　　[5] P. 234.

Tyrconnel became "the fifth of the Popish religion at the Board".[1] On Christmas Day the new Roman Catholic Chapel at Whitehall was opened, "which had no other form of consecration that I can hear of", says Bramston,[2] "but a marble stone consecrated at Rome and blessed by the Pope" which was "brought and placed under the altar"; and soon after the Benedictine Order was settled at St James's. Early in 1687 Rochester, whom the King had attempted to convert in vain, was driven from office, and Tyrconnel superseded Clarendon in the government of Ireland. In June, 1687, a Papal nuncio arrived in England and was conducted to Windsor Castle by a train of thirty-six coaches with six horses in each. Bramston[3] tells us that the King commanded the Duke of Somerset to conduct him into his presence, who begged to be excused. Thereupon he was removed from his post of Gentleman of the Bedchamber and the place given to the Earl of Dumbarton, a Scotchman and a Papist. On November 11 Father Petre himself was made a Privy Councillor, of which Bramston writes:[4] "This man is by Order a Jesuit, and the only man of that Order of the public council to any prince in Christendom". The supreme control of affairs now passed into the hands of a triumvirate, consisting of Petre, Sunderland, and Sir Nicholas Butler, a convert to Rome. (4) In 1686 the King took the first steps in a still more dangerous policy. He utilised the dispensing power for an attack on the Church of England itself, for he gave permission to a convert to Rome to retain his London benefice; he allowed another convert, Obadiah Walker, to remain Master of University College, Oxford; and a third convert, John Massey, was appointed Dean of Christ Church.

These measures had the effect of rousing the clergy, who began to warn their hearers from the pulpit against the errors of the Church of Rome. The King attempted to silence them, and ordered Henry Compton, Bishop of London, to suspend a London rector for controversial preaching. This the bishop refused to do until he had himself investigated the case, and in order to beat down

---

[1] Bramston, p. 248.   [2] P. 253.   [3] Pp. 280–1   [4] P. 300.

this resistance James armed himself with a new weapon. The Act of the Long Parliament which had abolished the High Commission Court forbade its revival, but James now revived it, arguing that as the old Court punished laity as well as clergy, the prohibition in the Act did not prevent him, in virtue of his ecclesiastical supremacy, from constituting a new Court with jurisdiction over the clergy alone. This Court, of which Jeffreys, now Lord Chancellor, was made President, was used, like its predecessor, to silence preachers, but it was now employed, not to punish attacks upon the bishops but attacks upon the Church of Rome. Its first business was to suspend Compton and to place the administration of the diocese of London in the hands of a commission of bishops. "Thus in the revolutions of time, a Catholic King made use of the ecclesiastical powers which the Tudors had appropriated from the papal armoury, in order to carry back to the papal allegiance the Anglican Church."[1]

On April 4, 1687, James II's First Declaration of Indulgence[2] suspended all penal laws against Dissenters and Roman Catholics alike, and allowed to both freedom of public worship. As the King had expected, many of the Dissenters received it joyfully, although signs were not wanting that in the long run their Protestantism might prove stronger than their Nonconformity.

It was almost immediately after the issue of the Declaration that an event took place which, although unimportant in itself, acquired importance by reason of its dramatic character—the expulsion of the Fellows of Magdalen College, Oxford.[3] It had been represented to James by some of his Roman Catholic advisers that the dispensing power might be conveniently used to throw open the Universities to learned Roman Catholics, and a royal mandate was sent to Cambridge in February, 1687, requiring the admission to a degree of Alban Francis, a

---

[1] Trevelyan, *Stuarts*, p. 434.

[2] Printed in Grant Robertson, pp. 388–91.

[3] *Cf.* also the Charterhouse case, in which the King attempted by dispensation to obtain the admission of a Roman Catholic as a pensioner (Feiling, p. 221).

Benedictine monk, without taking the oaths required by statute; and when the Vice-Chancellor refused to break the law, he was deprived of his office by the High Commission Court. Soon after, the office of President of Magdalen fell vacant at Oxford, and the Fellows received letters mandatory from the King requiring them to elect one Anthony Farmer, a man of bad character but of Romanising tendencies, as their President. This the Fellows refused to do, and elected one of their own number, Dr Hough. When summoned before the High Commission to answer for their disobedience, they had no difficulty in proving the unfitness of Farmer,[1] but the Commission declared the election of Hough null and void, and the King ordered the election of Samuel Parker, Bishop of Oxford. When the Fellows refused to make the election on the ground that the office was already filled, they were one by one expelled from their Fellowships; but their Vice-President's dignified reply to the Commissioners was quoted all over England: "Our statutes, which we are sworn to observe,...are agreeable to the King's laws, both ecclesiastical and civil, and as long as we live up to them we obey the King".[2] Their places were filled by Papists, and when Parker, the intruded President, died, the intruded Fellows elected as their Head the Romanist Bonaventura Gifford, the titular Bishop of Madaura. The College was then "filled apace with Popish priests and others of the Roman communion",[3] and the College Chapel was used for the Roman Mass.

The King had thus been Catholicising by means of his dispensing power the army, the civil service, the Privy Council, and the Universities; but he regarded all his measures as only provisional, until a new Parliament could be summoned to do what the old Parliament had refused to do—to repeal the Test Act and the penal laws. For this

[1] Among other things, Farmer "did misbehave himself in Trinity College in Cambridge"; had co-operated in the enterprise of throwing the Abingdon town stocks into the river "in the night time"; and the Porter of Magdalen had been heard to say "that Mr Farmer did very often come into the College late at night, so much in drink that he could scarce go or speak" (*State Trials*, xii. 11, 14, 15).

[2] *State Trials*, xii. 47.   [3] Quoted in Hutton, p. 226.

he looked to his policy of Toleration, for "the whole machine was phanatick; and the design was, to compass a phanatick Parliament". With this object in view, the remodelling of the corporations was carried still further, and Roman Catholics and Dissenters were admitted to those boroughs which returned members to Parliament; Roman Catholics were appointed as lords-lieutenant in the counties; and three questions were propounded to the deputy-lieutenants and the justices of the peace:[1] (1) Whether, if chosen to serve in Parliament, you will consent to the repeal of the penal laws and the Test Act? (2) Whether, if not standing yourself, you will vote for a member who will do so? (3) Whether you will be willing to maintain the Declaration of Indulgence? But so strongly was public feeling now running against James, that he found he could not trust even his own nominees to send tolerationists to Parliament, and the plan for a new Parliament was therefore abandoned for a time.

The next step was the issue, on April 27, 1688, of the Second Declaration of Indulgence, in terms almost identical with the First Declaration; but it was now ordered that this should be read in churches.[2] Even the First Declaration had caused searchings of heart among Royalist churchmen. The discreet and loyal Evelyn had written about it in his Diary, under date April 10, 1687:

This was purely obtained by the Papists, thinking thereby to ruin the Church of England, being now the only Church which so admirably and strenuously opposed their superstition.... What this will end in, God Almighty only knows; but it looks like confusion, which I pray God avert.

But the Second Declaration did far more than the First, for the order requiring it to be read in churches demanded the active personal co-operation of the clergy in the ecclesiastical policy of the King. They could no longer regard the Declaration as an act of authority, with which

---

[1] See Bramston, p. 301. A summary of the replies to these questions, which disclose a strong Royalist opposition to James in the counties, is given in Feiling, pp. 218–9.

[2] The Order in Council is printed in Grant Robertson, p. 391.

they were not concerned. To read it was to abandon their attitude towards Roman Catholics and Dissenters, and so to do violence in one way to their past professions; to refuse to read it was to give up the doctrine of non-resistance which they had preached so often, and so to do violence to their past professions in another way. James II was forcing upon the clergy a dilemma which they had no desire to bring upon themselves, and so driving them into an act of rebellion which they would gladly have avoided. He was under the delusion that the Declaration of Indulgence had so far won the Dissenters to his side, that he could attack the Church with impunity. But now the Dissenters themselves were beginning to repudiate the fatal gift.

When the day for reading the Declaration came, scarcely a single clergyman obeyed the King's order. When Bishop Sprat began to read it in Westminster Abbey, the whole congregation left the church; and one divine is said to have preached a sermon against the Declaration from the text, "Be it known unto thee, O king, that we will not serve thy gods, nor worship the golden image which thou hast set up".[1] And seven of the bishops presented a petition[2] to the King remonstrating against the Declaration, and praying that the clergy might be excused from reading it.

The importance of the Trial of the Seven Bishops[3] lies in this—that it is the point at which the principle of non-resistance definitely and finally broke down. To the conference at Lambeth of May 18, 1688, out of which the petition grew, were summoned eleven of the bishops and some of the deans—more particularly Stillingfleet, Dean of St Paul's, and Tillotson, Dean of Canterbury. It has been said of Tillotson, that "after the orgies of the saints and the orgies of the sinners, he made sanity acceptable to a whole generation";[4] and it was precisely

---

[1] This sermon has been ascribed to Samuel Wesley, the father of the great John Wesley; but at this time he was an undergraduate at Oxford. He was not ordained until August 7, 1688.

[2] Printed in Grant Robertson, p. 392.

[3] See note on "The Trial of the Seven Bishops, 1688", Appendix, p. 292 below. Extracts from the report of the Trial are printed in Grant Robertson, pp. 392–406.

[4] Dowden, quoted in Trevelyan, *Stuarts*, p. 349.

these men who were in wisdom, learning, and external reputation the leaders of the English Church. Their revolt is an indication, not only that moderate men in general were turning against James, but that the moderate clergy, who were all pledged to non-resistance, were being forced at last to reconsider their position. Not all those who were summoned were able to attend, and the signatures to the petition in its final form were those of Sancroft, Archbishop of Canterbury, Turner of Ely, White of Peterborough, Lloyd of St Asaph, Ken of Bath and Wells, Lake of Chichester, and Trelawny of Bristol. The King received the petition under the impression that it was a submission, for the bishops who brought it were known to be the most earnest advocates of non-resistance upon the Bench, but as soon as he had read it he exclaimed, "This is a standard of rebellion", and the bishops were soon after committed to the Tower on a Privy Council warrant and an information for seditious libel was lodged against them in the Court of King's Bench. "As they stepped on board the barge on which they were to be taken to the Tower", says Ranke[1], with his unfailing instinct for the historical significance of apparently unimportant things, "during the passage and on their landing, they were greeted by the assembled throng with acclamations in which religious reverence and political sympathy were combined. It was the moment at which Episcopacy concluded, as it were, its alliance with the people of London". If we compare with this the mobbing of the bishops by the Londoners at the time of the Long Parliament, we can measure the effect of James II's policy in uniting against him ancient foes. When the jury returned their verdict of acquittal, "there was a most wonderful shout, that one would have thought the Hall had cracked".

"All the way [the Bishops] came down", says Luttrell,[2] "people asked their blessing on their knees. There was continued shoutings for half an hour, so that no business could be done; and they hissed the Solicitor. And at night was mighty rejoicing, in ringing of bells, discharging of guns, lighting of candles, and bonfires in several

[1] iv. 354.
[2] *Brief Relation*, i. 448.

places though forbid, and watchmen went about to take an account of such as made them—a joyful deliverance to the Church of England".

The French Ambassador wrote disconsolately to Louis XIV, "They made bonfires, and the populace burned an effigy of the Pope".

In spite of all, the nation might have waited in patience for the death of James and the peaceful succession of his Protestant daughter, had it not been for an event by which the whole situation was changed. On June 10, 1688, a son was born to James, and all hope of a Protestant succession disappeared. Just after the battle of Sedgemoor, Lord Keeper North had told the King that "although the Duke of Monmouth was gone, yet there was a P. of O. on the other side of the water".[1] William of Orange was of princely rank, and a member of the royal family of England.

"If Charles was half a Frenchman", says Seeley,[2] "William was half an Englishman, and whereas the difference...of the English and French races was marked, the English and Dutch felt themselves to be closely akin....In both countries he represented monarchy", and "like all his House he was a Protestant. He stood forth at this time as the great representative of the Protestant cause in Europe".

On June 30, the day on which the Seven Bishops were acquitted, an invitation was despatched to William of Orange, signed by both Whigs and Tories, asking him to land an armed force to defend the liberties of England against his father-in-law.

The invitation to William of Orange was the result of a coalition of all parties against James, and it was signed by seven statesmen who were in a very special sense representative men. Admiral Russell and Henry Sidney represented the humiliated Whigs, and they were related to Lord Russell and Algernon Sidney—leaders and victims of the movement in favour of Exclusion. The Earl of Shrewsbury and Lord Lumley were themselves converts

---

[1] *The Lives of the Norths*, Ed. A. Jessopp, i. 358.
[2] ii. 216.

from Rome, and stood for that tendency which had been felt ever since the Reformation for the Church of England, as a great symbol of national unity, to "draw all men unto it". Compton, the suspended Bishop of London, represented the Church itself, now converted from the doctrine of non-resistance; while the presence of the two more famous names of Danby and Devonshire was evidence that the great party quarrel had come to an end for a time, for Danby was one of the founders of the Tory party while Devonshire was one of the oldest and most celebrated Whigs.

On rumours of the impending Dutch invasion, James tried to retrace his steps, but found that it was too late. The country gentlemen whom he had removed, refused to take office again, and Sir John Bramston remarked to the lord-lieutenant of his county who was trying to induce him to accept a commission in the militia, that "he would find gentlemen not forward to take commands; some would think one kick of the breech enough for a gentle-man".[1] Soon after he wrote, "I am weary of mentioning the particular persons that go over to the Prince of Orange".[2]

And so James fell, in spite of the fact that he "anticipated modern Liberalism in proclaiming the inalienable rights of conscience and in announcing the abandonment of all penal laws".[3] His fate was due, in a sense, to the in-capacity of his Jesuit advisers, educated in a sort of cosmopolitanism, to understand the character and pre-judices of the English people. He fell a victim, partly to his own complete want of that political tact and sensitive-ness with which his brother Charles had been so richly endowed, but partly also to Father Petre's fatal breadth of view.

The Convention Parliament of the Revolution, met on January 22, 1689, to deal with the technical and constitu-tional difficulties which a change of kingship involved.[4] The Tories were in a majority in both Houses, but the

---

[1] *Autobiography*, p. 326. [2] *Ib.* p. 337. [3] Seeley, ii. 254.
[4] See *Parliamentary History*, v. 36–108; Ranke, iv. 490–511; and the summary of the proceedings in H. D. Traill, *William the Third*, c. 5.

party was split into three sections, each of which had its own solution of the situation. The Whigs also had their solution, but they were unanimous, and this enabled them to outvote any of the Tory sections, although they were weaker than the Tories combined.

One of the Tory groups desired that negotiations should be opened with James, and that he should be invited to return, subject to such conditions as would effectually secure the civil and ecclesiastical constitution of the kingdom.[1] This solution had two weak points, for (1) it brought James back again, and this the nation was not prepared to endure; and (2) it could easily be shewn that such an arrangement was not really compatible with the Tory doctrine of non-resistance. If resistance was unlawful, then the Tories had no business to be imposing conditions upon an anointed King. The position that it was lawful to exclude James until he gave satisfactory guarantees involved the further position that, failing such guarantees, he might be excluded for ever. Moreover, it was not easy to see what fresh guarantees James had to offer. Thus this solution was felt to be illogical, and was dropped at an early stage.

Another plan, attributed to Archbishop Sancroft, had the merit of getting rid of James, while saving to all appearance the doctrine of non-resistance, and for a time it held the field. Sancroft's view was that the perverseness of the King entitled Parliament to treat him as if he were insane.

"The political capacity or authority of the King and his name in the government", he said, in the pompous language which philosophers affected in his day, "are perfect, and cannot fail; but his person being human and mortal, and not otherwise privileged than the rest of mankind, is subject to all the defects and failings of it. He may therefore be incapable of directing the Government... either by infancy, by lunacy, deliracy, or apathy—whether by nature or casual infirmity—or, lastly, by some invincible prejudices of mind, contracted and fixed by education and habit, with unalterable resolutions superinduced, in matters wholly inconsistent

[1] See William Sherlock, *A Letter to a Member of the Convention*, printed in Somers' Tracts, x. 185–90.

and incompatible with the laws, religion, peace, and true policy of the kingdom".[1]

The proper solution of the constitutional problem was therefore to appoint a Regent. The plausibility of this argument, combined with the Archbishop's great personal influence, obtained for it prolonged and careful consideration, but it contained at least three important defects: (1) Although it disposed of James it did not dispose of his son, who on Tory principles would still retain an indefeasible hereditary right to succeed him; (2) Its harmony with the doctrine of non-resistance was much more apparent than real, for it was only by a fiction that James could be regarded as insane, and if it was once conceded that "a king who is merely bad may be treated as though he were mad",[2] the position was practically surrendered to the advocates of resistance; (3) It was at any rate quite novel in theory and very inconvenient in practice to establish a Regency in the name of a hostile sovereign who was always plotting beyond sea to overthrow an authority which was nominally his own. This would be to reduce the distinction between the King *de facto* and the King *de jure* to an absurdity.

A small but very influential section of the Tories, headed by Danby, maintained that by leaving the country James had abdicated, and since the throne of England could not in law be vacant, the Crown had already devolved upon the next heir. But, since there was reason to suppose that the so-called Prince of Wales was a suppositious child, and since—owing to the King's withdrawal—further enquiry into the circumstances of its birth was impossible, the next heir was Mary of Orange, James II's elder daughter, whom it only remained to proclaim. This view would have been sound enough if it had not entirely depended upon the wholly untenable proposition that the Prince of Wales was a suppositious child.[3]

---

[1] Quoted in George D'Oyly, *Life of Sancroft*, i. 419.

[2] Traill, p. 44.

[3] Professor Gwatkin, who was no friend to James II, says, rather unkindly, that the suggestion that this son was a changeling did his father an injustice, for "the characteristic stupidity of the Pretender in later years is good evidence of his parentage" (p. 374).

The various attempts to make the Tory doctrine fit the actual facts were scarcely more than plausible; and very gradually and reluctantly the Lower House began to realise that the only possible solution was that put forward by the Whigs. They maintained that James II having, by a gross abuse of his power, broken the mutual contract between king and people[1]—expressed on the one side by the coronation oath, and on the other by the oath of allegiance—had forfeited the Crown; that the throne was thereby vacant; and that it was the right of the nation to elect a new king, and to impose upon him such conditions as would ensure the country against misgovernment in the future. This view, by openly asserting the right of resistance upon which the Revolution was really based, expressed far more precisely than any of the others the actual condition of affairs. The Tories could not by any device, however ingenious, evade the fact that on their principles James was still their king; but the Whigs, never having adopted these principles, were able, while admitting the unimpeachable hereditary claim of James, boldly to assert the right of the nation to expel a bad king.

The ultimate victory of the Whig view at the Revolution is a striking illustration of the value of public debate in Parliament. As soon as the other solutions were subjected to criticism, their inadequacy stood clearly revealed, and it became evident that common sense was destined to triumph over sentiment and an exaggerated respect for technicalities. The two famous Resolutions which embodied the Whig position were passed in the House of Commons on January 28 and 29, 1689, after less than a week's debate:

(1) "That King James II, having endeavoured to subvert the constitution of his kingdom by breaking the original contract between king and people; and, by the advice of Jesuits and other wicked persons, having violated the fundamental laws; and having withdrawn himself out of the kingdom; has abdicated the Government; and that the throne is thereby vacant"; and (2) "That it hath been found by experience to be inconsistent with the safety and welfare of this Protestant kingdom to be governed by a Popish Prince".[2]

[1] See note on "The Theory of Contract", Appendix, p. 294 below.
[2] *Commons' Journals*, x. 14, 15.

These Resolutions were carried against the extreme Tories by a coalition of the moderate Tories with the Whigs.

But when the Resolutions came before the House of Lords, it became evident that a different view was in the ascendency there.[1] The Lords accepted the second Resolution without hesitation, for James had no party there any more than in the Commons; but for the first Resolution it was proposed to substitute a declaration in favour of a Regency. This was only just rejected by fifty-one to forty-nine—a result entirely due to the fact that the Tory Danby and his supporters voted with the Whigs. Somewhat the same majority—fifty-three to forty-six—voted that there was an original contract between king and people; the House agreed without a division that James had broken it; and an unimportant change was made by the substitution of the word "deserted" for the word "abdicated". But the really important controversy was over the phrase, "that the throne is thereby vacant". The forty-nine peers who had voted for a Regency were now supported by Danby and his party, for it was their contention that Mary of Orange had already succeeded to the throne. It was therefore decided by fifty-five to forty-one that these words should be omitted. The Commons disagreed with the Lords' amendments, and a deadlock between the two Houses was the result.

But meanwhile the question was being settled out of court. Up to the date of the last division in the Peers, William had maintained an impenetrable silence, although the astute Halifax had made the remark: "I can only guess at his Highness's mind. If you wish to know what I guess, I guess that he would not like to be his wife's gentleman usher".[2] Such a result of the Revolution would be indeed intolerable. William of Orange had not come to England as William the Conqueror came—to obtain for himself a better inheritance, but to occupy one of the vital strategic positions in the area of the European conflict. His chief preoccupation all along had been to appropriate the resources and fleet of England for the benefit of the coalition against France, and it was impossible for him to

---

[1] *Lords' Journals*, xiv. 110–19.   [2] Macaulay, i. 642.

allow the constitutional power of controlling these resources thus to slip from his grasp. He therefore decided to intervene, and by a few sentences addressed to the chief political leaders he settled the controversy finally in favour of the Whigs.

"No man", he said, "could esteem a woman more than he did the Princess; but he was so made that he could not think of holding anything by apron-strings; nor could he think it reasonable to have any share in the government, unless it be put in his person, and that for term of life. If they did think it fit to settle it otherwise, he would not oppose them in it, but he would go back to Holland and meddle no more in their affairs".[1]

After this declaration, only one course was open to English statesmen, for the action of William would determine that of his wife, and Mary was indispensable to the Tories, as the next heir on their reading of hereditary right. The Lords gave way as a matter of course, and the Resolutions of the Commons were passed in their original form. It was then agreed without a division that the Prince and Princess of Orange should be declared King and Queen of England.

Thus, without bloodshed, without proscriptions, even without any important breach of public order, the Revolution of 1688 was carried through by the action of Parliament. Nor, although it is called a revolution, did it involve any interruption of historical continuity. We might almost say that the expulsion of James II is the counterpart in the seventeenth century of an episode of the sixteenth—the execution of his great-grandmother in Fotheringay Castle a hundred years before, because she was a Roman Catholic heiress to the throne of Elizabeth.

[1] Burnet, i. 820.

APPENDIX

I

[See p. 17]

THE UNION WITH SCOTLAND
(Calvin's Case, 1606)

IT was one of the dearest wishes of James I that the personal union between England and Scotland which his accession had established, should be converted into a real union. He expressed this view after his own fashion when he said, "I am the husband and all the whole Isle is my lawful wife.... I hope therefore no man will be so unreasonable as to think that I, that am a Christian king under the Gospel, should be a polygamist and husband to two wives".[1] But James aimed at too much—"one worship of God, one kingdom entirely governed, one uniformity of law".[2] Even unity of government did not come for a hundred years, and Scotland still has a different law and a different worship. One member said that the Scots were pedlars and not merchants.[3] Bacon, who was in favour of naturalisation, had to controvert "plausible similitudes", among which was the comparison of England to a rich pasture threatened by the irruption of a herd of famished cattle.[4] Another member indulged in "invective" against the Scottish nation, "using many words of scandal and obloquy, ill-beseeming such an audience and not pertinent to the matter in hand"; and, dipping into the history of Scotland, remarked, "They have not suffered above two kings to die in their beds these 200 years".[5]

The question of union was, however, fully considered in the session of 1606, and a scheme for an Act of Union was drawn up, but the plans of James and Bacon were wrecked upon the naturalisation question. The lawyers drew a distinction between the *Ante-nati*, born in Scotland before the King's accession to the throne of England, and the *Post-nati*, born after it, and they asked Parliament to pass an Act conferring naturalisation upon the *Ante-nati*, but only declaring it with respect to the *Post-nati*, on the ground that they were already naturalised at common law. The opposition which this proposal met with was partly due to blind hostility to the alien, but there was also a more solid objection. If Philip and Mary had left a son, and he had inherited Spain, would all Spaniards born after his accession be naturalised Englishmen at common law, capable of sitting and

---

[1] Speech of 1603 (*Works*, p. 272).   [2] Gwatkin, p. 265.
[3] *Parliamentary History*, i. 1082.   [4] *Ib*. i. 1086.   [5] *Ib*. i. 1097.

voting in Parliament and repealing the penal laws against the Roman Catholics? The lawyers argued in vain: the country gentlemen saw a real danger, and refused to pass the Bill. The whole question of naturalisation was therefore left to be settled by the law-courts, and although the *Ante-nati* had no case, the *Post-nati* brought a collusive action on behalf of a *Post-natus* named Robert Calvin, which was argued before all the judges in the Exchequer Chamber. It was urged by counsel engaged against the *Post-natus* that the King had two "ligeances"—the "ligeance of the King of his kingdom of England" and the "ligeance of the King of his kingdom of Scotland", and a person born in one "ligeance" was an alien in the other. Coke's Report of the case, filling fifty-two closely printed columns in the *State Trials*,[1] is a massive achievement of ponderous learning, touching on every subject connected, however remotely, with the matter in hand, from the legal status of the Samaritan leper down to the allegiance due to "Canutus the Danish King", with references to Glanville, Fortescue, Skeene, Bracton, Fleta, Littleton, Dyer, Griffith, Justinian, Virgil, Aristotle, Pomponius, "Tully", St Luke, and many other authors; but its conclusion is clear enough. The judges held that where a king inherited two kingdoms, though the laws might be different, there was only one "ligeance", and anyone born within the King's "ligeance" was his natural-born subject, and no alien in either of his kingdoms.

II

[See p. 50]

THE SUBSIDY ACT OF 1624

The novel clauses introduced into the Subsidy Bill of 1624[2] with a view to settling the money voted by Parliament upon a war with Spain, provide (1) that the money raised by it should be paid to treasurers appointed by Parliament, who should only pay it over on warrants from the Council of War; (2) that the money should be appropriated to certain specified purposes all directly or indirectly connected with the war which they hoped that James would declare upon Spain:—"The defence of this your realm of England; the securing of your kingdom of Ireland; the assistance of your neighbours the States of the United Provinces and others your Majesty's friends and allies; and for the setting forth of your royal navy"; (3) it was expressly declared that both the treasurers and the Council of War should be responsible to Parliament, which should have power to commit them prisoners to the

[1] ii. 611-58.   [2] 21 Jac. I, c. 33.

Tower of London in case of default; and (4) as a guarantee for their performance of the duties laid upon them, both the treasurers and the Council of War were to take oath faithfully to discharge their duties according to the tenor of the Act.

III

[See p. 60]

DARNEL'S CASE (1626)

Among the gentlemen committed to prison by the Privy Council for refusing the Forced Loan, were five men of ancient family and great influence in their counties—Sir Thomas Darnel, Sir John Corbet, Sir Walter Erle, Sir John Heveningham, and Sir Edmund Hampden. The offence for which they were committed was not known either to the common or to the statute law; and they therefore sued out a writ of *habeas corpus*,[1] requiring the Warden of the Fleet Prison to produce them before the judges of the Court of King's Bench, together with a return shewing the cause of their commitment, in order that the judges might decide whether they could or could not be bailed. The Warden of the Fleet made return that they were imprisoned *per speciale mandatum Domini Regis*;[2] and the question therefore arose whether this was in law a sufficient return to justify the judges in refusing to bail the prisoners. When the case was argued, counsel for the prisoners admitted—as indeed they were bound to do—that the Privy Council had the right to imprison; but they urged that the King in Council must, like any other magistrate, specify the cause of the commitment, in order that the judges might decide whether to bail or remand. (1) They argued that there were numerous precedents in which persons committed by the Council had afterwards been bailed by the judges. But "I conceive", said Serjeant Bramston "that our case will not stand upon precedents, but upon the fundamental laws and statutes of this realm, and though the precedents look the one way or the other, they are to be brought back unto the laws by which the kingdom is governed".[3] An appeal was therefore made (2) to the clause in Magna Charta which declared that "no man should be imprisoned except by the judgment of his peers or the law of the land". (3) Counsel also urged that if in the case of the King's prisoners cause need not be shewn, they would not be

---

[1] The writ could not yet be claimed as of right but only of grace. See a full discussion of the case in Relf, pp. 1–26.

[2] Gardiner, *Documents*, p. 57. Extracts from the *State Trials* are here printed (pp. 57–64).

[3] *State Trials*, iii. 10.

bailable by the judges, and their imprisonment might therefore be perpetual if the King so desired.

I beseech your Lordship to observe the consequence of this cause. If the law be that upon this return this gentleman should be remanded, I will not dispute whether or no a man may be imprisoned before he be convicted according to the law; but if this return shall be good, then his imprisonment shall not continue on for a time but for ever; and the subjects of this kingdom may be restrained of their liberties perpetually, and by law there can be no remedy for the subject, and therefore this return cannot stand with the laws of the realm or that of Magna Charta.... If your Lordship shall think this to be a sufficient cause, then it goeth to a perpetual imprisonment of the subject; for in all those causes which may concern the King's subjects and are applicable to all times and cases, we are not to reflect upon the present time and government, where justice and mercy floweth, but we are to look what may betide us in the time to come hereafter.[1]

It is easy for any reader of the report of the case to see that this last argument made a profound impression upon the judges, who were studiously fair and moderate throughout, and later on in the trial one of the judges specially directed the attention of the counsel for the Crown to this point. "Mr Attorney", he said, "if it be so that the law of Magna Charta and other statutes be now in force, and the gentlemen be not delivered by this Court, how shall they be delivered? Apply yourself to shew us any other way to deliver them".[2] "Yea", added another judge, "or else they shall have a perpetual imprisonment".[3]

But from a legal point of view the answer of the Crown was conclusive. (1) Heath, the Attorney-General, was able to shew that in all the precedents quoted by the other side of persons committed by the Council and afterwards bailed by the King's Bench, either the cause of imprisonment had been returned upon the writ or, if not, the Council had consented to the prisoners being bailed. (2) He was able to shew that the argument from Magna Charta proved too much, for if the clause about imprisonment prevented imprisonment by the Council it would prevent imprisonment before trial; and yet criminals were always being imprisoned before trial in virtue of precedents in the light of which the law was interpreted. Magna Charta forbade imprisonment before the verdict of a jury unless it was "by the law of the land", and imprisonment on a Council warrant had long been part of the "law of the land". The "due process of law" was not limited to the law-courts; it extended to commitments by the Privy Council on the one hand, just as it extended to commitments by the House of Commons on the other, and as long as the right was exercised in accordance with the precedents, no one could question its validity. (3) But the point on

<hr>

[1] *Ib.* iii. 8. [2] *Ib.* iii. 31. [3] *Ib.* iii. 32,

which Heath was strongest was the practical value of the right to imprison without shewing cause. It was the duty of the Council to track down and unravel conspiracies and assassination plots, and for such a purpose the power of imprisonment in secret and for an indefinite time was vital to the well-being of the State.

The King might be technically right, as he often was, for he had good legal advice at his command, but everybody knew that there was fiction and unreality at the heart of the argument. The power which the Tudors had used to unravel plots, was being employed by Charles I to punish men for refusing to contribute to the Forced Loan. The King claimed to possess the power for the benefit of a conspiracy-threatened commonwealth; it was being actually used by him to force men to pay taxes in an extra-Parliamentary way. Nevertheless, in these days of technical interpretations, the judges had no choice: they refused to consider general principles and based their judgments upon the law as interpreted by precedents. Chief Justice Hyde, in giving judgment for the Crown, referred with great respect to a resolution of the judges in the thirty-fourth year of Elizabeth's reign, by which they gave an authoritative opinion upon this very point, holding that the King's special command was such sufficient warrant for a commitment as to require no further cause to be expressed, and he then concluded his judgment in language that is not without a certain dignity:[1]

But the question now is, whether we may deliver this gentleman or not? You see what hath been the practice in all the kings' times heretofore, and your own records; and this resolution of all the judges teacheth us, and what can we do but walk in the steps of our forefathers? If you ask me which way you should be delivered, we shall tell you we must not counsel you. Mr Attorney hath told you that the King hath done it, and we trust him in great matters, and he is bound by law, and he bids us proceed by law—as we are sworn to do, and so is the King. And we make no doubt but the King, if you seek to him, he knowing the cause why you are imprisoned, he will have mercy; but we leave that. If in justice we ought to deliver you we would do it; but upon these grounds and these records and the precedents and resolutions we cannot deliver you, but you must be remanded. Now if I have mistaken anything, I desire to be righted by my brethren; I have endeavoured to give the resolutions of us all.[2]

[1] *State Trials*, iii. 59.
[2] The precise legal effect of the judgment is discussed in Relf, pp. 3–10.

IV

[*See* p. 77]

HAMPDEN'S CASE (1637)[1]

It may be said of the arguments in Hampden's case that their real interest is not so much legal as political; it lies less in the precedents quoted on either side than in the constitutional doctrine which lies behind them.

The most important of the speeches on behalf of Hampden was that of Oliver St John,[2] who is described by Clarendon[3] as "a man reserved, and of a dark and clouded countenance, very proud, and conversing with very few, and those men of his own humour and inclinations". This sombre and reticent lawyer anticipates a constitutional doctrine which is characteristically modern—the doctrine of the eighteenth century, that every official act of the Crown must be done in the way prescribed by law, and in no other way. He admits that defence against danger is the King's business, and of that danger the King is the sole judge. He goes even further, and abandons the distinction which he might have maintained between maritime towns and inland places. But granting all this, he argues that there are certain fixed or known ways in which the King is to proceed. Such rules or known methods, he says, govern all the actions of the King.

His Majesty is the fountain of justice; and though all justice which is done within the realm flows from this fountain, yet it must run in certain and known channels.... The justice whereby all felons and traitors are put to death proceeds from his Majesty, but if a writ of execution of a traitor or a felon be awarded by his Majesty without appeal or indictment preceding, an appeal of death will lie by the heir against the executioner.[4]

In the same way, although it is true that the King has power to provide for the defence of the realm, he can only do so in certain regular ways—as for instance by enforcing the obligations under which holders by military tenure enjoyed their lands. But suppose all these regular ways should prove insufficient! Then the law provides "other ways for a new supply": and these "other ways" are aids and subsidies granted in Parliament. And that Parliament is the proper source of extraordinary supplies appears from the actions of former kings, who frequently obtained supplies for the defence of the realm—not by writ, but by parliamentary grant. It

---

[1] Extracts from the speeches are printed in Gardiner, *Documents*, pp. 108–24
[2] The whole of St John's speech is printed in Rushworth, ii. 481–544.
[3] i. 246.   [4] Gardiner, *Documents*, p. 111.

would be inconceivable that if they could have legally obtained supplies by writ outside Parliament they should have taken the trouble to go to Parliament for them. "It is rare in a subject—and more in a Prince—to ask and take that of gift which he may and ought to have of right."[1] Why should kings have obtained loans and benevolences, and anticipated the rents of Crown lands for war expenses, if all the time they had possessed the legal right of levying ship-money to any amount? For

if his Majesty, as in the writ, may without Parliament lay twenty shillings upon the plaintiff's goods, I shall humbly submit it why by the same reason of law it might not have been £20, and so *in infinitum*; whereby it could come to pass that if the subject hath anything at all left him, he is not beholding to the law for it, but it is left entirely to the goodness and mercy of the King.[2]

The most important speech for the Crown was that of the Attorney-General, Sir John Bankes.[3] He collected a large number of precedents to prove that the Crown had levied aids for the defence of the realm without consent of Parliament, although he was unable to shew anything quite like ship-money in its present form—a regular contribution, demanded from year to year. He also made a good technical point by saying that if the other side admitted the King to be sole judge of the danger, then the Court had no right to enquire in what circumstances his discretion had been exercised. They must be content to know that the King had decided that the realm was in danger, and that a decree had gone forth from Caesar Augustus that all England should be taxed. But, like St John, Bankes had his constitutional doctrine, rising above precedents and mere technicalities—and this is the doctrine of "absolute power". The power to compel his subjects to set forth ships and men is "innate in the person of an absolute King, and in the persons of the Kings of England". This power "is not any ways derived from the people, but reserved unto the King when positive laws first began".[4] "Supreme jurisdiction, both by sea and land, was never yet impeached, and from him lieth no appeal."[5] And from this position Bankes drew that portentous inference of his age which always reduced the constitutional party to despair—that the rights of Parliament and the liberties of the subject are derived from the Crown only as matters of grace and favour. It was argued by a whole school of thinkers that sovereignty is at once indivisible and inalienable, and therefore that the sovereign power which grants a right or a privilege may at any time reclaim it. To these thinkers "it seemed natural to assert that because King John granted Magna Charta, all the powers resigned by him still inhere in the King and

[1] Gardiner, *Documents*, p. 114. [2] Rushworth, ii. 508.
[3] Printed in *ib.* ii. 544–90. [4] *Ib.* ii. 546.
[5] *Ib.* ii. 589.

may be recalled".[1] But Bankes's final appeal to the ultimate necessity of monarchy is not without dignity and eloquence.

My lords, if there were no law to compel this duty, yet nature and the inviolate law of preservation ought to move us. These vapours which are exhaled from us will again descend upon us in our safety and in the honour of our nation. And therefore let us obey the King's command by his writ, and not dispute. He is the first mover among these orbs of ours; and he is the circle of this circumference; and he is the centre of us all, wherein we all, as the lines, should meet; he is the soul of this body, whose proper act is to command.[2]

In placing their respective constitutional doctrines before the Court, both St John and Bankes were confronted by the same difficulty. The judges of the seventeenth century had been trained in a narrow school and were prejudiced in favour of technical interpretations. Thus the political arguments of counsel appear smothered in a mass of technicalities, and it is this that makes their speeches such dull reading. But Hallam, and the constitutional writers generally, very much overstate what they call the "servility" of the judges. It is true that the independence of the Bench had been grievously shaken by the dismissal of Chief Justice Coke in 1616, and even as lately as 1634 the judges had been reminded that they held office during the King's pleasure only, by the sudden dismissal of Sir Robert Heath, Chief Justice of the Common Pleas— once the counsel for the Crown in Darnel's case—"no cause being then nor at any time since shewed for his removal". But they were still trained lawyers of high standing; although their habit of mind, engendered by the legal training of that day, led them to attach great weight to technicalities. These were supplied in abundance. There was in this case something like an antiquarian revival upon both sides. Prodigious industry was displayed in collecting precedents, and even the extension of ship-money to inland places was not without legal support. So recent an investigator as Thorold Rogers[3] finds that in 1296 the estates of Merton College, Oxford, as far inland as Basingstoke, paid 6s. *pro warda maris*; and in 1338 Leatherhead paid 2s. for the ward of the sea at Shoreham. It was, perhaps, such precedents as these which Noy discovered and relied upon, when he searched the records in the Tower.

Of the five judges in favour of Hampden, two gave judgment upon merely technical grounds; and the other three are fairly represented by Sir George Crooke,[4] whom tradition depicts as having hesitated what to say, but to have been persuaded to speak out his real mind by his wife. This story must not be too eagerly accepted,

[1] Figgis, p. 248.   [2] Rushworth, ii. 590.
[3] *Agriculture and Prices*, v. 157. Rogers says that these entries "seem very like ship-money"; but they might conceivably refer to the maintenance of sea walls.
[4] *State Trials*, iii. 1127–81.

as it is in a manner common form, and begins with the dream of Pilate's wife. Crooke accepts in its main features the remarkably modern doctrine which St John had laid down, and in his judgment he makes three main points: (1) that the King cannot in an ordinary way tax the subject, save in Parliament. "The common law of England", he says, in words as clear and emphatic as any used by the constitutionalists at any time during this great controversy, "setteth a freedom in the subjects in respect of their persons and giveth them a true property in their goods and estates; so that without their consent, or implicitly by an ordinance which they consented unto by a common assent in Parliament, it cannot be taken from them nor their estates charged".[1] (2) That it is difficult to imagine a case in which the defence of the realm on an emergency could not be provided for in Parliament as expeditiously as by writ. (3) That there is no such thing as absolute power.

Whereas it hath been much urged and argued by Mr Solicitor and Mr Attorney that this writ is warranted by the King's prerogative and power-royal to send forth such writs for defence and safety of the kingdom in time of danger, to this I answer, That I do not conceive there is any such prerogative.[2]

It is true that Crooke is obliged to qualify this bold statement to meet the case of a real emergency arising in a way that could not be foreseen. "Royal power", he says, "...is to be used in cases of necessity and imminent danger, when ordinary courses will not avail,...as in cases of rebellion, sudden invasion, and some other cases where martial law may be used, and may not stay for legal proceedings".[3] But in such a case he seems to foreshadow another modern constitutional device: he appears to contemplate indemnity by statute, after the danger has passed away.

Just as Crooke accepts St John's constitutional doctrine, so the majority judgments accept, elaborate, and improve upon Bankes's doctrine of absolute power. In answer to the contention of Hampden's counsel that the King was bound by the "fundamental laws", Berkeley hit upon a phrase that has become famous. "The law", he said, "knows no such King-yoking policy".[4] But Finch in his judgment went much further than Berkeley. The law had laid upon the King the duty of defending the realm, and it therefore of necessity gave him the right of laying such charges upon the people as would enable him to fulfil the duties imposed upon him.

Sea and land make but one kingdom, and the King is *sponsus regni*.... The soil and the sea belong to the King, who is lord and sole proprietor of them, ...and without a navy this authority can do but little good. The King holds

---

[1] *State Trials*, iii. 1147.   [2] *Ib.* iii. 1161.   [3] *Ib.* iii. 1162.
[4] Gardiner, *Documents*, p. 121. Extracts from Berkeley's argument are here printed (pp. 115–24).

this diadem of God only: all others hold their lands of him, and he of none but God: but this is but to light a candle for others. From hence only I will observe that none other can share with him in his absolute power. A Parliament is an honourable Court; and I confess it an excellent means of charging the subject and defending the kingdom; but yet it is not the only means.[1] . . . Acts of Parliament may take away flowers and ornaments of the Crown, but not the Crown itself; they cannot bar a succession. . . . No Act of Parliament can bar a king of his regality, as that no lands should hold of him; or bar him of the allegiance of his subjects; or the relative on his part—as trust and power to defend his people. Therefore Acts of Parliament to take away his royal power in the defence of his kingdom are void. . . . They are void Acts of Parliament to bind the King not to command the subjects, their persons and goods, and I say their money too, for no Acts of Parliament make any difference.[2]

Thus, he concludes,

I conceive by the common law and the fundamental policy of the kingdom, that the King may charge his subjects for the defence of the kingdom, and that the King may charge his subjects towards the defence thereof when it is in danger; and I hold that the King is sole judge of the danger, and ought to direct the means of defence.[3]

Here, at any rate, was plain speaking. "Undoubtedly", wrote Clarendon long afterwards,[4] "my Lord Finch's speech in the Exchequer Chamber made ship-money much more abhorred and formidable than all the commitments by the Council Table and all the distresses taken by the sheriffs in England".

In earlier cases absolute power had come in as a subsidiary argument; in the case of ship-money it has grown to be the essential ground of the decision. The authority of the Crown and the authority of Parliament here come into collision over a fundamental issue, and the constitutional doctrine of the eighteenth century, appearing before its time, crosses swords with the doctrine of the Tudors, now somewhat belated and out of date.

V

[See p. 95]

THE TRIAL OF THE EARL OF STRAFFORD (1640)

The side on which Strafford was most vulnerable to attack, was his Irish administration. In some ways this was statesmanlike and efficient; even at the worst it may be said that Strafford

---

[1] *State Trials*, iii. 1225–6. [2] *Ib*. iii. 1235. [3] *Ib*. iii. 1243. [4] i. 89.

understood Ireland better than Pym, who could only prescribe parliaments and trial by jury.

In Ireland...there was indeed some use for the policy of "Thorough". A state of society so backward and so distracted could be best ruled as India was afterwards ruled by its English governors. Wentworth cleared his way through the opposition of self-seeking officials such as Mountnorris and Loftus, crushing them by methods akin to those used by Hastings against Nuncomar and Francis.[1]

He saw that the country was poor, that it was disorderly, and that it was Papist—and for each of these ills he had a remedy. (1) He met the poverty of Ireland by encouraging industry, and in particular by introducing the cultivation of flax. (2) He dealt with disorder by the method which the Tudors had found effective a century before, and set up in Dublin a Castle Chamber "to bridle stout noblemen and gentlemen"; but he supported this by the method which Cromwell was to find efficacious in dealing with rebellion a generation later—the maintenance of a well-paid, well-organised, and well-disciplined force. (3) He recognised the profound importance of the religious question in Ireland, in its bearing upon the difficulties of Irish government. "I plainly see", he said,[2] "that so long as this kingdom continues Popish, they are not a people for the Crown of England to be confident of"; and in an age when the reconciliation of a whole people to the Reformation did not seem as impossible as it does now, he adopted the measure that came most naturally to the statesmen of the day, and refurbished the official machinery of conversion—that corrupt and dilapidated organisation, the Irish Protestant Church.[3] In addition to these measures, and with the same end in view, he sought with his projected Plantation of Connaught to utilise the experience already gained in the Plantation of Ulster by James I.

Thus in Ireland Strafford set before himself great public objects, in striking contrast to the ordinary Irish politician, who was intent upon private gain. But in the achievement of his ends he had impatiently brushed aside legality, and the record of his administration teemed with acts of arbitrary power. It was easy for a parliamentary committee intent upon an impeachment to find material out of which to construct and to support the first count in the indictment—that Strafford had "traitorously endeavoured to subvert

---

[1] Trevelyan, *Stuarts*, p. 188.   [2] Quoted in *D.N.B.* lx. 274.

[3] "This poor Church, which hath thus long laid in the silent dark", "many ways distempered" (Wentworth to Laud, January 30, 1634; *Letters and Dispatches*, i. 187). The letter refers to the "unlearned clergy", non-residency, the ruinous state of the churches and parsonage houses, and "the rites and ceremonies of the Church run over without all decency of habit, order, or gravity",—"the Popish titulars exercising the whilst a foreign jurisdiction much greater" than that of the Irish bishops.

the fundamental laws and government of the realms of England and Ireland, and instead thereof to introduce an arbitrary and tyrannical government against law".[1]

Nor was it in Ireland only that material for the impeachment could be found. In England also Strafford was regarded as a personification of tyranny, an instigator of the methods of arbitrary government; and by taking advantage of his unfortunate phrase in Council, "You have an army in Ireland you may employ here to reduce this kingdom", Pym was able to introduce into the impeachment a suggestion almost as shocking as a charge of parricide—that Strafford had advocated the use of a Papist army to enforce arbitrary government in England itself. In Scotland also the man was execrated who had urged upon the King a vigorous prosecution of the war; and thus, as an historian of the time remarks, "Three whole kingdoms were his accusers, and eagerly sought in one death a recompense of all their sufferings".[2]

Part of the legal interest of Strafford's trial lies in the failure of the managers of the impeachment to shew that he was guilty of treason as treason was at that time understood. An attempt was made to establish a doctrine of cumulative treason, but as Strafford himself urged in his defence, "When a thousand misdemeanours will not make one felony, shall twenty-eight misdemeanours heighten it to a treason"?[3] The only speaker who handled cumulative treason in a manner that was in the least degree convincing was the able lawyer Glynne, who argued that a series of acts innocent in themselves might, when taken together, prove the existence of a treasonable design.

The greatest traitor in the memory of any that sits here to hear me this day had a better, a fairer excuse in this particular than my Lord of Strafford, and that is Guido Faux; for he might have objected that the taking of the cellar, the laying of the powder under the Parliament House, the kindling of the match and putting it near, are not so much as a misdemeanour, if you look no further; for it was no offence in him to lay barrels under the Parliament House, and to kindle the match, and to lay it near; but collect all together, that it was *ea intentione*, to blow up the King and the State— there is the treason,...so that the rule is the same.[4]

But Glynne's analogy was really too far-fetched, and the doctrine of cumulative treason did not long survive the criticism brought to bear upon it.

Again, in order to meet Strafford's contention that he had neither compassed the King's death, nor levied war against the King, nor committed any act which by any conceivable interpretation could be brought under the Statute of Edward III, it was

---

[1] Rushworth, *Tryal*, p. 8.   [2] May, i. 88.
[3] Rushworth, *Tryal*, p. 145. There were 28 articles in the impeachment.
[4] *Ib.* p. 708.

necessary for the managers of the impeachment to invent and set forth a wider conception of treason which was, to say the least of it, entirely novel. Pym argued that the worst traitor was not he who attacked the Sovereign's person or government, but he who attacked the Sovereign in his political capacity, and by undermining the laws which constituted his greatness, exposed him to disaster and ruin.[1] The chief objection to this view of treason was its want of definiteness. "Undermining the laws" was a charge which might be made to cover anything, from raising troops to attack Parliament, down to opposition to any measure which Parliament wanted to pass. If this conception of treason were allowed to take root, "the time might soon arrive", as Gardiner points out,[2] "when treason would be as light a word in the mouth of a member of Parliament as damnation had been in the mouth of a medieval ecclesiastic".

Although it was impossible to convict Strafford of legal treason, it was also impossible for the leaders of the Commons to let him go free, for he was not only the personification of absolutism in the past, but they deemed him dangerous to liberty in the present. They could never free themselves from the fear of military violence; and the Irish army was still at the orders of the man who had created it and possessed the authority to use it. His condemnation therefore appeared to them a matter of supreme necessity, and when the impeachment seemed certain to fail, the Bill of Attainder was brought in. It is possible that even now Charles might have saved his minister if he had thrown the sword aside, reduced the Irish army, and disbanded the army in the north; but he listened to the advice of his energetic, daring, and dangerous Queen, and embarked on a series of infatuated schemes, all of which involved the threat or the use of force. He sent money to the northern army and talked of taking the command in person; he planned to seize the Tower, to bring over the Irish army, to move the army of the north upon London, and to order the dissolution of the Long Parliament. The air of London grew thick with plots, and in the alarmed and sensitive state of the public mind the attainder made rapid progress. When it had been first introduced it was found that the Earl had many friends; the first resolution—that he had "endeavoured to subvert the fundamental laws"—was only carried in the teeth of vigorous opposition; and even in the debates on the attainder they did not all desert him. The poet Waller wanted to know what were the "fundamental laws", and the majority were put to it to find an answer. At last someone said that if Waller did not know, he had no business to sit in the House;[3] and by this no one was much enlightened. But as the situation developed under the King's hands, even Strafford's friends began to desert him.

---

[1] Gardiner, ix. 306.   [2] ix. 306–7.   [3] Gardiner, ix. 336.

"Truly, Sir,...", said the Royalist Lord Digby,[1] "...I confidently believe him to be the most dangerous minister, the most insupportable to free subjects, that can be charactered. I believe his practices in themselves have been as high, as tyrannical, as any subject ever ventured on; and the malignity of them are hugely aggravated by those rare abilities of his, whereof God hath given him the use but the Devil the application. In a word, I believe him still that grand apostate to the commonwealth, who must not expect to be pardoned in this world till he be dispatched to the other".

It is true that Digby added: "And yet let me tell you, Mr Speaker, my hand must not be to that dispatch", but there were others who would not be so scrupulous. The grim phrase let fall by Essex, "Stone dead hath no fellow",[2] was echoed by others. In the end the Attainder Bill passed the Lords, and with the City mob howling round the gates of Whitehall, and threatening the safety of the Queen and her children, Charles also surrendered, and gave the Bill the royal assent. When the news came that the King had deserted him, Strafford's only comment was, "Put not your trust in princes", and he set about preparing for death. One of the older historians[3] recognises the tragedy of his end when he writes, "And so fell this noble Earl, who if his master could have saved him might have been able to save his master. This was indeed the blow that by degrees reached up to the King's own head".

In condemning Strafford by attainder after a fair and open trial by impeachment had failed to secure the desired condemnation, the Long Parliament was turning against him that emergency power on which he had drawn so largely for a justification of the system of "Thorough". It was the Long Parliament which was now "loose and absolved from all rules of government". This being so, it is of peculiar interest to find that Pym's speeches against Strafford constitute throughout an eloquent vindication of the reign of law as the necessary condition for the maintenance of liberty. Let the people, Strafford had once said,[4] "attend upon the King's will, with confidence in his justice, belief in his wisdom, and assurance in his parental affections", instead of feeding themselves with "the vain flatteries of imaginary liberty". Contrast with this the line of parliamentary thought as indicated by Pym at the trial.

Good laws—nay, the best laws—are no advantage when will is set above law.[5]...The law is that which puts a difference betwixt good and evil, betwixt just and unjust. If you take away the law, all things will fall into a confusion. Every man will become a law to himself, which, in the depraved condition of human nature, must needs produce great enormities. Lust will become a law, and envy will become a law, covetousness and ambition will

[1] Rushworth, *Tryal*, p. 50.   [2] Clarendon, i. 320.
[3] Kennett; quoted in *State Trials*, iii. 1524 *n*.
[4] Quoted in Firth, *Cromwell*, p. 23.
[5] Rushworth, *Tryal*, p. 104.

become laws; and what dictates, what decisions such laws will produce, may easily be discerned in the late government of Ireland.[1]

To substitute arbitrary power for law was not hurtful to subjects only.

This arbitrary power is dangerous to the King's person, and dangerous to his crown.... If the histories of those Eastern countries be perused where princes order their affairs according to the mischievous principles of the Earl of Strafford,...they will be found to be frequent in combustions, full of massacres, and of the tragical ends of princes.[2]

"To alter the settled frame and constitution of government", he said in another place, "is treason in any State. The laws whereby all other parts of a kingdom are preserved would be very vain and defective, if they had not a power to secure and preserve themselves".[3] Finally, in his defence of liberty Pym rises to extraordinary heights of solemn eloquence.

"Such arbitrary courses", he says, "have an ill operation upon the courage of a nation, by embasing the hearts of the people.... Those that live so much under the whip, and the pillory, and such servile engines as were frequently used by the Earl of Strafford, they may have the dregs of valour;... but those noble and gallant affections which put men to brave designs, and attempts for the preservation and enlargement of a kingdom, they are hardly capable of. Shall it be treason to embase the King's coin, though but a piece of twelvepence or sixpence—and must it not needs be the effect of a greater treason to embase the spirits of his subjects, and to set a stamp and character of servitude upon them, whereby they shall be disabled to do anything for the service of the King and commonwealth?".[4]

Here Pym seems to recognise the psychological value of liberty which Seeley,[5] in his desire for the scientific definition of imponderables, so strangely ignores.

VI

[See p. 175]

OLIVER CROMWELL

The Admission Register of Sidney Sussex College, Cambridge, records Oliver Cromwell's admission in 1616 to the College as a Fellow-Commoner in the usual Latin form;[6] but between this and the next entry there has been inserted a Latin note[7] which has been translated thus:

[1] Rushworth, *Tryal*, p. 662. [2] *Ib.* p. 663. [3] *Ib.* p. 669. [4] *Ib.* p. 665.
[5] In his *Introduction to Political Science*, Lecture V.
[6] "Oliverus Cromwell Huntindoniensis, admissus ad commeatum sociorum Aprilis vicesimo tertio, tutore Magistro Richardo Howlet."
[7] "Hic fuit grandis ille impostor, carnifex perditissimus, qui, pientissimo rege Carolo primo nefaria caede sublato, ipsum usurpavit thronum, et tria regna per quinque ferme annorum spatium sub Protectoris nomine indomita tyrannide vexavit."

This was that arch-hypocrite, that most abandoned murderer, who having by shameful slaughter put out of the way the most pious King, Charles the First, grasped the very throne, and for the space of nearly five years under the title of Protector harassed three kingdoms with inflexible tyranny.

Here we have what Cromwell originally was, side by side with one view of what he afterwards became; and the gulf between the student at Cambridge and the man who held the destinies of England in the hollow of his hand is a wide one for the historian to bridge. We admit Cromwell's greatness, but the question has still to be asked and answered, Why did he become so great?

That Cromwell was a man of a very high order of ability goes without saying. It is true that he came very slowly to the front. Clarendon said of him that his powers seemed to increase with the demands of his high position, "as if he had concealed faculties until he had occasion to use them".[1] With parliamentary experience he came to be an influential speaker—not so much because he was eloquent as because he was in earnest.

"When he delivered his mind in the House", says a contemporary, "it was with a strong and masculine excellence, more able to persuade than to be persuaded. His expressions were hardy, opinions resolute, asseverations grave and vehement.... He expressed himself with some kind of passion, but with such a commanding, wise deportment till, at his pleasure, he governed and swayed the House, as he had most times the leading voice".[2]

But Cromwell was not only an able man: he was also peculiarly representative in the tone and temper of his mind of the characteristically English way of thinking and feeling about public affairs. His strong conservative instinct was associated with a singular sanity and soberness of judgment. In an age of visionaries Cromwell refused to dream dreams, and when other men were reaching after the impracticable, he always kept a firm hold upon the solid facts of life. Yet with all this sobriety, he was capable of an extraordinary breadth of view, and often delivered himself of a very wise philosophy.[3]

[1] vi. 92.
[2] Quoted in Morley, p. 75.
[3] *E.g.* his observations upon the *Agreement of the People* on October 28, 1647: "Therefore although the pretensions in it and the expressions in it are very plausible, and if we could leap out of one condition into another that had so specious things in it as this hath, I suppose there would not be much dispute, though perhaps some of these things may be very well disputed. How do we know if, whilst we are disputing these things, another company of men shall gather together, and they shall put out a paper as plausible perhaps as this? And if so, what do you think the consequence of that would be? Would it not be utter confusion?...But truly I think we are not only to consider what the consequences are (if there were nothing else but this paper), but we are to consider the probability of the ways and means to accomplish: that is to say, to consider if, according to reason and judgment, the spirits and temper of the people of this nation are prepared to receive and to go on along with it..." (*Letters and Speeches*, iii. 350).

It should be observed also that Cromwell's religious faith gave to all his actions some of the precision and confidence which William III drew from predestination and Napoleon from his trust in the star of Destiny. First and foremost he relied upon his own inward conviction of where the right course lay. "The true knowledge", he said, "is not literal or speculative; but inward, and transforming the mind to it".[1] But to the inward conviction he added the outward sign—the purpose of God made manifest in events. There was no such thing as chance or fate in Cromwell's scheme of life: of fate he says himself, "that were too paganish a word".[2] Things happened because God willed them, and thus all happenings were full of meaning. As the medieval astrologers read the stars, so Cromwell read events, and sought to wrest from them the message of Heaven.

"Victory or defeat", says one of his biographers,[3] "was not an accident; it was the working of 'the Providence of God in that which is falsely called the chance of war'. Therefore each successive triumph of his cause was a fresh proof of its righteousness. His victories in Ireland became a justification of the Republic. 'These', he told the Speaker, 'are the seals of God's approbation of your great change of government'".

There was something fatalistic about this view of life, but it gave him a confidence in himself and his cause which nothing else could have given.

But in order to answer the question with which we started, other factors must be taken into account besides those concerned with character. The greatest fact of the Civil Wars was the creation of the New Model; and it was Cromwell's connexion with the army which made him historically great. And it is not difficult to see how this connexion came about. Cromwell was born to greatness in this sense—that he was a born soldier, just at the time when a born soldier was bound to become great. Essex, though slow, was a general of solid power; Fairfax was a soldier of considerable reputation; Waller was in some respects a remarkable strategist—but Cromwell towered above them all. In the earlier part of his career he was one of the best cavalry leaders known to history, and to say that is to say a great deal.

"Infinite great", says one of Cromwell's contemporaries,[4] "are the considerations which dependeth on a man to teach and govern a troop of horse. To bring ignorant men and more ignorant horse, wild man and mad horse, to those rules of obedience which may crown every motion and action with comely, orderly, and profitable proceedings—*hic labor, hoc opus est*".

And not only was Cromwell great in war as a scientific soldier—if we may use so modern an expression with regard to that age—but he possessed precisely that vigour and energy which mark the leader

[1] Quoted in Trevelyan, *Stuarts*, p. 62.   [2] *Letters and Speeches*, ii. 424.
[3] Firth, *Cromwell*, p. 252.   [4] Quoted in Morley, p. 118.

of men. "He was of a sanguine complexion", says Baxter,[1] "naturally of such a vivacity, hilarity, and alacrity, as another man hath when he hath drunken a cup too much". Carlyle, paraphrasing Charles Harvey, puts the same point more poetically: "He was a strong man in the dark perils of war: in the high places of the field hope shone in him like a pillar of fire when it had gone out in all the others".[2] In the turmoil of the Great Rebellion such a leader of men was bound to come to the front, and when the country gentleman of Huntingdonshire was once at the head of a troop of horse, his supreme military qualities were sure in the long run to give him the chief command. And to crown all, Heaven itself set its seal upon him by giving him a succession of great victories in the field. Milton in his famous sonnet speaks of Cromwell as one

> Who through a cloud
> Not of war only, but detractions rude,
> Guided by faith and matchless fortitude,
> To peace and truth thy glorious way hast ploughed.

But we should be inclined to say rather that it was by means of war, and not in spite of it, that Cromwell became great.

But the fact that Cromwell was a great soldier just at the time when a great standing army was coming into existence, does not explain all his greatness. Not only was the army a military organisation, it was also an association of sects. And by some strange coincidence, the born soldier was also "the darling of the sectaries", for he had intervened at a crisis in their history to save them from Presbyterian persecution. Thus he had made himself in a special sense their champion, and to support Cromwell meant to make sure of Toleration.

Dryden, writing on the death of Cromwell, concludes his poem thus:

> His ashes in a peaceful urn shall rest,
> His name a great example stand, to shew
> How strangely high endeavours may be blessed
> Where piety and valour jointly go.

It is precisely this combination of piety and valour—though in a sense somewhat different to Dryden's—that is the secret of Cromwell's greatness. His piety, and his device of Toleration, made him the idol of the sects; his valour, and his five great battles, made him the idol of the army. But just at this time it so happened that the sects were the army; it was therefore natural that the highest civil office should fall to the Lord General when the army was holding supreme power.

---

[1] *Reliquiae Baxterianae*, i. 57. The sentence might, however, be read as applying to Harrison. It has been taken both ways.

[2] *Letters and Speeches*, ii. 91.

Andrew Marvell, in the same poem[1] in which he touches so delicately upon the tragic scene of the King's execution, also does full justice to the great usurper.

> And if we would speak true,
> Much to the man is due,
>
> Who from his private gardens, where
> He lived reservèd and austere,
> (As if his highest plot
> To plant the bergamot;)
>
> Could by industrious valour climb
> To ruin the great work of Time,
> And cast the kingdoms old
> Into another mould;
>
> Though Justice against Fate complain,
> And plead the ancient rights in vain;
> (But those do hold or break,
> As men are strong or weak).
>
> Nature, that hateth emptiness,
> Admits of penetration less,
> And therefore must make room
> Where greater spirits come.

But Marvell clearly understood where the true foundations of Cromwell's power lay, for he concludes his poem thus:

> But thou, the war's and fortune's son,
> March indefatigably on;
> And for the last effect,
> Still keep the sword erect;
>
> Besides the force it has to fright
> The spirits of the shady night,
> The same arts that did gain
> A power, must it maintain.

VII

[See p. 246]

THE FIRST EARL OF SHAFTESBURY

With the exception of Cromwell, Shaftesbury is perhaps the most interesting figure of the seventeenth century; but the contrast between them is striking. Cromwell was robust, both in physique and character; Shaftesbury was a puny, attenuated politician who belongs to the class of acute party managers. Cromwell

---

[1] *An Horatian Ode upon Cromwell's Return from Ireland.*

was a man of prayer; Shaftesbury was described by his contemporaries as a Deist,[1] and as such he would have been far more at home with the statesmen of the eighteenth century than among the crusaders of the Civil War.

> For close designs, and crooked counsels fit;
> Sagacious, bold, and turbulent of wit,
> Restless, unfixed in principles and place,
> In power unpleased, impatient of disgrace;
> A fiery soul, which, working out its way,
> Fretted the pigmy body to decay,
> And o'erinformed the tenement of clay.[2]

Three points in particular concerning Shaftesbury should be considered. (1) His political experience was unique, and in his own person he connects in the most remarkable manner the pre-Restoration and post-Revolution periods. No other man shared to the same extent in what Ranke calls the "great agonies of the seventeenth century". He was educated in one revolution, presided over a second, and was connected through his ideas and his friends with a third. He began his political life in the Short Parliament at the age of eighteen; and so he could say of the opening of his career, as his friend Locke did of his own birth: "I no sooner perceived myself in the world but I found myself in a storm". He moved among the men who fought the question of ship-money and took arms against the King; outlived these and co-operated with Cromwell; worked with Monk to bring about the Restoration; and even then found himself still young—one of the group of younger politicians who opposed the antiquated Clarendon in the Pension Parliament. And when Clarendon died, Shaftesbury had outlived the only English statesman whose experience was as varied as his own.

(2) Shaftesbury borrowed all his most important political ideas from the period of Cromwell, and applied to the politics of the Restoration what he had learned during his impressionable years. And here, as in most other things, he stands out in contrast to Clarendon. Clarendon stands for steadiness, stability, the restoration of the old order, hostility to new ideas—but Clarendon was old enough to be no longer impressionable when the Civil War broke out. Shaftesbury, on the other hand, had been educated in a period which had seen the collapse of all fixed principles and traditional ways of thinking, and the striking out of new lines in every direction to meet the new conditions which revolution established. Thus we

---

[1] "As to religion, he was a Deist, and seemed to believe nothing of Christianity but only that it contained good morals.... He had odd notions of a future state, and thought that our souls went into stars and animated them" (Burnet's MS.; printed in Ranke, vi. 85).

[2] Dryden, *Absalom and Achitophel.*

find Shaftesbury eagerly taking up the idea of Toleration, and becoming the Cromwell of the discredited sects. He realised, as those who had not seen the Cromwellian system at work could scarcely do, the possibilities of Dissent as a political force; and he endeavoured to exploit this force to give himself a supreme position. And after all, he only just failed to carry the Exclusion Bill; and when he failed it was the sects with whom he took refuge. In his exile at Amsterdam he associated chiefly with the Dutch Brownists, and it was in the house of one of them that he died.[1] Another idea which Shaftesbury borrowed from the period of revolution was the immense political importance of the City of London. He had seen the riots and demonstrations against Strafford and the bishops; he had seen the duel between the City and Cromwell's army—the only antagonist that was able to overcome it; and he had seen the precise method of the Restoration largely influenced by the views and actions of the City. Thus his earlier experience had led him to think of the City as a great reservoir of political force, which, if well-directed, could be used with overwhelming effect. A Presbyterian himself by tradition, he cultivated the City in every possible way—going to live in Aldersgate Street and becoming a member of one of the City guilds. In 1680 he sent the Lord Mayor and sheriffs in deputation to the King to make representations on behalf of the Exclusion Bill, and when the King triumphed, his life was saved by the fact that the sheriffs of London were among his supporters. They picked out a grand jury "from the very centre of the party",[2] and when they ignored the bill of indictment, "at night were ringing of bells, and bonfires in several parts of the City".[3]

(3) If Shaftesbury borrowed his main ideas from the past—from Cromwell and the Rebellion—he was also connected in a remarkable manner with the future—with the Revolution and the eighteenth century. One of the ideas of the future at the Restoration was the development of trade and plantations. Charles II himself, who was quite as sensitive as Shaftesbury to his social and political environment, had written to his sister in 1668, "The thing which is nearest the heart of the nation is trade and all that belongs to it";[4] and Colbert de Croissy wrote to Louis XIV, "Commerce is the idol of Great Britain's worship".[5] Here also Shaftesbury faithfully reflected the trend of his time, and with him the newer interest of trade replaced the older and more absorbing interest of religion. He was on the Council of Trade and Plantations; he was financially interested in the Bahamas; and he took a leading part in the plantation of Carolina, bringing his two ideas of Toleration and Trade together there when in 1669 he invited the philosopher Locke to draw up a constitution

---

[1] Christie, ii. 456.   [2] North, *Examen*, p. 110.
[3] Luttrell, i. 146; see also Christie, ii. 427.
[4] Julia Cartwright, *Madame* (edition of 1894), p. 272.   [5] *Ib.* p. 332.

for the colony in which religious toleration should be guaranteed.[1]
The Revolution of 1688 itself was in a sense the realisation of
Shaftesbury's schemes, for the expulsion of James II was the belated
triumph of the principle of Exclusion, and the Toleration Act of
William III did for Dissenters very much what Shaftesbury had
approved in the Declaration of Indulgence. Ranke regards him as
the principal founder of the Whig party of the eighteenth century,[2]
and as the statesman who first controlled a party in the Commons
from a seat in the Lords he certainly laid the foundation of that
alliance between the peers and the people which is characteristic of
the Georgian Whigs. If we leave out Pym as belonging to the
antediluvian days when there were no fixed parliamentary parties,
Shaftesbury is the first great party leader of modern politics. He is
also the first party-organiser and wire-puller, the modern demagogue,
and the modern parliamentary debater. North calls him the great
"prompter-general" of political clubs. Thus Shaftesbury belonged,
as it were, to two generations at once—to the generation of Pym
and Hampden, and to the generation of the Revolution of 1688.
And even after the dissolution of the Oxford Parliament, things
might have been different if Shaftesbury had not died. What might
not Absalom have accomplished if Achitophel had lived! But
Absalom was deprived of that counsel which was "as if a man had
enquired at the oracle of God", and he staked and lost everything
on the field of Sedgemoor.

VIII

[See p. 253]

GODDEN v. HALES (1686)

The defendant, Sir Edward Hales, holding a military office
under the Crown, had neglected to take the oaths of allegiance
and supremacy and to receive the sacrament according to the
rites of the Church of England, as required by the Test Act.
For this he was indicted at the Rochester Assizes in March,
1686, and convicted; and the informer Godden—his own coach-
man acting in collusion—thereupon sued him in the Court of
King's Bench for the £500 to which the informer was entitled under
the Act. In his defence Hales produced letters patent under the

---

[1] W. D. Christie, *Life of Shaftesbury*, i. 288. The constitution is printed in
Locke, *Works* (10th edition, 1801), x. 175–99. It permits "any seven or more
persons agreeing in any religion" to constitute a recognised Church. See also
Shaftesbury's memorial to Charles II, probably written in 1669, in which he
recommends the toleration of Dissent in the interests of trade (printed in *ib.* ii.
Appendix 1).

[2] iv. 167.

Great Seal by which the King, in virtue of his dispensing power, relieved him of the penalties which he had incurred by omitting to take the Test; and the question for the Court to decide was, whether this defence was good in law.

The limits of the dispensing power had already been laid down after a fashion by Chief Justice Vaughan in 1674 in the case of *Thomas* v. *Sorrell.* The old rule of law had been that the King might dispense with *malum prohibitum* but not with *malum in se*— that is to say, he might dispense with penalties for an offence created only by statute, but not for an offence at common law. This rule Vaughan rightly rejected as confusing, because, on the one hand, everything *malum in se* was also in a sense *malum prohibitum* and, on the other, it was not the case that with every *malum prohibitum* the King might dispense. He had therefore laid down more precise rules of his own, stating four negative propositions and one affirmative: (1) the King cannot dispense with laws affecting a man's life, liberty, or estate (*e.g.* he cannot grant a dispensation to commit murder, to imprison another, or to deprive him of his property); (2) he cannot grant a man a dispensation to annoy or damage another (*e.g.* to trespass on his lands); (3) he cannot grant a man a dispensation to exempt him from doing that which he is required to do for the public benefit (*e.g.* to omit repairing a bridge which he is legally bound to repair); (4) he cannot grant a dispensation so as to deprive a third person of any advantage which would accrue to him if the dispensation were not granted (*e.g.* he cannot allow a butcher to sell bad meat contrary to statute, for that would be to deprive the purchaser of his right to sue for damages—a case of special interest because under the old rule of law selling bad meat would be only *malum prohibitum* and not *malum in se*). But (5) the King may dispense with laws, said Vaughan, "by transgressing which the subject can have no particular damage, and therefore no particular action". The commonest instance of royal dispensation in the Restoration period, and one that was accepted as valid, is of the kind granted on October 13, 1662, to the Fellows of Emmanuel College, Cambridge,

for Dr William Sancroft, King's Chaplain, whom they have elected Master of the College, from the statute which requires that the Master shall not be absent from the College more than one month in a quarter of a year, under penalty of loss of office.[1]

Sir Thomas Powys, the counsel for Hales, accepted Vaughan's statement of the law in the case of *Thomas* v. *Sorrell,* and argued that the dispensation in the case now before the Court was valid because it damaged no one nor deprived any person of his right of action. "If it were any wrong", he said, "it were to the King

---

[1] *Calendar of State Papers (Domestic),* 1661–2, p. 514.

himself, and sure the King may very well dispense with that which only relates to himself".[1] He also dealt in a way of his own with the old distinction between *mala prohibita* and *mala in se*. He admitted that all *mala in se* are non-dispensable, and of *mala prohibita* those acts which concern property, but those which concern government, the King may dispense with,

and this for the great inconveniencies which may happen, or urgencies of State which may force him to it, and those unforeseen at the time of making the law; for it may happen, by a vicissitude of times, those laws that were made for the preservation of government should turn to the destruction of it, if the King could not dispense with them.[2]

We recognise here the old conflict between the technicalities of the law and the realities of the situation which appeared in the great constitutional cases of the period before the Long Parliament. The King could allow the Master of Emmanuel to be relatively non-resident: could he by the same argument destroy all the defences which Parliament had erected against the Catholicising of the army, the State, and the Church? And if the arguments of counsel in Hales's case remind us of Charles I's reign, still more do the judgments from the Bench. The King had already taken pains to make sure of the issue by tampering with the independence of the judges. An unofficial opinion had been asked of them before the case came on, and four who held that such a use of the dispensing power would be illegal had been dismissed to make room for men who had no such scruples. It was desirable, said James, that the judges should be "all of one mind". The result was that the judgments of the King's hirelings swept away all the careful distinctions which had been drawn by Chief Justice Vaughan and, reverting to the discredited doctrine of absolute power, laid it down that the Crown can dispense with any statute except those dealing with offences which are against the Law of God. "There is no law whatsoever", said Chief Justice Herbert, "but may be dispensed with by the supreme law-giver, as the laws of God may be dispensed with by God himself";[3] and all the judges except one, a man of no great reputation, agreed in a decision in favour of the dispensing power upon the following grounds: (1) that the Kings of England are sovereign princes; (2) that the laws of England are the King's laws; (3) that therefore it is "an inseparable prerogative" in the Kings of England to dispense with penal laws in particular cases and upon particular necessary reasons; (4) that of those reasons and those necessities the King himself is sole judge; and (5) that this is not a trust invested in or granted to the King by the people, but "the ancient remains of the sovereign power and prerogative of the Kings of England, which never yet was taken from them, nor can be".[4]

---

[1] *State Trials*, xi. 1193.   [2] *Ib.*   [3] *Ib.* xi. 1196.   [4] *Ib.* xi. 1199.

IX

[*See* p. 259]

THE TRIAL OF THE SEVEN BISHOPS (1688)

The case was heard on June 29. The indictment charged the distinguished prisoners with having conspired together to write and publish in the County of Middlesex "a certain false, feigned, malicious, pernicious, and seditious libel".[1] In order to sustain this indictment, the prosecution set out to prove (1) that the signatures to the petition were the signatures of the Bishops; (2) that they had written the petition in Middlesex; (3) that they had published it; (4) that this publication had also been in Middlesex; and (5) that the terms of the petition constituted a libel.

The first four of these questions were technical, and upon these the prosecution nearly broke down. It was not difficult to prove the signatures, although the Court took a long time about it, but it was not clear that the petition had been written in Middlesex, for the Archbishop of Canterbury, who had signed it, had not been outside the grounds of Lambeth Palace for months, and Lambeth was in Surrey. This count was not, however, essential, and the prosecution therefore fell back on the crime of publication, and argued that since the signatures were admitted, the mere fact of writing and signing the libel constituted publication; but the Court at once pointed out that if signing was publication, the publication was at Lambeth in Surrey and not in Middlesex as charged in the indictment. It was then argued that the coming of the petition into the King's hands at Whitehall in Middlesex was publication, and there was a presumption that, since the Bishops had signed the petition and the King had received it, it was they who had delivered it to him; but the judges, who would have been only too glad to see the case break down upon a technical point, again intervened. "No, brother", said the Lord Chief Justice to the Attorney-General, "we ought not to do anything by presumption here". "No, no, by no means", said Mr Justice Powell, "we must not go upon presumptions but upon proofs".[2] And the difficulty was to find proofs, for apparently no one had seen the Bishops deliver the petition, and the King himself could not be called. The whole case was just on the point of collapsing when "a person of a very great quality"— Lord Sunderland, the President of the Council—made an opportune appearance in the witness-box, and swore that the Bishops had applied to him for an audience, and had told him that they desired it for the purpose of presenting a petition. "Now this", said the

---

[1] *State Trials*, xii. 279.   [2] *Ib*. xii. 336.

Lord Chief Justice,[1] "with the King's producing the paper and their owning it at the Council, is such a proof to me as I think will be evidence to the jury of the publication".

The case now left the region of technicalities and broadened out into a great constitutional question, raising once more, in a new form, the question of the legality of the suspending and dispensing powers. The argument for the defence is neatly summed up by Lingard.[2] The Bishops contended

that their petition was not seditious, because it was presented in private; nor false, because the matter of it was true; nor malicious, because it was drawn from them by necessity and offered to the Sovereign with the most innocent intention.

And the truth of the petition was supported by the argument that the King had no legal power to suspend by a declaration the laws affecting religion.

"That is it", said Serjeant Pemberton, "which we stand upon for our defence. And we say that such a dispensing power with laws and statutes is a thing that strikes at the very foundation of all the rights, liberties, and properties of the King's subjects whatsoever. If the King may suspend the laws of our land which concern our religion, I am sure there is no other law but he may suspend; and if the King may suspend all the laws of the kingdom, what a condition are all the subjects in for their lives, liberties and properties! All at mercy!"[3]

The reply of the prosecution may be summed up thus. The petition was libellous, because it diminished the King's sovereign power and authority by accusing him of exercising illegal powers and therefore of committing illegal acts. If the dispensing power were really illegal, the truth of the petition would save it from being libellous; but the legality of the dispensing power had been clearly established by Hales's case. The prosecution added, that the Bishops were meddling with what did not concern them, for they had no right to petition the King save in Parliament. It is interesting to find that this doctrine was at once repudiated by the judges. Mr Justice Powell "spake aside" to the Lord Chief Justice and said, "My Lord, this is strange doctrine! Shall not the subject have liberty to petition the King but in Parliament? If that be law, the subject is in a miserable case".[4] And soon after, another judge took occasion to remark, "It is the birthright of the subject to petition".[5]

Two of the judges summed up in favour of the Bishops and two against them; and then, as it was already late, the jury were locked up until the next morning without food, fire, or candle, according to custom. As the Lord Chief Justice was a man of humane disposition, he enquired, as they were preparing to depart, "Gentlemen

---

[1] *Ib*. xii. 357.
[2] *History of England*, x. 11.
[3] *State Trials*, xii. 371.
[4] *Ib*. xii. 407.
[5] *Ib*. xii. 419.

of the jury, have you a mind to drink before you go?"[1] A stage direction follows, "Wine was sent for for the jury". In the strength of this light refreshment they had to go until 10 o'clock on the morning of Saturday, June 30, when the Court assembled to hear their verdict. At first the jury was divided, seven being for the Bishops and five against them, for with all his faults James never packed his juries, although the two judges who had summed up against the Crown were dismissed at the end of term. But the arguments of the seven prevailed, and a verdict of Not Guilty was returned.

From the purely legal point of view, as Sir J. F. Stephen points out,[2] the interesting feature of the trial is the way in which the Court regarded the falsehood of the matter alleged and the malice of the defendants as questions to be left to the jury. Even in the present day, when the province of the jury has greatly widened, the question whether the King had a dispensing power—that is, the question of the truth of the libel—would be clearly a point of law, to be decided by the judges; and yet the whole Court, perhaps as a way of shelving responsibility, agreed to treat it as a question of fact, and left it to the jury to decide. "It seems to me", says Stephen,[3] "...impossible to appeal to" the trial "as a precedent for any legal proposition whatever....The whole proceeding was coloured by passionate political excitement".

X

[See p. 265]

THE THEORY OF CONTRACT

The Whig theory of the Revolution of 1688 was not without its fiction. The Whigs justified resistance on the ground that James had broken "the original contract between king and people".

For this terminology it is not necessary for our purposes to go further back than the *Leviathan* of the philosopher Hobbes, who wrote in 1651 in defence of absolute monarchy. Hobbes had laid it down that States originate in a "covenant" between men by nature equal, each of whom surrendered to the "sovereign" some part of his private right, and consented to obey it for the sake of peace and defence. But a "sovereign" thus constituted by "covenant" became "absolute"—that is to say, there was no power to take back what was given. Subjects who had undertaken to obey the sovereign

---

[1] *State Trials*, xii. 429.   [2] *History of Criminal Law*, i. 414.
[3] *Ib*. ii. 315.

were bound by their compact for ever, and their children after them, to the utmost limits of recorded time. Thus the power of kings could not be questioned; it was an "absolute power". But Hobbes argued further that absolute government was the best. The State was a great body politic as *Leviathan* was a great body natural, and the body politic, like the body natural, could only be well ruled when all its members were subject to a single head.

The terminology of "contract" or "covenant" which Hobbes had used to argue to absolute monarchy, was employed by Locke and the Revolution Whigs to argue to the right of resistance. But Locke grafted Hobbes's terminology on to a very much older argument which had been used for quite a different purpose nearly a century earlier. Richard Hooker, writing in the *Ecclesiastical Polity* in 1593 on behalf of the Church of Elizabeth, had sought to shew that the Puritans were wrong in rejecting all methods of Church government which were not directly founded upon the New Testament Scriptures. To this end he shewed that all laws are products of Reason—means adapted to an end—and as circumstances and conditions change, Reason is justified in changing Laws to meet the changed conditions and so better to secure the end desired. Hooker had in his mind Laws Ecclesiastical, and his object was to shew that the Elizabethan Church Settlement, even if it was not to be found in the New Testament, was an adaptation by Reason of the system of the Early Church to the changed conditions of the sixteenth century. But this argument of Hooker's upon the Ecclesiastical Polity was capable of being applied to the Civil Polity also, and in the course of his book he did something to make the application. "Laws", he said, "are available by consent; utterly without our consent we could be at no man's commandment living". It was the merit of Locke, (1) that he saw clearly the force of Hooker's argument in its bearing on the Revolution doctrine of resistance, and stated it afresh in a clearer and more popular form; and (2) that in order to secure this clearness of statement, he borrowed the "contract" terminology of Hobbes. Thus he laid it down, as Hobbes had done, that government originates between king and people, but unlike Hobbes, he made the contract, as the lawyers would call it, "bi-lateral"—binding on both parties, and susceptible of breach from both sides. By it the king was bound to good government as much as the people were bound to obedience, and any serious failure on his part to provide the one absolved them from the obligation of rendering the other.

Of course it is easy enough to shew that the doctrine of an "original contract between king and people" is wildly unhistorical; that States as a matter of fact do not originate in contract; that the very conception of contract arises comparatively late in the history of a State, and depends entirely upon the fact that the State has been for a long time firmly established. The old notion of primitive man at a public meeting engaged in forming a State succumbed very early to historical criticism. But although the theory of Locke was historically absurd, it afforded the necessary philosophical justification for resistance at the Revolution, and so was of the greatest possible service to the Whig party. It did not affect the value of that service that Locke's Treatise on Civil Government was not actually published until early in 1690—after the event.

BIBLIOGRAPHICAL NOTE

*The following are the full titles and editions of the
works referred to in the footnotes.*

ABBOTT, WILBUR, C. "The Long Parliament of Charles II." In *English
Historical Review*, xxi. 21, 254. 1906.
Acts and Ordinances of the Interregnum 1642–1660. Ed. [Sir] C. H. Firth
and R. S. Rait. 1911.
ANSON, Sir WILLIAM. *Law and Custom of the Constitution.* Fourth edition.
1909.
BACON, Sir FRANCIS, Viscount St Albans. *Works.* Ed. James Spedding.
1857–9.
—— *Letters and Life.* Ed. James Spedding. 1861–74.
BAILLIE, ROBERT. *Letters and Journals....* 1637–42. Ed. D. Laing.
Bannatyne Club Publications. 1841–2.
BARLOW, WILLIAM, afterwards Bishop of Lincoln. *The Sum and Substance
of the Conference...at Hampton Court, January* 14, 1603. Edition
of 1625.
BASTWICK, JOHN. *The Litany of John Bastwick.* 1637.
BAXTER, RICHARD. See *Reliquiae Baxterianae.*
BRAMSTON, Sir JOHN. *Autobiography.* Camden Society's Publications.
1845.
BURNET, GILBERT, Bishop of Salisbury. *History of his Own Time.* Edition
of 1724.
Calendar of State Papers (Domestic).
CARLYLE, THOMAS. *The Letters and Speeches of Oliver Cromwell.* Ed.
Mrs S. C. Lomas. 1904.
CARTWRIGHT, JULIA. *Madame: A Life of Henrietta, Daughter of Charles I
and Duchess of Orleans.* 1894.
CHRISTIE, W. D. *A Life of Anthony Ashley Cooper, First Earl of Shaftes-
bury,* 1621–1683. 1871.
CLARENDON, EDWARD HYDE, first Earl of. *The History of the Rebellion and
Civil Wars in England begun in the Year* 1641. Re-edited by W. D.
Macray. 1888.
Clarke Papers. Ed. [Sir] C. H. Firth. Camden Society's Publications.
1891.
COKE, Sir EDWARD. *Twelfth Report.*
Commons' Journals.
COWELL, Dr JOHN. *The Interpreter....* 1607.
CREIGHTON, MANDELL, Bishop of Peterborough, afterwards Bishop of
London. *Queen Elizabeth* (1896). Edition of 1900.
DICEY, A. V. *The Law of the Constitution.* 1885.
Dictionary of National Biography. First edition.
DOWELL, S. A. *A History of Taxation and Taxes in England.* Edition of
1884.
D'OYLEY, GEORGE. *Life of Archbishop Sancroft.* 1821.
DRYDEN, JOHN. *Absalom and Achitophel.*

DUNCAN-JONES, A. S. *Archbishop Laud*. Great English Churchmen Series. 1927.

EDWARDS, THOMAS. *Antapologia*.... 1644.

ELLIS, Sir HENRY. *Original Letters Illustrative of English History*.... 1824–46.

English Historical Review.

EVELYN, JOHN. *Diary*. Ed. Austin Dobson. 1906.

FEILING, KEITH. *A History of the Tory Party* 1640–1714. 1924.

FIGGIS, J. N. *The Divine Right of Kings*. Second edition. 1914.

FILMER, Sir ROBERT. *Patriarcha: or the Natural Power of Kings*. Written 1642; published 1680.

FIRTH, [Sir] C. H. *Oliver Cromwell and the Rule of the Puritans in England*. Heroes of the Nations Series. 1900.

—— *Cromwell's Army*. Ford Lectures for 1900–1. 1902.

—— *The House of Lords during the Civil War*. 1910.

—— *The Last Years of the Protectorate* 1656–1659. 1909.

FORSTER, JOHN. *The Arrest of the Five Members by Charles the First*. 1860.

—— *Sir John Eliot: a Biography*. Edition of 1872.

FRERE, W. H. afterwards Bishop of Truro. *A History of the English Church in the Reigns of Elizabeth and James I*, 1558–1625. 1904.

FROUDE, J. A. *The Reign of Elizabeth*. Everyman Library.

FULLER, THOMAS. *The Church History of Britain*. Edition of 1837.

—— *Ephemeris Parliamentaria*.... 1654.

—— *The History of the Worthies of England*. Ed. P. A. Nuttall. 1840.

GARDINER, S. R. *History of England* 1603–1642. Edition of 1883–4.

—— *History of the Great Civil War* 1642–1649. 1886–91.

—— *History of the Commonwealth and Protectorate* 1649–1660. 1894–1903.

—— *The Constitutional Documents of the Puritan Revolution* 1625–1660. Second edition, 1900.

—— *Student's History of England*. 1890–1.

—— *Cromwell's Place in History*. 1897.

GNEIST, R. *The History of the English Constitution*. Translated by P. A. Ashworth. 1886.

GOLDWIN SMITH. *The United Kingdom: a Political History*. 1899.

GOOCH, G. P. *English Democratic Ideas in the Seventeenth Century*. Thirlwall Prize Dissertation for 1897. Cambridge Historical Essays. 1898.

GRANT ROBERTSON, [Sir] C. *Select Statutes, Cases, and Documents* 1660–1832. Second edition. 1913.

GREEN, J. R. *History of the English People*. 1881–3.

GWATKIN, H. M. *Church and State to the Death of Queen Anne*. 1917.

HACKET, JOHN, Bishop of Coventry and Lichfield. *Scrinia Reserata: a Memorial offered to the Great Deservings of John Williams, D.D.* 1693.

HALIFAX, GEORGE SAVILE, first Marquess of. *A Character of King Charles II*.... 1750.

HALLAM, HENRY. *The Constitutional History of England from the Accession of Henry VII to the Death of George II*. Edition of 1876.

HALLIWELL, J. O. *Letters of the Kings of England....* 1848.

HAYWARD, Sir JOHN. *Annals of the first four years of the Reign of Queen Elizabeth.* Ed. John Bruce. Camden Society's Publications. 1840.

HEATH, JAMES. *A Chronicle of the late Intestine War...*(1663). Edition of 1676.

HEYLYN, PETER. *Cyprianus Anglicus: or the History of the Life and Death of William Laud, Archbishop of Canterbury.* 1668.

HEYWOOD, OLIVER. *Autobiography, Diaries....* Ed. J. Horsfall Turner. 1881.

HUNT, JOHN. *Religious Thought in England from the Reformation....* 1870.

Hutchinson, Memoirs of Colonel. Ed. [Sir] C. H. Firth. 1885.

HUTTON, W. H. *The English Church from the accession of Charles I to the death of Queen Anne 1625–1714.* 1903.

JAMES I. *Political Works.* Ed. C. H. McIlwain. 1918.

JENKS, E. *The Constitutional Experiments of the Commonwealth.* Thirlwall Prize Dissertation for 1889. Cambridge Historical Essays. 1890.

JESSE, J. H. *Memoirs of the Court of England during the Reigns of the Stuarts.* Edition of 1840.

KELLISON, MATTHEW. *The Gag of the Reformed Gospel.* 1623.

KERSHAW, R. N. "The Elections for the Long Parliament." In *English Historical Review,* xxxviii. 496. 1923.

LAUD, WILLIAM, Archbishop of Canterbury. *Works.* Ed. W. Scott. 1847.

LEIGHTON, ALEXANDER. *An Epitome or brief discovery....* 1646.

—— *Sion's Plea against the Prelacy.* 1628.

L'ESTRANGE, HAMON. *The Reign of King Charles.* 1656.

LINGARD, JOHN. *History of England.* Edition of 1883.

LIPSON, E. "The Elections for the Exclusion Bill Parliament 1679–1681." In *English Historical Review,* xxviii. 59. 1916.

LOCKE, JOHN. *Works.* Tenth edition, 1801.

LODGE, EDMUND. *Illustrations of British History....* 1838.

Lords' Journals.

LUDLOW, EDMUND. *Memoirs.* Ed. [Sir] C. H. Firth. 1894.

LUTTRELL, NARCISSUS. *A Brief Historical Relation...*1678 *to...*1714. 1857.

MACAULAY, T. B. *History of England.* Edition of 1880.

MACY, J. *The English Constitution: a Commentary on its Nature and Growth.* 1897.

Manchester and Cromwell, The Quarrel between. Camden Society's Publications. 1875.

MANWARING, ROGER, afterwards Bishop of St David's. *Sermons on Religion and Allegiance.* 1627.

MASSON, DAVID. *Life of Milton....* 1859–80.

MAY, THOMAS. *History of the Long Parliament....* Edition of 1647.

MELVILL, JAMES. *Autobiography and Diary.* Wodrow Society. 1842.

MILTON, JOHN. *Prose Works.* 1848–53.

MONTAGU, RICHARD, afterwards Bishop of Chichester. *A Gag for the New Gospel? No: A New Gag for an Old Goose.* 1624.

—— *Appello Caesarem.* 1625.

MONTAGUE, F. C. *The Political History of England 1603–1660.* 1907.

MORLEY, JOHN, afterwards Viscount Morley. *Oliver Cromwell.* 1900.

NEAL, DANIEL. *History of the Puritans.* Edition of 1754.

NICHOLS, JOHN. *The Progresses...of King James I.* 1828.

NORTH, ROGER. *Examen....* 1740.

Norths, The Lives of the. Ed. A. Jessopp. 1890.

NOTESTEIN, WALLACE. *The Winning of the Initiative by the House of Commons.* Raleigh Lecture for 1924.

—— and FRANCES HELEN RELF. *Commons' Debates for* 1629. Publications of the University of Minnesota. 1921.

PARKER, SAMUEL, Bishop of Oxford. *History of his Own Time.* 1727.

Parliamentary History. Ed. William Cobbett. 1806–20.

PARSONS, ROBERT (writing under the pseudonym of R. Doleman). *A Conference about the next Succession to the Crown of England....* 1594.

PEPYS, SAMUEL. *Diary.* Ed. H. B. Wheatley. First edition, 1902.

PIKE, L. O. *A Constitutional History of the House of Lords.* 1894.

PORRITT, E. *The Unreformed House of Commons.* 1903.

PROTHERO, [Sir] G. W. *Select Statutes and other Constitutional Documents* 1558–1625. Third edition, 1906.

PRYNNE, WILLIAM. *Histriomastix.* Edition of 1633.

RALPH, JAMES. *History of England....* 1744–46.

RANKE, LEOPOLD VON. *A History of England, principally in the Seventeenth Century.* 1875.

RELF, FRANCES HELEN. *The Petition of Right.* Publications of the University of Minnesota. 1917.

Reliquiae Baxterianae.... 1696.

ROGERS, JAMES EDWIN THOROLD. *A History of Agriculture and Prices in England.* 1866.

RUSHWORTH, JOHN. *Historical Collections.* Edition of 1682.

—— *The Tryal of Thomas, Earl of Strafford.* 1680.

SEELEY, Sir J. R. *The Growth of British Policy.* 1895.

—— *Introduction to Political Science.* 1896.

SHAW, W. A. *A History of the English Church* 1640–1660. 1900.

SHERLOCK, WILLIAM. "A Letter to a Member of the Convention (1688)." Printed in *Somers' Tracts,* x. 185.

SIBTHORP, ROBERT. *Sermon on Apostolic Obedience.* 1627.

Somers' Tracts.

Star Chamber and High Commission Court, Cases in the. Ed. S. R. Gardiner. Camden Society's Publications. 1886.

State Trials. Ed. Thomas Bayly Howell. 1809.

Statutes of the Realm.

STEPHEN, Sir J. F. *A History of the Criminal Law of England.* 1883.

STRAFFORD, Earl of. *Letters and Dispatches.* 1739.

STRYPE, JOHN. *Annals of the Reformation.* Edition of 1824.

TASWELL-LANGMEAD, T. P. *English Constitutional History.* Eighth edition, 1919.

THURLOE, JOHN. *A Collection of State Papers.* 1742.

TRAILL, H. D. *Social England.* 1893–97.

—— *William the Third.* Twelve English Statesmen Series. 1888.

TREVELYAN, G. M. *History of England.* 1926.

—— *England under the Stuarts.* 1904.

Trevelyan Papers.

TURNER, E. R. "Parliament and Foreign Affairs 1603–1760." In *English Historical Review*, xxxiv. 172.

—— "The Privy Council of 1679." In *English Historical Review*, xxx. 251.

WHITELOCKE, BULSTRODE. *Memorials of English Affairs*...(1682). Edition of 1853.

—— *A Journal of the Swedish Embassy in the Years* 1653 *and* 1654. Ed. H. Reeve. 1855.

WILLIAMSON, Sir JOSEPH. *Letters*. Camden Society's Publications. 1874.

INDEX

Abbot, George, Archbishop of Canterbury, 13, 53

"Abhorrers," 245

Agitators, 143, 144, 146; election of (Apr. 1647), 142; sent back to their regiments (Nov. 1647), 149; Levellers' design to reappoint (1649), 161

Agreement of the People, of 1647, 156; of 1649, 156, 156 n., 157, 186

Albemarle, Christopher Monk, 2nd Duke of, 252 n. *See also* Monk

Altar controversy, 15

Anabaptists, 127 n., 129

"Anarchy, Year of," 205

Andrewes, Lancelot, Bishop of Winchester, 12, 13, 51

Apology of 1604, 19, 29–31

Appello Caesarem, 53

Appropriation of supply, in 1624, 50; in 1665, 233

Argyle, Archibald Campbell, 8th Earl of, 86, 108

Argyle, Archibald Campbell, 9th Earl of, his insurrection (1685), 251

Arlington, Henry Bennet, 1st Earl of, a member of the Cabal, 234

Arminianism, Arminians, 68, 80, 100, 104; origin of the term, 12; supported by the Stuart Kings, 13, 54; points of controversy with the Puritans, 14–16; its strength and weakness, 51–2; resolution of 1629 against, 69

Army of the Parliament, a professional career, 136, 163, 183; arrangements for disbanding in 1647, 141; the members appeal to force against (1647), 143; its political organisation, 144; army democracy, 159; its difficulties in 1648, 149; Pride's Purge, 152; it brings the King to trial, 152–4; further intervention in politics (1653), 164-6; arrears of pay, 145, 209, 211. *See also* New Model

Army of the younger Stuarts, 241, 251, 252; its formation, 224; its precarious position, 224–5; objections to, 225; modelling of, by James II, 254

Army, Council of the, 144, 146, 148, 156; abolished (1647), 149; the Levellers design its reappointment (1649), 161

Army, Declaration of the (1647), 144

Army Plot (1641), 107

Articuli Cleri (1605), 35

Arundel, Thomas Howard, 2nd Earl of, case of privilege (1626), 58

Astley, Sir Jacob, 134

Attainder, of Strafford, 95, 280–1; of Laud, 95

Authorised Version of 1611, 28

Bacon, Sir Francis, afterwards Lord Chancellor, 31, 39, 40, 46; favours concessions to the Puritans, 27; contrasted with Coke, 41; his impeachment (1621), 50, 58

Bancroft, Richard, Archbishop of Canterbury, 28, 34, 35, 36

Bankes, Sir John, his speech in Hampden's case (1637), 274–5

Barebones Parliament, *see* Parliament of Saints

Bastwick, John, released and compensated, 92–3

Bate's case (1605), 43, 44

Baxter, Richard, 136, 137, 226, 228

Benedictine Order, settled at St James's (1686), 255

Benevolences, 215, 222

Berkeley, Sir Robert, his speech in Hampden's case (1637), 276

Berwick, 150, 207

Berwick, Treaty of (1639), 87

Biennial Parliaments, 147

Births, marriages, and deaths, Acts for the registration of (1653), 171

Bishops, Digby's speech in defence of (1641), 102; coercive power to be taken away from (1647), 148. *See also*, Seven Bishops, The

Bishops' Exclusion Bill (1641), 105, 113, 115

Bishops' War, 248; of 1639, 86–7, 88; of 1640, 90

"Black box," 246

Blake, Robert, 119, 134, 163

"Bloody Assize" (1685), 251, 252

Book of Rates (1608), 43

Book of Sports, 15

Bradshaw, John, 119, 155, 166, 167

Breda, Declaration from (1660), 209, 211, 215

Bristol, 125, 133

Bristol, John Digby, 1st Earl of, case of privilege (1626), 58, 217

"Brotherly Assistance" voted to the Scots, 92